CONVICTING THE INNOCENT

CONVICTING THE INNOCENT

DEATH ROW AND AMERICA'S BROKEN SYSTEM OF JUSTICE

Stanley Cohen

Skyhorse Publishing
A HERMAN GRAF BOOK

Visit our website at www.skyhorsepublishing.com.

10 9 8 7 6 5 4 3 2 1

Library of Congress Cataloging-in-Publication Data is available on file.

Cover design by Anthony Morais

Print ISBN: 978-1-63220-646-6
Ebook ISBN: 978-1-63220-813-2

Printed in the United States of America

ALSO BY STANLEY COHEN:

The Game They Played (1977, 2001)
The Man in the Crowd: Confessions of a Sports Addict (1981)
A Magic Summer: The '69 Mets (1988, 2003)
Dodgers! The First 100 Years (1990)
Willie's Game (with Willie Mosconi (1993)
Tough Talk (with Martin Garbus, 1998)
The Wrong Men (2003)
The Execution of Officer Becker: (2006)
Beating the Odds (with Brandon Lang) (2009)
The Man in the Crowd (a revised, expanded edition, 2012)

For my wife, Betty,
    who, for sixty years,
    healed all the wounds,
    bridged all the gaps, and,
    in myriad ways,
    transformed the frail thread of reality
    into the hard coin of reality

Contents

"The degree of civilization in a society can be judged by entering its prisons."

—Fyodor Dostoyevsky, *The House of the Dead*

"There will be no lasting peace, either in the heart of individuals or in social customs until death is outlawed."

—Albert Camus, *Reflections on the Guillotine*

Introduction

O N APRIL 3, 2014, Tommy Lee Sells was put to death at the Texas State Penitentiary in Huntsville for fatally stabbing a thirteen-year-old girl in Georgia fifteen years earlier. The execution, carried out by lethal injection, went smoothly. Sells closed his eyes and took a few deep breaths. Thirteen minutes later he was pronounced dead. The efficiency of the procedure surprised no one. The death house in Huntsville is the place to go if one wishes to see executions carried out to perfection. Texas, after all, is the capital punishment capital of America. Since 1976, the state has been home to nearly half of the 1,382 executions in the United States. Executing prisoners is a Texas pastime whose popularity is exceeded only by football.

The story of Sells's execution was noteworthy only because it was the first to follow a decision by the United States Supreme Court rejecting the right of the condemned to know the source or the contents of the drug being used to kill them. Just a few weeks later, the issue of lethal injection and the question of the death penalty itself began tugging at the nation's conscience when a botched execution resulted in the prolonged, agonizing death of an Oklahoma inmate.

Late in the afternoon of April 29, Clayton D. Lockett was wheeled into the death chamber at McAlester, Oklahoma, to be executed for the murder of a nineteen-year-old woman in 1999. Second only to Texas in applying the death penalty, Oklahoma might have been expected to carry it off without incident. But things started going wrong within just a few minutes. At 6:23, a sedative, midazolam, which the state had not previously used, was injected into Lockett's arms. About five minutes later, Lockett started blinking and his eyes turned glassy and then closed, according to reports from the scene by Ziva Branstetter, an editor at *The Tulsa World*, and Dean Sanderford, the condemned man's attorney. At 6:33, the physician in charge said Lockett was unconscious and the team began to administer two lethal drugs, one to paralyze the prisoner and one to make his heart stop. Within three minutes, Lockett's body started twitching; he rolled his head from side to side. He mumbled something inaudible and tried to lift his upper body from the gurney. At 6:39, sixteen minutes after the procedure had begun, the state's director of corrections halted the execution when the physician found that Lockett's vein had ruptured. Following another twenty-seven minutes of what some described as torture, Lockett was declared dead of a "massive heart attack" by Department of Corrections Commissioner Robert Patton. About six weeks after the incident, an independent autopsy commissioned by Lockett's attorneys concluded that the problem was caused by the failure of the executioners to place the injection properly in a vein in Lockett's groin. As a result, the drugs were not pumped directly into the prisoner's bloodstream. According to the autopsy, Lockett's vein had not collapsed, as the Oklahoma prison official had reported.

The "botched execution," as it has been called, attracted notice not only throughout the country but around the world, particularly in Europe. The death penalty is banned in the European Union which also has restricted the export of drugs used in lethal injections. Members of the EU view the United States' addiction to the death penalty with disdain. An anonymous tweet on Twitter seemed to capture the prevailing feeling on the continent. It read: "How could Oklahoma botch an execution? If there's one thing I would expect Americans to know how to do by now, it's kill somebody."

But apparently they did not, at least not those who were in charge of executing prisoners. For just a few months later, in July, an even more horrific execution was conducted in Arizona. It took the state nearly two hours to kill Joseph R. Wood III who, according to witnesses, repeatedly gasped while the execution was carried out. During that time, Wood's attorney filed an emergency appeal to a Federal District Court and placed a call to US Supreme Court Justice Anthony M. Kennedy asking that the procedure be halted because it was in violation of the "cruel and unusual" clause of the Eighth Amendment. Kennedy turned down the request and Wood died before the district court responded. Arizona officials said they used the same combination of drugs that had been used in Ohio months earlier on Dennis McGuire, who also suffered through an execution that lasted longer than expected. The day after Wood's execution, the attorney general of Arizona called a temporary halt to executions in the state.

Lethal injection was adopted as the procedure of choice in the United States beginning in 1977. It replaced, in reverse chronological sequence, the electric chair, the gas chamber, hanging, and the firing squad. Deemed to be the most humane form of execution, estimates nonetheless indicate that 7 percent of such executions have gone bad. As recently as 2008, a divided Supreme Court ruled that death by lethal injection did not violate the Eighth Amendment's prohibition of "cruel and unusual" punishment. In his decision, Chief Justice John Roberts wrote: "Simply because an execution method may result in pain, either by accident or as an inescapable consequence of death, does not establish the sort of objectively intolerable risk of harm that qualifies as cruel and unusual." Justice Antonin Scalia, the court's leading advocate of the death penalty, offered even more extreme views on more than one occasion. "Where does it come from that in the execution of a person who has been convicted of killing people we must choose the least painful method possible? Is that somewhere in our Constitution?" The court, he said, was considering "an execution, not surgery." In another instance, Scalia mused, "How enviable a quiet death by lethal injection," as he contrasted the death of a condemned killer with that of his victim.

The dispute over "cruel and unusual" puts the United States in the ironic position of striving to perfect a procedure that has become obsolete in most of the civilized world. Of the 195 independent states that are UN members or have UN observer status, 100 (51 percent) have abolished capital punishment completely; 7 (4 percent) retain it for ordinary crimes in exceptional circumstances, such as war; 48 (25 percent) permit its use for ordinary crimes but have not used it for at least ten years and are considered de facto abolitionist states. In 2013, five countries joined the abolitionist ranks—Chad, DR Congo, Cuba, Qatar, and Zimbabwe. Only forty countries, 20 percent of the total, maintain the death penalty in both law and practice. In 2012, according to statistics compiled by Amnesty International, the United States ranked fifth worldwide in the number of executions behind China, Iran, Iraq, and Saudi Arabia.

But even in the US, the appetite for capital punishment, though still robust, has shown signs of abating. In 2004, twelve states had abolished the death penalty. Ten years later, the number had grown to eighteen and in two others—Oregon and Washington—that formally retain the death penalty, the governors have pledged never to impose it. A 2014 poll found that the percentage of the public that supports capital punishment, though still a majority, has dropped to 56 percent from 80 percent in 1996. The loss of favor is driven chiefly by the number of wrongful death row convictions that have been uncovered in recent years, largely through the use of DNA evidence.

In an earlier book, *The Wrong Men* (Carroll & Graf, 2003), I cited 102 cases of what was described as America's epidemic of wrongful death-row convictions. Since then, more than 40 new cases of exoneration from death row have been recorded. Of course, no one knows for certain whether any of the average of forty-plus people executed annually in the United States between 2010 and 2013 have been innocent or wrongfully convicted. What we do know is that since 1973 more than 150 prisoners on death row have been exonerated. Many were freed after serving long terms, sometimes several decades, in solitary confinement. Some escaped execution just hours before their dates with death. Given the sheer weight of numbers and the random play of chance, it is not unreasonable to assume that a fair number of those put to death were either actually innocent or wrongfully convicted. A recent independent study estimates that 4.1 percent of all inmates on death row were convicted on false charges. Other estimates run as high as 10 percent.

It was the advent of DNA technology that turned the light on the glaring inadequacies of a system that convicts innocent people by the hundreds and sentences a substantial number of them to death. DNA evidence was first used in United States courts in 1987, but did not make its way into popular use until the mid-nineties. By 2003, more than eighty wrongfully convicted people had been exonerated by DNA evidence, at least a dozen of them freed from death row. That number has increased exponentially in the past decade.

The Wrong Men, which documented each of those cases, attracted a good bit of attention, some of it from unexpected sources. I received letters from several prisoners seeking my help in one way or another. One naively asked if I would come to Florida and represent him on appeal, as he felt his attorney was not sufficiently diligent in his defense. Another asked if I could help him locate a specific attorney in North Carolina who successfully represented a fellow prisoner. In each instance I responded as best I could. It was unlikely that I made much of a difference. But the correspondence served to put a human face on what in time and number threatens to become an abstraction.

In this new venture, *Convicting the Innocent*, I will describe in detail the forty-plus cases of death-row exoneration that have occurred since 2002. Some of the earlier cases, in which there have been new developments, will be reviewed more briefly. Also included will be a number of wrongful convictions that did not involve the death penalty, but in which the prisoner served many years of a life sentence. Every case is an illustration of the grim consequences that ensue when the legal mechanism has gone awry. And every case is haunted by the specter that an innocent man, under other circumstances, might have been put to death. The reasoning is elementary: If it has been established with scientific certainty that dozens, if not scores, of people have been wrongly convicted and sentenced to death, can one reasonably doubt that others were no less innocent, just less fortunate?

Justice Scalia, who appears to view capital punishment as a recreational activity, seems little troubled by the prospect of executing an innocent man. Considering the fate of Troy Davis who was executed in 2011 despite the apparent crumbling of the prosecution's case over the previous ten years, Scalia offered the suggestion that the guilt or innocence of the condemned man is not of paramount importance. "This court," he said, "has never held that the Constitution forbids the execution of a convicted defendant who has had a full and fair trial but is later able to convince a court that he is 'actually' innocent." That opinion was consistent with a 2006 pronouncement by the good justice that "not a single case—not one—[exists] in which it is clear that a person was executed for a crime he did not commit."

Scalia was wrong on two counts. He was factually incorrect; the actual innocence of a person who has been executed has been established more than once. More critically, his remark was intentionally misleading. For the justice is well aware that following an execution all further investigation is halted. Neither the state nor the defense has a stake in proving the innocence of a man already put to death. The execution of the innocent is not a chimera that troubles the imagination of the faint of heart. It is part of a broken system of justice.

Executing the Innocent

JUSTICE IS AN idea that is best understood in its absence. Throughout the ages, its substance has eluded the close study of scholars and the musings of poets, prophets, and philosophers. They were perhaps the wrong people looking in the wrong places. Experience tells us we can most easily identify justice in places where it never existed; we discern its nature in circumstances where it was applied too loosely or not at all. The ultimate irony is that justice is comprehended most clearly by those who have been denied its benedictions.

Even at its best, fine-tuned through a network of statutory and constitutional laws, viewed through a prism that refracts the light of evolving moods and shifting attitudes, justice is at best an inexact process. It depends on too many variables for it to function with precision: the quality of the defense attorneys, the intensity of the prosecution, the disposition of the judge, the reliability of witnesses, the makeup of a jury whose members rarely resemble the defendant's peers. Guilt or innocence is determined in an atmosphere of competition, a contest in which each side is committed to a particular outcome rather than to a concept as abstract as justice. It is little wonder, then, that the judicial process is as quixotic and unpredictable as any other contest. What troubles one's sleep is that here the stakes are so much higher.

It is no secret of course that the guilty are sometimes acquitted while innocent people are often convicted and sent to prison. The possibility of error is built into the system. But the random nature of the process becomes acute when the crime is a capital one and the innocent person is sentenced to death. It is not an uncommon occurrence. The Death Penalty Information Center, which gathers statistics on capital cases at its Washington, DC, headquarters, lists 154 cases between 1973 and 2015 in which innocent people were freed from death row. Many had spent more than a decade in isolated death-watch chambers before they were exonerated of the crimes with which they were charged. An unfortunate few suffered the torments of solitary for nearly four decades before being freed.

The problem of wrongful conviction is not a new one in America. The first documented case in the United States dates to 1820 when the presumed victim of a murder, for which two men had been sentenced to death, turned up alive and well in New Jersey. Since then, hundreds of additional cases, many of them involving a death sentence, have come to light. Not until recently, however, did the gravity of the issue attract sustained national attention. It had been ignored perhaps not because of public indifference but because the depth of the problem—the sheer volume of numbers—was unknown. The turning point came in the fall of 1998 when the National Conference on Wrongful Convictions and the Death Penalty was held at the Northwestern University School of Law in Illinois. The meeting featured the appearance of twenty-eight innocent former prisoners from all over the country who had been sentenced to death for crimes they did not commit.

A few months later, Illinois death-row prisoner Anthony Porter was exonerated just two days before his scheduled execution. The reprieve prompted Northwestern Professor David Protess and several of his students at the Medill School of Journalism to probe deeper into the circumstances surrounding Porter's conviction, and they uncovered conclusive evidence of his innocence. The two events stirred further interest and the Center on Wrongful Convictions was launched with private funding at the start of the 1999–2000 academic year. Its mission was to identify and rectify wrongful convictions and other serious miscarriages of justice. Soon, a nationwide examination of the death penalty was under way.

The most compelling argument against capital punishment is that innocent people will inevitably be put to death. While few can doubt that such executions have occurred, it is difficult to document the cases. The courts do not entertain claims of innocence when the defendant is dead. Attorneys move on to new cases. They do not seek fresh evidence that would exonerate those whose fate has already been sealed. All the same, there are a significant number of cases in which subsequent findings strongly suggest that an innocent man has been executed. Often, such cases involve a defendant with a criminal background that makes him a likely suspect and might inure the jury, and even the judge, to the possibility of error. He is, in the end, convicted not by the evidence but by his past.

Dennis Stockton
North Carolina

Dennis Stockton insisted on his innocence from the very beginning. There was, after all, no physical evidence to tie him to the murder with which he was charged. In fact, he was convicted solely on the testimony of an ex-con who in many respects was a more likely suspect in the killing and who later championed a campaign to save Stockton when he was awaiting execution. But despite mounting evidence that he was innocent, Stockton was executed by lethal injection on September 27, 1995, more than ten years after his conviction.

The victim of the crime was a friend of Stockton's, a young man named Kenny Arnder. Arnder's body was found in a gully near a dirt road in North Carolina not far from the Virginia border, on a July day in 1978. His arms were splayed wide in the form of a cross and his hands were chopped off at the wrist. He had been shot between the eyes. The body was covered with branches and had begun to decompose, making identification difficult.

Stockton had been with Arnder shortly before he was murdered. Arnder had called him at his home and asked Stockton to drive him to Kibler Valley, a remote, wooded area in southwestern Virginia. Arnder said he was worried because a man he feared had seen him stealing tires off a car. Stockton drove him to Kibler Valley and dropped him off at about 6 p.m. Arnder's body was discovered five days later. It was assumed that he had been killed in Virginia and his body moved across the border.

The police questioned Stockton because he was one of the last people to see Arnder alive. He was the type of suspect who was easy pickings for the authorities. At age thirty-eight, he had spent most of his adult life in criminal custody. As a juvenile, he was held in jail over a weekend for passing bad checks. At seventeen, he served three-to-five years on similar charges. When he was released, he was already prison-tough. He became involved with drugs, both as a user and dealer, and did time on a variety of charges including arson-by-contract, safecracking, and carrying a gun. He was at the top of the police's "usual suspects" list. During one investigation, police said they found a human body part preserved in a jar in Stockton's home. He told them he had gotten it from a biker gang and kept it to show to his friends. When police questioned him about the Arnder murder, he readily showed them the selection of guns he kept at home. None of them matched the murder weapon. The police left, apparently satisfied that Stockton was not their man.

His involvement in the case might have ended right there had he not responded to jailhouse rumors two years after Arnder's death by going to the police. In prison on other charges, Stockton heard it bruited around the prison that the police suspected him of committing the murder. He believed he knew the source of the rumors and decided to act on his own. He went to the police and told them he had new information on the crime. The police accompanied him to his house where he showed them letters he had received from a prominent citizen offering to pay him to commit a murder. He said he had received $3,000 but never killed anyone and suspected that the man who paid him might be circulating the rumors as a means of taking revenge. The letters, in police custody, never surfaced again; they apparently had been lost. But Stockton, who had tried to deflect suspicion, was again a prime suspect.

Two years later, he was charged by the Commonwealth of Virginia with the murder-for-hire killing of Kenny Arnder. The basis for the charge was the offer of testimony by a convict named Randy Bowman who was serving a prison sentence for larceny and possession of firearms. Bowman claimed to have been at a meeting during which Stockton was hired to kill Arnder for a fee of $1,500 by a man named Tommy McBride. McBride allegedly was angry with Arnder for crossing him on a drug deal and wanted him killed as a message to other dealers.

Stockton was tried in the rural town of Stuart, Virginia in 1983. Bowman testified that he was at McBride's house trying to sell some stolen goods when he overheard the deal being made. He also said he had not been promised anything in return for his testimony. His was the only evidence linking Stockton to the crime. Nonetheless, Stockton was convicted of murder-for-hire, a capital charge. At a separate sentencing hearing, he was sentenced to death.

In 1987, a federal judge set aside the death sentence when he learned that the jury deliberations had been tainted. The judge offered Stockton the choice of life imprisonment or a new sentencing hearing. Insisting on his innocence, Stockton opted for the new hearing. It was a mistake. Federal law does not allow evidence concerning guilt or innocence to be heard at a re-sentencing procedure, and Stockton again was sentenced to death.

During his twelve years on death row, Stockton kept a detailed diary on life in what he called "the monster factory." He also helped plan the only mass escape from a death row in American history, although he did not take part in the plan's execution. He remained in his cell during the breakout and documented the event carefully, still hoping he would someday be granted a new trial. It appeared that his hopes were not unfounded. Questions continued to emerge regarding the credibility of Bowman's testimony. There was speculation that he had been offered incentives to testify against Stockton, but the prosecution denied it. Anthony Giorno, the prosecuting attorney, sent a letter to Stockton's defense attorneys in 1990, in which he said: "I am not aware of any promises made to Bowman other than that I told him I would endeavor to see that he would be transferred [to a different penitentiary]." Giorno also enclosed a letter written by Bowman to the prosecution two weeks before the trial in which he said: "I am writing to let you know that I'm not going to court [to testify] unless you can get this 6 or 7 months I've got left cut off where I don't have to come back to prison." So it was clear that Bowman expected to be rewarded for his testimony, but the prosecution denied making any deal.

In 1994, Stockton's attorneys obtained affidavits from law enforcement officials stating that Bowman had become angry after Stockton's trial "because promises allegedly made to him were not kept." According to the affidavits, Bowman said he had been promised a reduction in sentence or a transfer to another prison in return for his testimony.

Seventeen days after Stockton was sentenced to death, prosecutors dropped charges against Bowman for obtaining stolen property. Fourteen months after the trial, Bowman was released on parole.

On September 25, 1995, a district court judge ordered a sixty-day stay of execution when defense attorneys presented separate affidavits from Bowman's former wife, his son, and a friend, stating that Bowman had admitted committing the murder. A Virginia newspaper reported that Bowman had confessed his guilt to a journalist. The Virginia federal court apparently found the new evidence to be unconvincing. The district court's stay was lifted a day after it had been ordered. The following day Dennis Stockton was executed. Though it probably will never be known for certain, the likelihood is that an innocent man was put to death that day.

Cameron Todd Willingham
Texas

The same might be said of Todd Willingham, who was executed in February 2004 for murdering his three young children by arson at the family's home in Corsicana, Texas. Ten months later, Gerald Hurst, a nationally known fire investigator, reviewed the case documents, including the trial transcriptions and an hour-long videotape of the fire scene and determined that not only was Willingham innocent but that no crime had been committed. "There's nothing to suggest to any reasonable arson investigator that this was an arson fire," he said. "It was just a fire."

Relatives of Willingham decided to seek a posthumous pardon from state officials. The Innocence Project, a non-profit organization dedicated to exonerating wrongfully convicted people, kept the case alive. Founded in 1992 by Barry Scheck and Peter Neufeld and affiliated with the Benjamin N. Cardoza School of Law at Yeshiva University in New York City, the Innocence Project filed a lawsuit against the state of Texas seeking a judgment of "official oppression."

In 2010, Judge Charlie Baird wrote an order that would have exonerated Willingham. It read: "This Court orders the exoneration of Cameron Todd Willingham for murdering his three daughters. In light of the overwhelming, credible, and reliable evidence presented by the Petitioners, this Court holds that the State of Texas wrongfully executed Cameron Todd Willingham." However, Baird's order never became official because, as reported in the *Huffington Post*, "a higher court halted the posthumous inquiry while it considered whether the judge had the authority to examine the capital case."

In 2011, Texas Attorney General Greg Abbott responded to questions from the Texas Forensic Science Commission about jurisdiction and authority. His opinion prohibited the commission from investigating "specific items of evidence that were tested or offered into evidence prior to" September 1, 2005. Barry Scheck offered a rejoinder, saying that "the reasoning of the opinion is wrong and contrary to the clear intention of the legislature when it formed the Commission."

The awareness that the judicial machinery is imperfect and that the consequences of the death penalty can never be remedied has led to a re-examination of capital punishment at both the federal and state levels. The Center on Wrongful Convictions (CWC) has proposed a series of reforms that would reduce the possibility of innocent people being executed. The reform measures include modifying eyewitness identification procedures, requiring police to videotape interrogations and confessions, and banning testimony by informants who will be rewarded for their cooperation. These procedures clearly would reduce the number of wrongful convictions but would not come close to eliminating them.

The justice system in the United States is complex and its many parts rub against one another in ways that are hardly conducive to finding the truth. The various parts—prosecution, defense, judiciary—not to mention law enforcement, where the process begins, each have their particular biases, and in every case the stakes are high. Elections must be considered, reputations protected, and, of course, prospects for a brighter future ensured. Convictions are the coin of the realm. Except for the defense attorneys, when they are not appointed by the state, few careers are advanced by finding suspects to be innocent. Wrongful conviction has a long history in the US, beginning in 1820 with the mistaken presumption that a Vermont farmhand who disappeared had been murdered. According to Rob Warden, Executive Director of the CWC, this early case violated virtually every precept of independent judgment.

The Boorn Brothers
Vermont

One day in 1812, Russell Colvin disappeared from his home in Manchester, Vermont, where he had worked on his father-in-law's farm along with his wife's two brothers, Jesse and Stephen Boorn. It was no secret that he and his brothers-in-law were not on the best of terms. The brothers had complained often and loudly that Colvin did not pull his weight and was taking advantage of their father's largesse. Few who knew the family were surprised when Colvin didn't return, and the Boorns were suspected of having a hand in his disappearance. But it took the specter of divine intervention to seriously raise suspicions of homicide.

The missing persons case lay dormant for seven years until Amos Boorn, an uncle of the brothers, claimed that Colvin appeared at his bedside during a recurring dream. The ghost informed Amos he had been slain but did not identify his killer. He did confide that his remains had been put into an old cellar hole in a potato field on the Boorn farm. The cellar hole was excavated and found to contain pieces of broken crockery, a button, a penknife, and a jackknife, but no body parts. Colvin's wife, Sally, identified the items as having belonged to her husband. It was, in a sense, in her interest to do so. Sally had given birth to a child more than nine months after Russell was gone from the scene. Under Vermont law, a child born to a married woman was presumed to be fathered by her husband, making Sally ineligible for state financial support; unless, of course, her husband was dead. She may not have understood at the time that her husband's demise would sharpen the focus of suspicion on her brothers.

Subsequent events kept the case under public scrutiny. Soon after the cellar hole had been searched, a mysterious fire destroyed the sheep barn on the Boorn property. A few days later, a dog unearthed several bone fragments beneath a nearby stump. Three local physicians said they were human bones. Seven years after he had vanished, it appeared clear to the local citizenry that Colvin had been murdered, his body buried and moved on several occasions, and the barn burned down to destroy evidence of the murder. On the basis of such speculation, Jesse Boorn was taken into custody and a warrant was issued for the arrest of Stephen, who had recently moved to New York.

In jail, Jesse shared a cell with a forger named Silas Merrill, who had a tale to tell the authorities. Merrill said that Jesse had admitted taking part in the murder after a visit from his father, Barney. As the story went, Jesse told him that during an argument, Stephen had knocked Colvin to the ground with a club. Barney then came by, and seeing that Colvin was still alive, slit his throat with Stephen's penknife. They buried the body in the cellar hole, then moved it to the barn, and finally to the stump area when the barn burned down. Merrill agreed to tell his story to a jury in exchange for his immediate release. It sounded like a good deal to State's Attorney Calvin Sheldon. Merrill was set free.

With a death sentence looming, Jesse decided to confess in order to minimize his own role in the crime while at the same time exculpating his father and placing the blame chiefly on his brother, whom he doubtless believed to be outside the reach of Vermont's jurisdiction. However, when a Manchester constable visited Stephen in New York, he agreed to return in an effort to clear his name. Jesse immediately recanted, saying he had falsely confessed in an attempt to save himself and his father from execution. Confession or not, the state's attorney chose to seek the death penalty.

During the trial, witnesses emerged to testify they had heard the Boorn brothers threaten to kill Colvin. Others recalled that after his disappearance, the brothers had said they knew Colvin was dead. But there was one bit of new evidence that had served the defendants' interest. Before the trial started, the largest of the bones the dog had uncovered was compared with an actual human leg bone that had been preserved after an amputation, and the dissimilarities could not be ignored. The same three doctors who originally had deemed it to be a human bone now agreed it was of animal origin. But the damage had already been done. Were it not for the inaccurate identification of the bones, the brothers would not likely have been arrested, and the case would have continued to be little more than grist for the rumor mill.

The exclusion of the bone evidence now was of little consequence. The testimony offered at trial weighed heavily against the brothers. Stephen decided to follow his brother's lead. Hoping to slip the hangman's noose, he confessed that he had taken part in the killing but insisted that he acted in self-defense. It was to no avail. The jury quickly found the brothers guilty, and the three-judge panel sentenced them to death. In a specially convened session, the Vermont General Assembly considered a plea for clemency. Jesse's sentence was commuted to life because he appeared to be less culpable. Stephen would be hanged.

The brothers had been convicted, as it were, on the basis of a tip provided by a ghost, the misidentification of a bone as being human, the trumped-up testimony of a jailhouse snitch, the seven-year-old recollections of some neighbors, and two false confessions. Nevertheless, justice sometimes finds a way of slipping back in through the cracks. If the spectral appearance of an unexpected visitor was, at least in part, responsible for the brothers' arrest, a confluence of events almost as unlikely would lead to their salvation.

On a late November day in 1819, an item in *The New York Evening Post,* noting how divine intervention had helped bring Colvin's killers to justice, was being read out loud by a guest in the lobby of a New York hotel. A traveler from New Jersey, Tabor Chadwick, overheard the story. Chadwick knew a man named Russell Colvin who often spoke of Vermont and who had worked the last few years as a farmhand in Dover, New Jersey. He immediately sent a letter to *The Post* and one to the Manchester postmaster. In each letter he described Colvin as "a man of rather small stature—round forehead—[who] speaks very fast, has two scars on his head, and appears to be between 30 and 40 years of age."

Chadwick received no response from Manchester, perhaps because the postmaster, Leonard Sergeant, also happened to be the junior prosecutor in the case. *The Post* published the letter on December 6, 1819. James Whelpley, a native of Manchester living in New York at the time, read it and went to Dover where he found Colvin alive and well but unwilling to return to Vermont. Apparently familiar with the case, Whelpley knew Stephen's execution was scheduled for January 28, 1820. He enlisted the help of an attractive young woman to lure Colvin back to Manchester. She enticed him to accompany her to New York, but once there she abandoned him and Whelpley found it necessary to devise a new scheme. The War of 1812 had left a British presence around New York, and Whelpley told Colvin, who now wanted to return to New Jersey, that British ships were offshore and they would have to take a circuitous route back to Dover. He then urged Colvin onto a stagecoach headed in the opposite direction. It was bound for Manchester.

They arrived on December 22, 1819. Having heard of his impending arrival, a crowd of Colvin's former neighbors, including local officials, were waiting to greet him, no doubt interested to see if another ghost might be on the loose. Having convinced the authorities it was indeed the original Colvin who emerged from the stagecoach, the Boorn brothers were released. They had served seven years in prison; Stephen had come within a month of being hanged.

The first death-penalty exoneration in United States history had little overall effect. It was looked upon as a glitch in a criminal justice system that otherwise functioned pretty well. But as the years went by, it became apparent that the glitches were part of the system. Corrections were made, new laws were passed aimed at protecting the innocent from wrongful conviction, but each refinement turned a brighter light on the heart of the problem: it was not possible to achieve a high degree of certainty in a system that depended so heavily on the imperfections of human response and perceptions. Despite forensic advances, such as the use of fingerprinting in the latter part of the nineteenth century, the judging of guilt and innocence remained more an art than a science.

A significant shift in that balance occurred in 1989 with the awareness that DNA, which is in effect a molecular fingerprint, can be used to provide dead-certain evidence of a suspect's innocence. Since then, the scientific technique of DNA comparison has been used to free hundreds of innocent persons, many of them from death row. Perhaps of even greater consequence, the certainty introduced by DNA evidence has exposed the inefficiencies imbedded in the system. For if the innocence of hundreds of suspects wrongfully convicted could be firmly established by the presence of DNA, dare we contemplate how many others, perhaps thousands, have been convicted on false grounds when no DNA was present?

The causes of wrongful conviction are many. Most studies place eyewitness error or false accusation at the head of the list. Others are the snitch testimony of jailhouse informants; false confession, false forensics, sometimes called junk science; lack of credible evidence; and some form of official misconduct—prosecutorial, judicial or police— and, not infrequently, the absence of an adequate defense. Each of these causes will be examined in what follows, though it should be noted that virtually every case, regardless of the proximate cause of wrongful conviction, contains the taint of official misconduct. The incentive to cheat, to bend the rules in favor of conviction, is built into the system.

The principal focus of this book is on the exoneration of prisoners who have been freed from death row as that is where the stakes are highest. A later section deals with cases in which the wrongfully convicted served long terms, perhaps part of a life sentence, before being freed. Many of those cases played out in states that have abandoned capital punishment, but nonetheless sent innocent people to the penitentiary for extended periods of time, more often than not a product of some form of official corruption. Every case is an illustration of the grim consequences that ensue when the legal mechanism has gone awry. Freeing innocent people who have been incarcerated unjustly is no indication that the system really works. It shows only that it is badly broken and in serious need of repair.

PART I

Official Misconduct

THOSE WHO DO the arithmetic attest that eyewitness error accounts for more than half the wrongful convictions in the United States. If the identifications of jailhouse snitches are added to the mix, the total would be nearly two-thirds. But while false eyewitness testimony may be the proximate cause in most cases where the wrong man is sent to the death house, it is rarely sufficient to get a conviction. Corrupt practices, usually prosecutorial misconduct, are present in almost every instance, greasing the rails on which hundreds of innocent people are sent to death's door. Misidentifications are not always the honest mistakes of well-meaning citizens doing their civic duty. They are prompted by police eager for an arrest, orchestrated by prosecutors hungry for a conviction, nourished by judges who owe their seats to a public that has not outgrown its wistful nostalgia for frontier justice.

The corrupt practices of those who run the machinery of justice are not the aberrations of an otherwise sound system. They have been woven into the fabric of a social structure that often appears to presume guilt rather than innocence. The ideal of justice that once favored our best instincts has been turned against itself. The great fear of a politician or prosecutor is not that an innocent man may be convicted but that a guilty one might walk free. Which candidate seeking public office today will be ready to chance the prospect of being called soft on crime?

By most educated estimates, about 10 percent of the inhabitants of death row or inmates serving life sentences are innocent. They were put where they are by a combination of such corrupt practices as: police perjury, which has become so commonplace that defense attorneys often refer to testimony by police as "perjumony;" the false testimony offered by those who themselves are in trouble with the law—sometimes suspects, often already incarcerated—who receive favors in return for their fabrications; prosecutors who withhold evidence that might benefit the defense; incompetent or overworked defense lawyers, some of whom have been known to sleep through their clients' trials while presenting virtually no defense at all; and confessions that have been prompted or coerced from suspects who have little or no understanding of how the law works.

When a defendant is acquitted on the basis of such misconduct, there invariably ensues a public outcry that a guilty man may have been turned loose on a technicality. But in truth there are no technicalities, only laws designed to protect the innocent that have been skirted or twisted by those whose power has corrupted the system badly, albeit not yet absolutely.

The Death Row 10
Illinois

They became known as The Death Row 10. Their renown was not of long duration nor did it spread very far, but it earned them at least a footnote in the nation's grim struggle with its penal system. They were all prisoners on Illinois' death row who were alleged to have been beaten and tortured by former Chicago Police Commissioner Jon Burge and his detectives. Although they were not charged at the time, Burge and the detectives were forced into taking early retirement in 1993. Five years later, the ten men joined together inside prison and asked the Campaign to End the Death Penalty (CEDP), a national organization that worked at the grassroots level for the abolition of capital punishment, to help them organize.

The CEDP took their cases, and along with volunteer help from other groups including attorneys and students from the Bluhm Legal Clinic of the Northwestern University Law School, four of the men were exonerated. On January 10, 2003, Illinois Governor George Ryan pardoned Aaron Patterson, Madison Hobley, Leroy Orange, and Stanley Howard on the grounds that they had been physically coerced into confessing to crimes they did not commit. The following day, convinced that the four represented a system that had become totally corrupted, the governor commuted the sentences of all of the remaining 167 prisoners on Illinois' death row. On March, 9, 2011, he signed legislation ending capital punishment in the state of Illinois.

Ryan's action, audacious by any political standard, prompted a new debate regarding the application of capital punishment. Although only four of the ten were exonerated, the case of the Death Row 10 gave impetus to the abolition movement.

Aaron Patterson
Illinois

Back in the old neighborhood no one wanted to mess with Aaron Patterson. He was as tough as they came and his reputation as leader of Chicago's Apache Rangers street gang further embellished his tough-guy image. It was that image, no doubt, that contributed to his spending more than fifteen years of his young life on death row for a crime he did not commit.

The crime was the murder of an elderly couple, Vincent and Rafaela Sanchez, who were found stabbed to death in their home on the south side of Chicago in 1986. Patterson was arrested on the basis of a tip provided by a woman named Marva Hall who was the cousin of another suspect. Hall told the police Patterson had admitted to her that he had committed the murders. He was arrested eleven days after the victims' bodies were found. Four hours later he signed a confession. Indicted by a grand jury, he was eligible for the death penalty because there were multiple murders and the crime had taken place during the commission of a burglary, another felony.

Before the trial began, Patterson filed a motion to suppress his confession on the grounds that it had been coerced after four hours of police interrogation during which he had been severely tortured. The motion was denied in Cook County Circuit Court. Patterson's allegation of police abuse was made, in its own crude fashion, at the time of his interrogation. Left alone for about an hour after he promised to confess, Patterson had used a paper clip to etch a message into a metal bench. The message read: "Aaron 4/30 [the date of the interrogation] I lie about murders. Police threaten me with violence. Slapped and suffocated me with plastic. No lawyer or dad. No phone. Signed false statement to murders."

At trial, Patterson testified that he had been intermittently beaten and smothered with a plastic typewriter cover before agreeing to confess. After the brief respite during which he etched his note, Patterson said an officer brought Assistant State's Attorney Kip Owen into the room. Patterson asked if he could speak to Owen alone and the officer left. He told Owen that he had been tortured and asked for an attorney. Owen then left and summoned the officer to return. Patterson testified that the officer threatened him with further torture until he agreed to sign the confession drafted by Assistant State's Attorney Peter Troy. The officer, who was not named in court, was later identified as Jon Burge, at the time a lieutenant and later commander of the police unit. The three men involved in extracting the confession—Burge, Owen, and Troy—were not directly involved in the torture.

The jury wasted little time in returning a verdict of guilty. They also found no mitigating circumstances to prevent the imposition of the death penalty. An appeal to the Illinois Supreme Court brought no relief. It paid little heed to Patterson's charge of physical coercion. Yet, aside from Hall's dubious identification, there was no other evidence on which he could have been convicted, let alone sentenced to death—no forensic evidence, no murder weapon, no physical evidence of any kind. Further, his charge of torture by Burge and his crew could not have been seen as entirely baseless. Substantial evidence had accrued from as far back as the 1970s that they had used torture to extract confessions from scores of prisoners. Just five years before denying Patterson's appeal, the Supreme Court had ordered a new trial for Andrew Wilson, who had confessed to the murder of two Chicago police officers. Wilson said he had been physically coerced into confessing. He maintained that he had been cuffed to a hot radiator and that "electrical shocks had been administered to his gums, lips, and genitals." A doctor who examined him found "multiple bruises, swellings, and abrasions" and several "linear blisters."

Indications continued to grow that torture on the part of Chicago's police department was a common practice. In a civil rights case that followed, a jury found that the City of Chicago has a de facto policy allowing police to physically abuse suspects in cases in which police officers were killed or injured. In 1991, the year before Patterson lost his appeal, the Chicago Police Department's Office of Professional Standards had suspended Burge and two of his assistants following allegations of torture. The month after Patterson lost his appeal, US District Court Judge Milton I. Shadur ordered the release of a secret Chicago Police Department internal report, prepared in1990 by the Office of Professional Standards (OPS) cataloging more than fifty instances of "methodical" and "systematic" torture involving Burge's unit. Specific officers were named in thirty-five of the cases; Burge was personally named in more than half of them. A month later, the Chicago Police Board forced Burge to retire.

At around the same time, Patterson finally caught a break. G. Flint Taylor Jr., an attorney who six years earlier had helped prove that torture had been used in the Wilson case, stepped in and offered to represent Patterson. Marva Hall, whose identification of Patterson was the only evidence other than his confession to implicate him in the crime, had signed an affidavit saying that she had initially fabricated her testimony to protect her cousin. She also said she had tried to recant before testifying but decided against it when Assistant State's Attorney Jack Hynes threatened her with jail if she did.

Taylor filed a petition for post-conviction relief, asking Judge John E. Morrissey for an evidentiary hearing on Patterson's torture allegations growing out of the OPS report. Morrissey denied the petition, saying, "any nexus between Area 2 Chicago Police Department headquarters' alleged systemic torture of people and Aaron Patterson is highly tenuous at best." Taylor appealed, and in 2000 the Illinois Supreme Court concluded that "substantial new evidence supports defendant's claim that his confession was the result of police brutality" and ordered Morrissey to hold the hearing. However, months passed without a hearing being scheduled. At that point, a group of attorneys led by Locke E. Bowman of the Macarthur Justice Center at the University of Chicago Law School entered the case and demanded the appointment of a special prosecutor to investigate the allegations of torture. In April 2002, Presiding Judge Paul E. Biebel, of the Criminal Division of the Cook County Circuit Court, granted the request. In the meantime, Taylor had filed a petition with the Illinois Prisoner Review Board requesting a pardon for Patterson based on innocence. On January 10, 2003, Governor Ryan granted the request, touching off the clearing of Chicago's death row and the abolition of capital punishment in the state of Illinois.

In 2006, Cook County special prosecutors Edward Egan and Robert Boyle released the results of an independent investigation into the torture allegations against Burge. They found that Burge approved the torture of criminal suspects for two decades using methods such as electric shock, radiator burns, guns to mouth, and bags pulled over the head. In 2010, Burge was convicted of perjury and obstruction of justice for denying he had engaged in misconduct even though, according to the judge, there was a "mountain of evidence" indicating he had. Patterson and the three other Death Row 10 inmates who were freed settled their separate law suits against the city, agreeing to share a $19.8 million payout. But it was not all good news for Patterson. By the time the settlement had been reached, he had returned to prison on a federal gun and drug conviction.

Madison Hobley
Illinois

At about two in the morning on January 6, 1987, Madison Hobley was awakened by the smoke alarm in his apartment on East 82nd Street in Chicago. When he opened the door he saw a hall full of smoke. He told his wife, Anita, to get their fifteen-month-old son, Philip, and flee the apartment, but they never made it out. Hobley, shoeless and wearing only his underwear, got out safely. He went to his mother's home, about one mile from the scene. His wife and son perished, along with five other residents of the building.

Early the following morning, two detectives, Robert Dwyer and James Lotito, appeared at his mother's apartment. They told Hobley that the fire had been caused by arson and that they wanted to ask him some questions. Perhaps, they suggested, he might be able to help them identify the arsonists. According to police, Hobley was ready to cooperate and went with them to local police headquarters. Hobley later claimed he was given no choice about accompanying the detectives. At that point, their stories diverged markedly and events started to quickly move beyond Hobley's control.

The police said that following brief questioning at the Area 2 station, Hobley voluntarily went downtown with them to central police headquarters where he confessed to setting the fatal fire. Hobley's version of events was far different. After being taken downtown, he said, he was handcuffed to a chair and kicked by Sergeant Patrick Garrity; then Dwyer, Lotito, and Detective Daniel McWeeney placed a plastic typewriter cover over his head and suffocated him until he blacked out. He said he never confessed.

The case against Hobley was, at best, fragile. Most critically, there was no evidence of a confession. Dwyer said he took notes as Hobley admitted his guilt but inadvertently spilled something on the pages and threw them away when the ink ran. At trial, no tangible evidence of a confession, neither written nor recorded, was submitted. The police testified that Hobley told them that on the night of the fire he took a can to a nearby filling station, bought a dollar's worth of gasoline, and emptied the can in the hallway outside his third-floor apartment and down the stairwell. Then he set a match to the gasoline and tossed the can down in the second-floor hallway.

The gasoline can being the only physical evidence linking Hobley to the crime, the prosecutors produced two witnesses who testified that they saw Hobley buying the gasoline. Andre Council, a customer at the station, testified that he was pumping gas when he saw a man make the purchase. About an hour later, he went to the fire scene, about half a mile from the station, where he saw the man who had purchased the gas. The next day, he saw a photo of Hobley on television, recognized him as the same man, and called the police. The station attendant, Kenneth Stewart, testified that a man had bought a gallon of gas at his station, but failed to identify Hobley in a police lineup. Coaxed by police to choose someone, Stewart selected Hobley as the most likely but said he was uncertain.

With no tangible evidence and only a tenuous identification to support their case, the prosecution produced a two-gallon gas can that another detective, John Paladino, said he found at the fire scene. But even that turned out to be problematic. Detective Virgil Mikus, who testified as an arson expert, told the jury that a burn pattern on the floor in front of the Hobley apartment indicated that gasoline had been poured there, but tests had shown no traces of gasoline in the area. He surmised that it must have been washed away by firefighters when they extinguished the blaze. Critically, Hobley's fingerprints were not found on the can, but that bit of information was withheld by the prosecution until some years later.

The jury found Hobley guilty and found no mitigating circumstances that would preclude the death penalty, which the judge imposed. Four years later, in 1994, the Illinois Supreme Court upheld the conviction and the sentence. The following year, Hobley's appellate attorneys—Professor Andrea Lyon, of the DePaul University College of Law, and Kurt H. Feuer—filed a petition for post-conviction relief in the Circuit Court alleging that the authorities had illegally withheld a forensic report stating that Hobley's fingerprints were not found on the gasoline can. The existence of such a report had been denied by police witnesses during the trial. The defense team also charged that other reports, one of which claimed that police had destroyed a second gasoline can found at the scene, had been suppressed. In total, the reports suggested that the can introduced into evidence had been planted there and that the fire had been set by someone other than Hobley. All the same, Circuit Court Judge Dennis J. Porter denied the petition without a hearing. In 1998, however, the Illinois Supreme Court reversed Porter and remanded the case for an evidentiary hearing. The court stated: "At defendant's trial, the defense theory was that another person had started the fire. The negative fingerprint report and the existence of a second gasoline can found at the fire scene certainly would have offered concrete evidentiary support to that defense theory."

The hearing sputtered along for more than two years. Bits and pieces of new evidence, most of it marginal, were introduced. The only defense chip of real consequence was the claim that the gasoline can introduced at trial had been planted at the scene. That case was made by an arson expert retained by the defense, Russell Ogel, of Packer Engineering. Ogel testified that the can showed no signs of exposure to the extreme heat that had destroyed other items in the area. Even the plastic cap was unharmed. Ogel also challenged the prosecution's contention that there were burn patterns on the third floor of the building. In fact, Ogel said, tests indicated the fire had started in a stairwell on a lower floor. Judge Porter was unmoved. "There is no showing," he said, "the favorable evidence could reasonably be taken to put the whole case in such a different light as to undermine confidence in the verdict." He denied Hobley a new trial.

Lyon and Feuer appealed and filed a petition with the Illinois Prisoner Review Board seeking a full pardon based on innocence. The board heard Hobley's petition in October 2002. Three months later, Governor Ryan granted the pardon. "Madison Hobley was convicted on the basis of flawed evidence," he said. "He was convicted because the jury did not have the benefit of all existing evidence, which would have served to exonerate him."

Hobley had spent thirteen years on death row.

Leroy Orange
Illinois

Leroy Orange didn't stand a chance. He was initially implicated in the murder of four people by his half brother, Leonard Kidd, and then virtually led to death row by his attorney, Earl Washington. In between, he was subjected to the same treatment as the other members of the Death Row 10, his confession physically extorted by Jon Burge and his crew by means of beating, suffocation, and electroshock. The crime he was convicted of was the murder of four people—two women, a man, and a child whose bodies were found in an apartment on Chicago's South Side. They had been bound and stabbed, and two fires had been set in the apartment.

Orange was convicted primarily on the basis of his confession. The only corroboration was a statement by Kidd which said Orange was responsible for the murders. Kidd recanted his statement prior to the trial, saying it was made following a torture session similar to the one accorded Orange. He also testified as a defense witness at Orange's trial and, against the advice of counsel, admitted that he himself was guilty of the murders.

Orange and Kidd had been arrested on January 12, 1984, the day after the bodies of Renee Coleman, Michelle Jointer, Ricardo Pedro, and Coleman's ten-year-old son, Tony, were found bound and stabbed. Kidd initially told police that he and Orange had been in Coleman's apartment in the early hours of January 11 and that Orange and Pedro had gotten into a heated argument. Fearing the argument might turn violent, Kidd said he left the apartment and waited outside. He said he saw "two dudes" armed with knives enter the apartment and later saw them leave, one wearing a jacket drenched in blood. Soon after Kidd made his statement, Orange confessed. The police then brought the two men face to face, and Kidd changed his story. He said he had lied about seeing the two other men and that Orange had killed the victims. He led police to garbage cans where they found two knives used in the crimes. Both men were indicted by a Cook County grand jury and remanded to jail. Orange continued to proclaim his innocence. He told his cellmate, a physician who examined him, relatives and friends who visited him, the public defender assigned to the case, and the judge before whom he was arraigned that he had been tortured and forced to confess.

Both Orange and Kidd were qualified to be represented by the public defender's office, but their family chose to retain private counsel. It was a mistake. They retained Earl Washington to represent both defendants despite an obvious conflict of interest. Three months later, Washington withdrew from the Kidd case and, to all appearances, he might just as well have withdrawn from Orange's case. He filed a motion to suppress his client's confession, but it was denied as being inadequate. Give the opportunity to file a more detailed motion, he failed to do so.

At the 1985 trial, Orange testified that he had been with the victims earlier that night, but had left at around 2:30 a.m., when all were alive. Kidd then testified on Orange's behalf and said he had committed the murders after Orange had left the apartment. The only evidence remaining against Orange was his confession. To no one's surprise, the police officers denied torturing either suspect. A jail physician testified that she had discovered no signs of torture. The jury found Orange guilty. Washington stipulated to his client's eligibility for the death penalty. Asked to offer any evidence in mitigation, Washington said there was none. The judge sentenced Orange to death.

At this point, Thomas F. Geraghty, director of the Bluhm Legal Clinic of Northwestern University Law School, along with clinic students, entered the case. They filed a petition for a new sentencing hearing. The hearing was pending when Governor Ryan granted Orange a full pardon based on innocence, criticizing prosecutors and the judiciary for relying on "procedural technicalities at the exclusion of the quest for truth" throughout the case. As for Kidd, he spent much of the next eighteen years on a rollercoaster ride through the judicial system. His death sentence was overturned and then reaffirmed. He remained on death row until Ryan commuted his sentence in 2003 to life in prison without the possibility of parole.

Stanley Howard
Illinois

Like Leroy Orange, Stanley Howard had to wait until Ryan cleared death row in 2003 before being exonerated. He served more than eighteen years for the 1984 murder of Oliver Ridgell, who was shot to death while sitting in his car on the South Side of Chicago. Also, like Orange, Howard's conviction was based on a confession extracted in like manner and a faulty eyewitness identification. The identification was provided by Tecora Mullen, who was seated alongside Ridgell at the time of the crime and with whom she was believed to be having an affair. Howard was not arrested until six months later when he was picked up on an unrelated charge, the armed robbery of two Chicago police officers two years earlier. He was not suspected of the Ridgell murder until two days after his arrest, when police noted he fit the description provided by Mullen.

Howard was first tried and convicted on the armed robbery charge and sentenced to twenty-eight years in prison. At his murder trial, the judge denied Howard's motion to suppress his confession which, Howard contended, had been beaten out of him. Aside from the confession, the only evidence the prosecution had was Tecora Mullen's identification, which was clearly suspect as it might have been fabricated to protect her husband. The jury returned a verdict of guilty and Howard was sentenced to death.

While on death row, Howard helped organize the Death Row 10.

Although pardoned on the murder charge, he remained convicted in the armed robbery case and faces imprisonment until 2023.

Glenn Ford
Louisiana

"My sons, when I left, was babies. Now they're grown men with babies . . . I've been locked up almost thirty years for something I didn't do."

Glenn Ford, one of the longest-serving death row inmates in modern American history, spent three decades in the maximum-security prison at Angola, Louisiana, before being exonerated in 2014 at the age of sixty-four. According to the Capital Post Conviction Project of Louisiana, new information corroborated what Ford had said from the beginning: he was not present or involved in the November 5, 1983 slaying of Isadore Rozeman.

Rozeman, a fifty-six-year-old jeweler and watchmaker, was found shot to death behind the counter of his shop in Shreveport, Louisiana. He appeared to be the victim of a robbery. Ford, who did yard work for Rozeman, was among the first to be questioned. Thirty-four years old at the time, married and the father of two sons, Ford said he had been in the vicinity of the store earlier in the day and several witnesses told police they saw him there.

Events started closing in on Ford a few months later, in February, when some items from Rozeman's store turned up in a pawnshop and a handwriting analyst said it was Ford's signature on the pawn slips. More critically, a woman by the name of Marvella Brown came forth and told police her boyfriend, Jake Robinson, along with Jake's brother, Henry, and Ford were at her house when Ford asked the other two men if they were going with him. They left together, she said, and Ford was carrying a brown paper bag. When they returned later that day, Ford was carrying a different bag which contained some watches and rings. He had a gun in his waistband. Jake also was carrying a gun. Later that month, Ford, Jake and Henry Robinson, and a fourth man, George Starks, were arrested and charged with capital murder and conspiracy to commit armed robbery.

From that point on, what had been a bad dream for Ford morphed into a nightmare. He was the first of the four to be tried. The case against him was virtually non-existent. No murder weapon was ever found. There were no eyewitnesses to the crime. Glenn Ford was about to fall victim to the charade that often passed for justice in the South, particularly when it was a black man who was on trial. Prosecutors used their jury challenges to eliminate any black candidates and an all-white jury was empanelled. Ford was represented by two court-appointed defense attorneys. His lead attorney had never tried a case before a jury. His assistant, two years out of law school, worked at an insurance firm and had never been involved in a criminal case of any kind. They failed to hire any expert witnesses because they believed, incorrectly, that they would have to pay their expenses themselves. A state expert who testified about the victim's time of death had never examined the body. One of the prosecution witnesses testified at trial that police had helped her make up her story.

As weak as the state's case was, the testimony of its witnesses seemed to compound its frailty. Under cross-examination, Marvella Brown, the state's key witness, said detectives had led her to shape her responses. Brown told the court she had been shot in the head some years ago, that the bullet had never been removed, and that she had difficulty thinking and hearing. A gunshot residue expert said Ford had voluntarily come in for questioning and he found gunshot residue on his hands. A fingerprint analyst said he lifted a single print from a paper bag found at the scene and the print contained a "whorl" pattern consistent with a Ford print, while prints from the Robinson brothers showed no such pattern. Dr. George McCormick, the parish coroner who failed to examine the corpse, testified that the position of Rozeman's body and a duffel bag with a bullet hole in it found next to the body led him to conclude that the victim was shot by someone who held the gun in his left hand; Ford was left-handed, the Robinson brothers were not. Testifying on his own behalf, Ford denied any involvement in the crime. He admitted selling some items of jewelry to the pawnbroker but said he had gotten them from the Robinson brothers.

The prosecution's case was good enough for the jury. Ford was convicted of capital murder and conspiracy to commit armed robbery on December 5, 1984 and, on the jury's recommendation, he was sentenced to death. The prosecution dismissed the charges against the Robinson brothers and Starks. A round of appeals by Ford was unsuccessful until 2000 when the Louisiana Supreme Court ordered a hearing on a post-conviction petition for a new trial filed by the Capital Post-Conviction Project of Louisiana. The hearing was not held until 2004, but Ford's new attorneys, Gary Clements and Aaron Novod, were well-prepared. An array of defense witnesses contested virtually every piece of evidence presented at trial.

An expert testified that the coroner's reconstruction of the crime was based entirely on speculation and bore no connection to the facts. Another defense expert noted that the gunshot residue was irrelevant because it was gathered more than a day after the crime and could easily have been picked up elsewhere, including the police station when Ford was arrested. Yet another said that the prosecution's fingerprint expert misidentified the print on the paper bag and that it could well have belonged to one of the Robinson brothers. Ford's trial lawyers also testified and were of more help to him than they were at his trial. They testified that between them they had little or no experience in criminal cases. The more experienced of the two, who specialized in oil and gas law, had never tried a case before a jury. His criminal work was limited to handling two guilty pleas. His associate had spent his two years since graduating from law school dealing with personal injury cases. Both acknowledged that they knew nothing about the funding of expert witnesses and did not know how to issue a subpoena. Members of Ford's family, who lived in California, were not brought to testify on his behalf at either the guilt or punishment phase of the trial because the attorneys were unaware that the state would pay their travel expenses.

In addition to the expert testimony, the defense produced a number of reports that had been withheld at trial which would have served Ford's interest. The reports showed that Shreveport police had received two tips from informants indicating that only the Robinson brothers were involved in the crime. Other reports suggested that some detectives had falsely testified at trial about statements made by Ford during his interrogation. Still others contained conflicting statements by Marvella Brown and by witnesses who said they had seen Ford near the store at the time of the crime. Despite the exculpatory evidence presented at the hearing, the post-conviction motion was denied.

Eight years later, in 2012, the Capital Post-Conviction Project filed a federal petition for a writ of habeas corpus. While the petition was pending, the district attorney's office initiated a new investigation. It discovered that a confidential informant for the sheriff's office had told authorities that Jake Robinson had admitted shooting Rozeman. In March 2014, the prosecution filed a motion to vacate Ford's conviction on the basis of the new evidence provided by the informant. A judge complied, the prosecution dismissed the charges, and Ford was freed. Under Louisiana law, he received $330,000 in compensation, an average of $11,000 a year, for serving thirty years in prison.

A year short of retirement age on his release, Ford was asked by a reporter if he harbored any resentment. "Yeah," he said, "because I was locked up almost thirty years for something I didn't do. Thirty years of my life, if not all of it; I can't go back and do nothing I should have been doing when I was thirty-five, thirty-eight, forty, stuff like that." He also said, "My mind's going all kinds of directions, but it feels good."

Ford was the 144th death row prisoner to be exonerated since 1973 when a de facto moratorium on capital punishment went into effect. His case was among those featured on CNN's series *Death Row Stories* in 2014.

Ford died of lung cancer on June 29, 2015. His death led to an examination of Louisiana's criminal justice system and, on a broader scale, an initiative calling for the abolition of the death penalty.

Joe D'Ambrosio
Ohio

The case of Joe D'Ambrosio was another of CNN's Death Row Stories. D'Ambrosio, an Army veteran, spent twenty years on Ohio's death row for the 1988 murder of nineteen-year-old Tony Klann, whose body was found in a Cleveland Creek. He had been stabbed to death. D'Ambrosio was convicted largely on the testimony of another suspect in the case, Ed Espinoza, who also implicated a third man, Michael Keenan. Keenan was given a twelve-year-sentence; D'Ambrosio was sent to death row. The three men were involved in a sordid series of events involving a mutual acquaintance by the name of Paul "Stoney" Lewis who they said had stolen drugs from them. Believing Klann could help them find Lewis, the trio forced him into their truck and drove around the neighborhood in search of their quarry. When they failed to locate him, Espinoza said, Keenan slashed Klann's throat and then D'Ambrosio stabbed him to death in a creek in Cleveland. D'Ambrosio was convicted and sentenced to death by a three-judge panel.

The appeal process ground through the judicial system to no avail. It was D'Ambrosio's good fortune that his case came to the attention of a Roman Catholic priest by the name of Neil Kookoothe. Kookoothe was a man of many disciplines, all of which were brought to bear on D'Ambrosio's behalf. He had graduated with a communications degree in the early 1980s. He then went to nursing school and worked as a licensed nurse at a hospital intensive care unit in Toledo. While working at the hospital, he put himself through law school and later worked as an attorney in Indiana. From the beginning, however, Kookoothe had been attracted to the priesthood, and after practicing nursing and law he went to seminary school and settled in as a man of the cloth. In his capacity as a cleric, he counseled a man on death row and served as a witness to his execution. As described by CNN, Kookoothe watched "the man's face turn beet red as lethal fluid ran through his veins. Beads of sweat glistened on his forehead. Strapped to a table, his chest and stomach heaved three or four times." Then, he was gone. "It's surreal when you know that the state is killing him," Kookoothe said. Having watched several other executions, he became a student of "state-sanctioned death" and an opponent of the death penalty.

It was his medical training that first drew him into D'Ambrosio's case. He noted that Klann's knife wounds were inconsistent with Espinoza's story. He understood, too, that Klann could not have screamed after his throat was cut, as Espinoza had testified. "If this is wrong, what else might be wrong?" he wondered. Kookoothe interested a local newspaper reporter, Martin Kuz, in the case. Klann's father told Kuz that shortly before his son's death, he had been subpoenaed as a witness in a rape case. Now, Kookoothe put his legal training to work. He searched the case files and learned that the suspect in the rape case, for which Klann had been summoned to testify, was Paul "Stoney" Lewis, the man Espinoza said they were looking for on the night of the murder. Klann apparently had been a witness to the rape.

Further investigation by Kookoothe found that D'Ambrosio had no motive to kill Klann and there was nothing connecting him to the murder. In 2006, a US Appeals Court judge ruled that prosecutors had "failed to disclose that Lewis was being investigated, and had earlier been indicted, for a rape to which Klann was a witness." The evidence the state withheld, the court wrote, "would have . . . increased a reasonable juror's doubt of D'Ambrosio's guilt." The judge overturned his conviction.

The prosecution attempted to retry the case, but the same Federal District Court that threw out his conviction barred the state from retrying him because the prosecutors' misconduct had biased D'Ambrosio's chances for a fair trial. District Court Judge Kathleen O'Malley wrote: "For 20 years, the State held D'Ambrosio on death row, despite withholding evidence that would have substantially increased a reasonable juror's doubt of D'Ambrosio's guilt. Despite being ordered to do so by this Court . . . the State still failed to turn over all relevant and material evidence relating to the crime of which D'Ambrosio was convicted. Then, once it was ordered to provide D'Ambrosio a constitutional trial or release him within 180 days, the State did neither. During those 180 days, the State engaged in substantial inequitable conduct, wrongfully retaining and then delaying the production of yet more potentially exculpatory evidence . . . To fail to bar retrial in such extraordinary circumstances sure would fail to serve the interests of justice."

The case finally was brought to conclusion on January 23, 2012, when the US Supreme Court declined to hear an appeal by the state of Ohio. Even before the Supreme Court ruling, the D'Ambrosio case had far reaching consequences. It initiated calls for Ohio to adopt "open-discovery laws" to force prosecutors to share more of its findings with defense attorneys. New legislation went into effect in 2010.

Nathson Fields
Illinois

When it comes to official misconduct, few cases can match the conviction of Nathson Fields, a member of a Chicago street gang, who served almost twenty years in prison, more than half of it on death row, for the shooting death of two rival gang members. The judge in the case was convicted of taking a bribe; the two eyewitnesses who identified Fields were members of the same gang as the victims; his co-defendant testified against him in exchange for a lighter sentence; two key trial witnesses said they had been coerced into testifying by police and prosecutors; and a police officer was found to have tampered with the evidence.

The killings took place in April 1984. Talman Hickman and Jerome Smith, members of the Black Gangster Disciples street gang, were shot dead on the streets of Chicago. No arrests were made for more than a year. In June 1985, Fields, a thirty-one-year-old member of the rival El Rukn gang, was arrested after being identified in a police lineup although he bore little resemblance to the description police had been given of the shooter. Fields was wearing a short-sleeve shirt, and an El Rukn tattoo was prominently displayed on his forearm. The police were unaware at the time that the two men who picked him from the lineup belonged to the Black Gangster Disciples.

Fields was charged with first-degree murder, along with a fellow El Rukn gang member, Earl Hawkins. Both men were convicted in a 1986 bench trial and sentenced to death by Judge Thomas Maloney. A year later, Hawkins received a reduced sentence and was freed from death row when he agreed to testify against other gang members in unrelated cases. Fields, who negotiated no deal, remained on death row and, in 1990, the Illinois Supreme Court upheld his conviction and sentence.

Then, in an incredible turn of events, both Fields's conviction and sentence were called to question when Judge Maloney was convicted of taking bribes following a federal judicial corruption investigation. Among other things, Maloney was charged with accepting $10,000 from Hawkins's lawyer, William Swano, to acquit his client of murdering Smith and Hickman. According to FBI evidence, Maloney, having learned of the investigation during the trial, returned the money to Swano and convicted Hawkins along with Fields.

Given Maloney's conviction, Cook County Circuit Court Judge Vincent Gaughan ordered a new trial for Fields in 1996. While the trial was pending, two witnesses who had testified against Fields recanted. Gerald Morris and Randy Langston, who stated they had seen Fields and Hawkins gun down the two victims outside a public housing project, signed affidavits saying their testimony had been coerced by police and prosecutors. They now said they had witnessed the shooting but could not identify the killers because both men wore masks.

Continued appeals by the prosecution delayed the retrial for another six years. Fields remained in custody until he was released on bond in 2003 while awaiting the new trial. When it finally took place, Hawkins testified against Fields in exchange for a plea to a lesser charge and a lighter sentence. However, his testimony did not serve him well. Under cross-examination by Fields's attorney, Jean Maclean Snyder, Hawkins admitted that he had been involved in at least fifteen homicides during his years as an El Rukn member. As a result, Judge Gaughan found his testimony unworthy of belief. He said: "If someone has such disregard for human life, what regard will he have for his oath? I find him incredible."

Fields was given a Certificate of Innocence in 2009. He had served eighteen years in prison, eleven of them on death row. Fields filed a federal lawsuit against the City of Chicago for wrongful conviction. Years after he was cleared, a police file connected to his case, which was said to be missing, was discovered in an old filing cabinet in the basement of a South Side police station. Police and prosecutors had denied the file existed, but Fields's lawyers claimed it was deliberately hidden because it contained evidence that might have cleared Fields sooner. The newly discovered file was in a file cabinet with unsolved cases dating back to 1944. In April 2014, the jury rejected Fields's claim that he was framed as a result of policies and practices of the Chicago police. Charges against the City, two policemen, and a prosecutor were denied, but the jury found that one cop, David O'Callaghan, had violated Fields's right to due process by withholding or fabricating evidence. Trial testimony suggested that police had backdated statements and may have manipulated lineups in an effort to convict Fields. In the end, Fields was awarded $199,150 by the Illinois Appellate Court.

Judge Maloney, who was sentenced to fifteen years for fixing three murder trials, served more than twelve years. A few months after his release in 2008, he died at the age of eighty-three.

Harold Wilson
Pennsylvania

For Harold Wilson, the third time was the charm. After a trial in which he was convicted of three first-degree murders and sentenced to death; after a second which ended in a mistrial; he was finally acquitted and set free. But by that time he had spent more than sixteen years in prison, most of the time on death row.

Wilson, thirty years old, was accused of committing three grisly murders on April 10, 1988. The three victims—sixty-four-year-old Dorothy Sewell; her thirty-three-year-old nephew, Tyrone Mason; and Mason's forty-year-old girlfriend Cynthia Goines—had been hacked to death with a carpenter's ax and stabbed with an ice pick in Sewell's Philadelphia home. Wilson, who had been staying with Sewell the previous few days, was arrested the day after the bodies were discovered when he was found to have cuts on his hands and an envelope stuffed with cash that was believed to be drug-related. Although he admitted using drugs, Wilson denied any connection to the killings. There was little evidence linking him to the crimes. At his 1989 trial, police testified that they had found a jacket spattered with the victims' blood in the basement of Wilson's home. Wilson testified that he had found the victims' bodies while he was high on drugs and that he had gotten the blood on his jacket while trying to remove an ice pick from Mason's chest. He was given three death sentences, one for each of the murders.

Wilson's salvation, delayed though it was, came by way of the back alleys of Philadelphia politics. He had been prosecuted by Philadelphia District Attorney Jack McMahon, a circumstance that would grease the skids to his being freed from death row. In 1997, eight years after Wilson's conviction, the courts began an examination of Philadelphia's jury-selection process. The investigation was prompted when Lynne Abraham, who was running against McMahon in a tight re-election campaign, released a training video to the media showing McMahon instructing new prosecutors to keep poor blacks off juries because they were less likely to convict. An excerpt from the video was broadcast by investigative journalist Amy Goodman on *Democracy Now!*, a non-profit, syndicated news hour that airs simultaneously on satellite and cable television, radio, and the Internet. The videotape, which was played during an interview with Harold Wilson, shows McMahon instructing his colleagues on the proper selection of a jury:

"[Inaudible] to get a competent, fair and impartial jury. Well, that's ridiculous. You are there to win, and in order to win—and the defense is there to win, too—and the only way you're going to do your best is to get jurors that are as unfair and more likely to convict than anybody else in that room. Let's face it again. There's the blacks from the low-income areas are less likely to convict . . . There's a resentment for law enforcement, there's a resentment for authority, and as a result, you don't want those people on your jury, and it may appear as if you're being a racist or whatnot, but again, you are just being realistic, you're just trying to win the case."

While the actions of the prosecuting attorney might have precipitated a deeper examination of Wilson's conviction, it was the inaction of his own attorney, Willis Berry, that freed Wilson from death row. In 1999, Wilson's death sentence was set aside on the grounds of ineffective counsel when a trial-level court determined that his attorney had failed to investigate and present mitigating evidence during the penalty phase of his original trial. Although his death sentence was overturned, Wilson's convictions on the murder charges were not, and he remained on death row.

In 2003, Wilson was granted a new trial when a judge found that McMahon had exercised his peremptory challenges in a discriminatory manner to keep blacks from serving on the jury. The new trial ended in a mistrial; the third trial began on October 31, 2005. It lasted less than a month. Now armed for the first time with DNA evidence, the defense showed that the blood on the jacket was that of the victims and an unidentified male. Wilson's DNA was nowhere to be found. Since the blood on the jacket was the only evidence linking Wilson to the murders, the jurors wasted little time in returning a verdict of not guilty.

Wilson described his feelings on hearing the verdict to Amy Goodman:

"Yeah, I'm standing, my two defense attorneys are standing, the district attorney is standing. And the floor person reads the verdict, and I believe the court crier says, 'On the charge of first-degree murder . . . how do you find the defendant? Say you are not guilty or guilty?' They said, 'Not guilty.' They say, 'On the second count of first-degree murder, say how do you—say how do you find the defendant, guilty or not guilty?' They said, 'Not guilty.' And I never heard anything else. My attorneys just asked the court could I be seated because I broke down. And I was seated. The next time I remember I was being escorted out of the courtroom into a holding cell. And the verdict was not guilty, three counts of first-degree murder, and not guilty of possession of an instrument of crime. So, my prayers were answered, my family's prayers, my mother's, my sister's, my brother's prayers were answered."

When Wilson was sent to prison, his son was two years old. When he was released, his son was a member of the Marine Corps, having served a tour of duty in Iraq. His daughter, a year younger, was a prison guard in Arizona. Wilson, now a middle-aged man, left prison with sixty-five cents and a token in his pocket. "Where does that leave you today?" Amy Goodman asked him.

"That leaves me as an exonerated former death-row prisoner. That leaves me to fend for myself, to survive at a level higher than a homeless person, because at this time I don't know where my next meal coming from, other than the support of family. I don't have any financial income. I don't have any work. It wasn't like I was being released and placed in a halfway house. It's not like being told that you have to report to a parole officer in seventy-two hours or you will be re-arrested. It's like, you know, after eighteen years of dealing with the injustice system, all the abuse—the physical, mental abuse—I'm placed back in society with nothing, just the shelter of my family."

When Wilson was freed, Willis Berry, the attorney whose ineffective counsel sent him to prison, was serving as a judge.

Gordon "Randy" Steidl
Illinois

"I'm laying this cross down today. I'm not carrying it anymore." Those were the words of Gordon "Randy" Steidl when he left Danville Correctional Center in Danville, Illinois, in the spring of 2004. The cross he bore was of no slight dimension. Steidl, now fifty-two years old, had spent seventeen years behind bars, including a dozen on death row, for a crime he did not commit. The crime was the brutal murder of a couple of newlyweds, Karen and Dyke Rhoads, whose bodies were found in their bedroom in downtown Paris, Illinois, in July of 1986. They had been stabbed to death and their house had been set afire following the attack, presumably to destroy any evidence. Steidl's conviction was based on the erratic testimony of two alcoholics and a jailhouse snitch, and sealed by shoddy police work and the ineffective counsel of his attorney.

The police had no viable leads in the case for two months. That changed in September when a local alcoholic and petty criminal, Darrell Herrington, came forth and told them that he had accompanied Steidl and a man by the name of Herbert Whitlock when they went to the Rhoads's home that July morning. Herrington said he heard the various parties arguing, and later saw a knife, blood, and the bodies of the victims. The police did not take Herrington's story seriously and for good reason. He admitted he was stone drunk when the crimes occurred and he removed all doubt when he failed a lie detector test.

Five months later, in February 1987, police heard a more credible story from Deborah Rienbolt, a certified nurse's aide, who told them that on the night before the murders she had seen Whitlock, whom she knew, in a bar arguing with Dyke Rhoads about backing out of a deal they had made. She also said that later that night, in another bar, she saw Whitlock with a knife she had previously loaned him and which he returned the day after the murders. More tellingly, she said she heard him say he was going to "take care of a few people [who] knew too much" and mentioned the name of Karen Rhoads. Rienbolt further said that later that night, at yet another bar, she met Whitlock and Steidl and went with them to the Rhoads house where she witnessed the killings. She added that she had seen one of the killers beat one of the victims with a broken lamp.

Given Rienbolt's statements, which in some respects, corroborated those of Herrington, the police felt they had enough of a case to charge the two suspects. Three weeks after their arrest, both Steidl and Whitlock were indicted by a grand jury for the murder of both victims. The two men were tried separately. Both testified that they had nothing to do with the murders. They admitted that they had been to several bars looking for women, but they said they had not seen either Rienbolt or Herrington. The women they were with confirmed their accounts of the night's events. Aside from the testimony of Rienbolt and Herrington, the jury heard from a jailhouse snitch, Ferlin Wells, who said Steidl had told him about the murders and said that if he thought Herrington would go to the police, "he would have definitely taken care of him." The testimony of Herrington, Rienbolt, and Wells was the heart of the prosecution's case. The only bit of forensic evidence was the broken lamp which was found at the scene of the crime.

As weak as the state's case was, the defense offered virtually nothing in Steidl's behalf. His attorney failed to call a number of witnesses whose testimony almost certainly would have buttressed his case and Whitlock's as well: a supervisor who would have said that Rienbolt was at work on the night in question, not out carousing in bars; a friend of Rienbolt's who also would have contradicted her account of where he was that night; and a forensic pathologist who would have told the jury that the knife Rienbolt said she had given Whitlock could not have been the murder weapon because the blade was too short. Steidl was convicted of both murders and sentenced to death. Whitlock was convicted of killing Karen Rhoads but acquitted of Dyke's murder. He was sentenced to life in prison.

After a series of state appeals were denied, Steidl's case began to take on the feel of a carnival atmosphere. Herrington and Rienbolt both recanted their testimony. In November 1988, Herrington testified under oath before a court reporter that his testimony was not completely true. Police, he said, had encouraged him to change critical parts of his story. Two months later, Rienbolt came forward and confessed that her story also had been fabricated. But within two weeks, both recanted their recantations and signed affidavits that their original stories were true. Fortunately for Steidl, help was on the way.

A new attorney, Michael Metnick, and his investigator, began reviewing his case. Rienbolt contacted them in 1996 and said she was ready to offer yet another version of the crime, this time, she assured them, the unvarnished truth. They videotaped her statement on February 17 and part of the video was shown on an episode of *48 Hours* on CBS. Nonetheless, five days later she recanted all the statements she had made on network television.

But yet another group of investigators was now on the case. A team of students from Northwestern University's Medill School of Journalism found several witnesses police had failed to interview. Complicating matters further, Lieutenant Michael Callahan of the Illinois State Police, had been assigned to reinvestigate the case, and he concluded that both Steidl and Whitlock were innocent. He also noted that the prosecutors had not considered other suspects. In addition, fire investigators determined that the broken lamp, the state's only piece of hard evidence, had been intact during the crime and was broken by firefighters while attempting to extinguish the blaze.

On December 11, 1996, the Illinois Supreme Court denied Steidl's appeal for a new trial but granted a new sentencing hearing on the ground that his attorney provided ineffective counsel at the sentencing phase of the trial. On February 18, 1999, Steidl was resentenced to life in prison when prosecutors declined to pursue the death penalty. Both he and Whitlock filed petitions for writs of habeas corpus. Whitlock's request was denied, but on June 17, 2003, US District Court Judge Michael McCuskey ruled that in Steidl's case "acquittal was reasonably probable if the jury had heard all of the evidence." Declaring that Steidl's trial attorney, S. John Muller, failed to purse exculpatory evidence, Judge McCuskey ordered the state to either retry Steidl or release him. The prosecution chose not to pursue the case and dismissed the charges against him on May 28, 2004. Whitlock remained behind bars for more than three additional years until the Illinois Appellate Court reversed his conviction, holding that exculpatory evidence had been withheld in his case as well. The charges against him were dropped in January 2008.

Upon his release, Steidl, now fifty-two years old, filed a federal civil lawsuit against several law enforcement agencies, arguing that his constitutional rights were violated in a seventeen-year conspiracy involving the Paris Police Department, the Illinois State Police, and the Edgar County State's Attorney's Office. Whitlock joined the suit later. The multiple defendants argued that the lawsuit should be thrown out; the judge for the federal Seventh Circuit Court of Appeals demurred. "If their claims are true," the court's opinion read, "a grave and nearly unbelievable miscarriage of justice occurred in Paris, Illinois. Two innocent men will have to deal with its consequences for the rest of their lives."

In October 2011, the Illinois State Police portion of the suit was settled, with Steidl being awarded $2.5 million. On March 28, 2013, a federal judge entered a $3.5 million agreed-upon judgment against Paris police chief Gene Ray, former lead detective James Parrish, and former Edgar County State's Attorney Michael McFatridge, making for a total award of $6 million. Commenting on the settlement, Flint Taylor, one of Steidl's attorneys, said, "I think it affirms what the evidence has shown, which is that Steidl was innocent of the crime which he was convicted for and that he suffered terribly for being wrongfully convicted."

Despite the settlement agreement, none of the defendants admitted any wrongdoing.

Seth Penalver
Florida

The crime was there for all to see, all three murders right there on the tape. Casmir Sucharski, one of the victims, had installed a video surveillance system in his Miramar, Florida home eight days earlier, and the tape told the tale. At 7:18 on the morning of June 26, 1994, two men, one wearing a shirt over his head and the other a cap and sunglasses, entered the house through a sliding door. There, they confronted Sucharski, forty-eight, the owner of Casey's Nickelodeon, a restaurant in Pembroke Park; twenty-five-year-old Marie Rogers, and a friend of hers, Sharon Anderson, also twenty-five. Sucharski was beaten by the two intruders for more than twenty minutes. Then, the man with the shirt over his head shot all three victims in the head. The man with the sunglasses shot Anderson and Rogers in the back. Before the men left, the man wearing the shirt was seen uncovering his face.

Early the next morning, the mother of Marie Rogers reported her daughter missing. She told police that Rogers and Anderson had gone to Casey's the previous evening. The police learned that the two women had left the restaurant with Sucharski shortly after midnight. When the officers arrived at Sucharski's home, they found the three bodies.

The surveillance tapes were an unexpected gift. Still photographs were created from the tapes and circulated among police departments in South Florida. Three weeks later, the Metro-Dade police department notified Miramar detectives that they had arrested three men in a home invasion and that one of them resembled the man who had uncovered his face at the Sucharski home. The man was identified as twenty-two-year-old Pablo Ibar. Ibar told the Miramar police that he had spent the night of the murders with two friends, one of whom was named Jean Klimeczko. Klimeczko said that the man who uncovered his face was Pablo Ibar. He also told them that the man with the cap and sunglasses resembled a man he knew by the name of Seth Penalver. Police obtained a photo of the twenty-one-year-old Penalver and Klimeczko identified him as the second gunman. When Penalver learned that there was a warrant out for his arrest, he voluntarily turned himself in on August 5. He and Ibar were soon indicted and the two men went on trial in Broward County Circuit Court in June 1997.

The case against Penalver was clearly defined: Was he the man in the sunglasses seen on the grainy surveillance tape? The problem was no one seemed able to identify him with any degree of certainty. Melissa Munroe, a former girlfriend of Penalver's, signed her name to his photograph but said that did not indicate she could identify him as the second gunman. The police, she said, had pressured her into signing the photo. Klimeczko said he was under the influence of alcohol and drugs when he made his earlier identification but now could not be certain. The police had also influenced him to sign, he said. Two facial reconstruction experts—one for the prosecution and one for the defense—both testified that the photo was of too poor a quality to make a definite identification. Such forensics as were found at the scene also were inconclusive. A bloody footprint did not match any of Penalver's shoes. A shirt found outside the murder scene contained some human hair, but again, it bore no resemblance to either Ibar's or Penalver's hair. Dozens of fingerprints at the scene did not match either of the suspects'.

The only testimony that implicated Penalver at all came from a woman by the name of Kimberly San, and it was itself suspect. San, who had lived with Penalver not long before the crime, said that while she could not identify him from the video, she recognized him by the way he walked. She said that on the day after the murders she had gone to Penalver's house to pick up some of her belongings; she saw the washing machine overflowing with pink bubbles, indicating that there were bloody clothes in the machine. San also admitted that she had offered her testimony in exchange for leniency for her new boyfriend, who was facing a charge of aggravated battery on a pregnant woman. Paul Manzella, the lead detective in the case, testified that no witnesses had been offered anything in exchange for their testimony. Finally, the prosecution presented evidence that when Penalver turned himself in he declined a police request to remove his shoes and that they had to be forcibly removed. Penalver allegedly responded, "I might as well be dead," suggesting, police maintained, a consciousness of guilt. That was the sum of the prosecution's case. After seven months at trial and twenty-seven hours of deliberation, the jury voted 10-2 for conviction, and on January 25, 1998, a mistrial was declared. But the prosecution was not yet done. The cases of Penalver and Ibar were severed and each was tried separately. Though no new evidence was introduced, both men were convicted and sentenced to death. For Penalver, however, the wheels of justice were still grinding.

In February 2006, six years after he was dispatched to death row, the Florida Supreme Court reversed his conviction and death sentence. In its decision, the court said its members had reviewed the videotape and concluded that it was "difficult to determine whether Penalver is the individual with the hat and sunglasses." Because the tape was inconclusive and there was no physical evidence connecting Penalver to the murders, the testimony of the eyewitnesses was critical, the justices ruled; they also found it to be flawed. Penalver would be tried a third time but not before another six years passed.

This time, help was to come from an unexpected source. Ibar, still under a sentence of death, had retained a new attorney who appeared to be more diligent than his predecessor. He obtained evidence through public record act requests that had not been previously disclosed to Penalver's trial lawyer. The records included raw notes of detectives' interviews with witnesses indicating that they had identified Penalver only after police had applied pressure. At trial, they had denied making the identification at all. It was also revealed that Detective Manzella had authorized reward money to be paid to Klimeczko for identifying Penalver, although Manzella had testified that no reward money had been paid to any of the witnesses.

The trial lasted eight months. Beginning in the spring, the trial continued into December and concluded four days before Christmas. There were numerous delays for a variety of reasons, including the death of the defense attorney's mother during jury selection, illnesses among jurors and the defendant, the death of the sheriff's deputy who discovered the bodies of the victims, and a gas leak that shut the courthouse as deliberations were about to start. The case went to the jury on December 12. After five days of deliberation, the jury reported that it was deadlocked with two jurors set on conviction. In an unusual move, both sides agreed to replace those jurors with two alternates and deliberations resumed the following day. The change was possible because alternate jurors are not excused in cases involving the death penalty until there is an acquittal or the penalty phase is completed. As it turned out, the two alternates agreed with the ten-member majority and Penalver was acquitted.

As for Ibar, prosecutors maintained that he could be seen clearly on the video unmasking himself. He remained on death row.

Wesley Quick
Alabama

It went bad for Wesley Quick in a hurry and it soon got worse. He was only eighteen when he was arrested and charged with committing three burglaries in a rural section of Alabama. He had been implicated by his friend, Christopher Scarborough, who was arrested on November 3, 1995, for pawning several items stolen in a series of home break-ins. Scarborough, whose signature appeared at the bottom of several pawn shop sale receipts, pointed police in Quick's direction. It was just the beginning of Quick's troubles. Two days after his arrest, as he sat in his cell in the county jail, he was informed by officers that he was also being charged with two counts of capital murder for the shooting deaths of John Hughes and Nathan King.

On October 26, 1995, the bullet-riddled bodies of Hughes, eighteen, and King, twenty, were found outside a truck in the remote wilderness of Turkey Creek Falls. The 9mm semiautomatic pistol used in the shootings was said to be among the objects stolen by Scarborough and Quick. The murders were described by police as drug-fueled, satanic thrill killings. Quick admitted to using drugs and said he had read some of the satanic bible years earlier. Charged with Quick was his friend Shellie Kitchen. Both had been fingered by a mutual friend named Jason Beninati who told police they had bragged to him about committing the murders. Kitchen wasted no time in resolving her case. She pleaded guilty to conspiracy to commit murder and was sentenced to two years in prison.

Quick went to trial, more than once. His first trial, in September 1997, did not last long. A mistrial was declared when it was learned that several jurors had violated the judge's orders not to discuss the case. At the second trial, four months later, Beninati was the chief witness for the prosecution. He testified that Quick and Kitchen had come to his house right after the shootings and Quick said he had killed two young men while Kitchen watched. He said Quick later took him to the crime scene, by then cordoned off by police, to prove he had done it. In his testimony, Quick admitted he had been at the creek but said he had been so high on LSD that he had no recollection of what happened on that day. He was convicted and sentenced to death.

Quick's attorney, Charles Salvagio, appealed to the Alabama Court of Criminal Appeals, arguing that Quick had been denied a free copy of the transcript of his first trial, to which he was entitled because he was indigent. The court agreed. On May 21, 2001, it vacated the conviction and remanded the case for retrial.

For Quick's third trial, Salvagio teamed up with Los Angeles defense attorney Thomas Mesereau to represent Quick pro bono. Salvagio and Mesereau had worked together pro bono twice before to win acquittals in high-profile capital murder cases in Alabama. The new defense team took an entirely different approach from that used in the previous trial. Now, Quick said that although he was high on LSD at the time, he did recall the shootings and he was not the trigger man. It was his high school friend, Beninati. He said he had not pointed the finger at him earlier because Beninati threatened to kill him, Kitchen, and their families if he did. Beninati insisted he was not at the scene when Hughes and King were shot but that Quick had taken him there to show him that both of the victims were dead. But under intense cross-examination by Mesereau, it was shown that Beninati knew the crime scene in the finest detail. He had offered to draw diagrams of where the bodies and vehicles were positioned at the time of the murders. He described the logos on the victims' shirts, the expressions on their faces, and other details the defense argued he could not have known unless he was at the scene. "He gave them so much detail that it was almost hard to imagine he was not there," Mesereau said. "He knew way too much about the murder and behaved like the killer."

After a week-long trial, a Jefferson County jury acquitted Quick on April 21, 2003. But his moment of relief was fleeting. Almost immediately after the verdict was announced, prosecutor Teresa McClendon made it clear that he still had three burglary charges pending against him. In short order, he was tried, convicted, and sentenced to seventy-six years in prison.

Lemuel Prion
Arizona

Given Lemuel Prion's past, it did not stretch the imagination to think police might have cast him as a suspect in a brutal murder case. His troubles with the law had begun with his failure to attend school when he was thirteen years old, but it was not long before he started to compile a rap sheet of some significance. He was arrested several times for burglary while in his late teens. He was convicted of aggravated assault and battery in a sexual case in Rock Hill, South Carolina, in his early twenties. Not long after, he spent five years, from 1986 to 1991, in prison in Pima County, Arizona, for attempting to rape a fifteen-year-old girl whom, according to court records, he threatened to "put to sleep" if she did not comply with his sexual demands. Prion moved from Arizona to Utah in 1993 at the age of twenty. There, he was convicted of aggravated assault for trying to beat his father over the head with a baseball bat. It was not the product of a sudden impulse. His father had brutally abused, one might even say tortured, Prion and his stepbrothers when they were children. It was while he was in a Utah prison that he was charged with the murder of Diana Vicari in Tucson, Arizona, a charge that eventually landed him on death row.

On October 24, 1992, the severed arms of the nineteen-year-old Vicari, a student at Pima Community College, were found poking out of a trash bag in a dumpster in an alley north of downtown Tucson. The rest of her body was never found. She was last seen the day before in the parking lot of the Tucson Convention Center. Shortly after her arms were discovered, a thirty-five-year-old prostitute, Tabitha Armentha, was kidnapped and sexually assaulted by a man at knifepoint. Police believed the two crimes were connected and Lemuel Prion emerged as a suspect. In August 1993, investigators questioned Troy Olson, a bartender who worked in the area of the convention center. They showed him photos of Vicari and Prion. He identified Vicari and said she had been at the bar a few days before her arms were found. He could not identify Prion. Neither could Armentha when shown a mug shot of the suspect. In 1995, local newspapers revisited the case and printed a photo of Prion. After seeing the photo, Olson called the police and said he now recognized the suspect. On October 31, 1997, while he was incarcerated in Utah, and exactly five years after Vicari's arms were found, a grand jury indicted Prion for murdering Vicari and on charges of kidnapping and aggravated assault in the Armentha case.

Prion was tried for murdering Vicari and assaulting Armentha at the same trial in 1999. The prosecution's case was less than flimsy. There was no forensic evidence—no fingerprints or blood stains; no murder weapon; nothing of any type that would place Prion at the scene of the crime. Prion would be convicted solely on the basis of the testimony of witnesses that had no first-hand evidence of his involvement with Vicari, none of whom could offer testimony on how or where the murder was committed; there was not even a body to which the arms belonged. The most damaging testimony, hardly of a compelling nature, was Olson's who said he had seen Prion and Vicari together on the night of the murder. An inmate at the Utah prison told the court that Prion had spoken to him about committing violent acts against women. Police said that Prion had described the size of Vicari's breasts which, a detective noted, he could not have known from the pictures he was shown. A former prostitute testified that Prion had threatened her life and told her he fantasized about raping and dismembering women. Other evidence submitted by the prosecution was the fact that the victim's car was found less than two blocks from where Prion was living; that he possessed weapons that could have been used to dismember Vicari, including a machete and a large fishing knife; that he frequented nightclubs Vicari also favored. That was the sum of the state's case.

The defense, effectively on notice that reasonable doubt would not work in its favor here, felt it was its burden to prove Prion's innocence, and their best hope was to show that another man committed the crime. And, in fact, there was a live suspect whom police had basically chosen to ignore. His name was John Mazure. Mazure, known to have a violent temper, had been with Vicari on the night of her disappearance. Questioned by police, he was found to have concealed information, and according to the defense, he had "appeared at work the day after Vicari's disappearance so disheveled and disoriented that he was fired." For reasons not quite known, the judge did not allow that evidence to be submitted at trial. On January 28, 1999, Prion was convicted of first-degree murder for killing Vicari and of kidnapping and aggravated assault in the case of Armentha. The judge sentenced him to death.

In August 2002, the Arizona Supreme Court unanimously overturned the conviction, ruling that the trial court was guilty of judicial error for excluding the evidence regarding Mazure. The court stated that the third-party evidence "supports the notion that Mazure had the opportunity and motive to commit this crime . . ." The Supreme Court also held that the trial court had committed prejudicial error for allowing Vicari's and Armentha's cases to be tried at the same time. The ruling noted that "any connection between the two crimes is attenuated at best."

On March 14, 2003, the Pima County Attorney's Office dismissed all charges against Prion, but while his life had been spared, he was still a long way from being a free man. He was immediately returned to Utah to serve out the remainder of his previous sentence.

Daniel Wade Moore
Alabama

In a real sense, Daniel Wade Moore had his life spared and his freedom restored by the same judge who overruled a jury's recommendation of a life sentence and sent him to death row. The judge, Glenn Thompson, called the murder of which Moore was convicted one of the worst he had ever encountered. The victim, Karen Tipton, was found dead in her home in Decatur, Alabama, on the evening of March 12, 1999. Her husband notified police and told them he had found the body. Tipton had been sexually assaulted and stabbed twenty-eight times. There were no signs of a break-in, but a number of items were missing from the apartment, including jewelry, a video camera, and the victim's purse.

Moore was not arrested until nearly two years later when his uncle notified the police that Moore had told him that he was in Tipton's house when she was murdered but that he was not involved in the killing. It was not much to go on, but the police had no other suspects. What they did have were two hairs found at the crime scene and they checked the DNA against Moore's. Unfortunately for Moore, the DNA ruled out 99.8 percent of the population, but not him. There was no other physical evidence linking Moore to the crime, but his record was not in his favor. He was a known drug addict and had been in trouble with the law more than once. He admitted telling his uncle that he was present at the time of the killing but said he had done so because his uncle had been badgering him about some of his other legal problems. On the basis of his uncle's testimony and the DNA found on the hairs, Moore was tried and convicted in November 2002 and sentenced to death two months later. However, things quickly turned in his favor.

Shortly after the trial, the judge learned that a 256-page FBI file on the case had not been turned over to the defense by the prosecution. The file contained evidence that Tipton had been carrying on an extramarital affair and pointed to her husband as a possible suspect. Judge Glenn Thompson, who originally had sentenced Moore to death, now weighed in in his favor. He overturned Moore's conviction in February 2003 because the prosecution had withheld the file from the defense. Indignant in his ruling, Judge Thompson said, "Orders were entered in any capital case, that whatever the state has, whatever the prosecutor has, whatever the investigation has, they should provide that to the defendant. The prosecution, Mr. [Don] Valeska specifically, looked me in the eye and said, quote, 'There ain't no such thing as an FBI report.' Well, there probably wasn't a report, but there were 256 pages of information collected by Decatur police officers that were sent to the FBI." Judge Thompson went on to say that Assistant Attorney General Don Valeska later came to him and acknowledged that such information was withheld. "It frustrated and angered me that he would be willing to lie to the court."

The Alabama Court of Criminal Appeals responded by ordering Judge Thompson to stand down from the case while continuing to allow Valeska to continue as prosecutor. A motion by the defense that retrying Moore for the same crime would violate his constitutional protection against double jeopardy was initially granted by the trial court and Moore was released from prison. But not for long. Five days later an appellate court overturned the trial court's decision and ordered a new trial. That trial, not held until 2008, ended with the jury deadlocked 8-4 for acquittal. A third trial was held in May 2009 and Moore was acquitted of all charges and released from prison the same day. Upon hearing the verdict, Judge Thompson said, "I felt it was the only conclusion that a jury could reach if they actually followed the law."

Commentary: Culture of Corruption

The perversion of the criminal justice system is not, as some would have it, the product of a random handful of miscreants who are looking for an express trip to the top. It runs much deeper than that. It is part of a culture of corruption that has infected the entire system, top to bottom, inside and out. It involves not only the police, the prosecution, and the judiciary; it is embedded in the machinery of the system itself: a bail structure that punishes poverty by locking up suspects who have not yet been convicted but are unable to raise as little as two hundred dollars; jails that are not fit for human habitation; lengthy periods of solitary confinement in which prisoners are deprived of all human contact; mandatory sentences that keep convicts incarcerated for longer periods than reason would allow; public defenders whose case loads keep them from providing their clients with adequate representation—in sum, a system that favors retribution over rehabilitation and political expedience over justice.

Entire jurisdictions, including whole cities, large and small, have been found to be operating in corrupt environments that poison even the possibility of achieving justice. The case of Chicago has been well documented. Burge's reign of terror lasted for nearly two decades. It is estimated that between 1972 and 1991, Burge's "midnight crew" picked up about 120 men, chiefly African Americans, who were tortured until they confessed to crimes of which they were innocent. Convicted and sentenced for lesser infractions, Burge was spared being charged with abuse because the statute of limitations had run out. As recently as the spring of 2015, Mayor Rahm Emanuel was seeking to pay reparations to scores of people who were among Burge's victims.

The brutal practices of the Los Angeles police department came to light in 1992 when television cameras captured the bludgeoning of Rodney King, but that was just the start of an investigation into police corruption. Later that decade, what became known as the Rampart Scandal touched off what has been called one of the most widespread cases of police misconduct in the history of the United States. All told, around seventy police officers were implicated; fifty-eight were brought to trial; five were ultimately fired; seven resigned, and twelve officers were suspended. The officers involved were all members of the Community Resources Against Street Hoodlums (CRASH) unit within the Rampart Division.

The depth of corruption was profound. Trial documents indicated that several police officers were in the direct pay of drug dealers and other heavyweights in the city's criminal hierarchies. They were involved in shootings, beatings, the framing of innocent people, a bank robbery, drug dealing, and the planting of evidence at crime scenes. The Rampart Scandal resulted in more than 140 civil lawsuits against the City of Los Angeles, costing the city an estimated $125 million in settlements. As of 2015, the extent of the scandal was still not fully known.

More recently, in December 2014, a two-year investigation of the Cleveland Police Department by the US Department of Justice uncovered a pattern of "unreasonable and unnecessary use of force" with black residents as the primary targets. In addition to abuses involving firearms, the report cited the use of Tasers, chemical spray, and fists. Such tactics, the report said, escalated potentially non-violent encounters into dangerous confrontations.

The city, long a hotbed of antagonism between the police force and the black community, was brought to a boil on November 22 by the fatal shooting of Tamir Rice, a twelve-year-old African American boy, when a rookie patrolman mistook a toy gun in the boy's waistband for a semi-automatic pistol. The situation was grave enough to prompt President Obama to dispatch Attorney General Eric H. Holder to Cleveland to announce his findings. He determined that the city's police problems stemmed from "systemic deficiencies, including insufficient accountability, inadequate training and equipment, ineffective policies, and inadequate engagement with the community."

The Cleveland report climaxed a two-week period fraught with tensions between communities and their police departments, some of which escalated into riots that went on through the night. The day before the Cleveland report was released, a grand jury in Staten Island, New York, declined to indict a white police officer in the choking death of Eric Garner, an unarmed black man who was accused of selling cigarettes illegally. The Garner case burst open less than two weeks after the small town of Ferguson, Missouri, became the site of round-the-clock rioting when a grand jury failed to indict a white police officer who shot to death Michael Brown, an unarmed black man. Both the Garner and Brown cases ignited violent demonstrations in major cities around the country, including New York, Boston, Chicago, and Washington.

The culture of corruption that permeates the local criminal justice systems throughout the country, critical as it is, seems to pale when one contemplates the infestation of law enforcement at the federal level, the very highest level, the sacrosanct Federal Bureau of Investigation, at its very peak. Peter Limone was the victim of such a travesty.

Peter Limone
Massachutts

The case of Peter Limone is like no other. His thirty-three years in prison—four and a half on death row—places him high on the longevity list among those wrongfully convicted who were later exonerated. But that is just the beginning of his story. Limone, convicted of a gangland hit, was framed by an unlikely cadre of racketeers and rogues. Some were members of the Mafia; others were FBI agents. One was the long-time, once-revered director of the bureau, J. Edgar Hoover.

On March 12, 1965, a small-time hood by the name of Edward "Teddy" Deegan was shot to death in an alley in Chelsea, Massachusetts, a suburb of Boston. The murder remained unsolved for more than two years. Then, a high-up Mafia hit man, Joseph "The Animal" Barboza, who moonlighted as an FBI informant, put the finger on Limone and three others—Joseph Salvati, Henry Tameleo, and Louis Greco. Barboza was a well known figure in the Boston area, and his appearance on the witness stand attracted its share of attention. US marshals surrounded the courthouse every day he testified, and of course all of his testimony was given under a grant of immunity.

It served Barboza's interest to have the case cleared because he himself was involved in the killing. He knew the four men he named were innocent and so did the FBI. The FBI's interest was served as well. Barboza was one of their top Mafia informants, and agents of the bureau were as protective of their snitches as they were of the reputation of their director. Solely on the strength of Barboza's testimony, which had been orchestrated and rehearsed in cooperation with FBI agents, Limone and the three others were convicted of capital murder and sentenced to die in the electric chair. They escaped death when Massachusetts abolished the death penalty in 1974, and their sentences were commuted to life. Both Tameleo and Greco died in prison. Salvati was released in 1997 when the governor commuted his sentence. Only Limone, whose criminal record included a youthful offense for an attempted break-in and a few gambling-related charges for running a dice game, continued to serve time. He had been denied parole in 1987, some twenty years into his sentence, and there appeared to be little hope he would ever set foot outside the prison gates. Thirteen years later, his outlook would change.

In 2000, the US Justice Department opened an investigation into corruption in the Boston office of the FBI. The investigation was to reach back to the 1960s, and what it began to uncover was not pretty. It turned up documents showing that officials at FBI headquarters, including Hoover, were aware that Boston agents were employing killers and gang leaders as informers and were protecting them from prosecution. Among the copious files relating to the Deegan case was a report showing that, two days before Deegan was killed, an FBI informant told Special Agent

H. Paul Rico that Vincent "Jimmy the Bear" Flemmi, the brother of another informant, planned to kill Deegan and that then-New England Mafia boss Raymond L.S. Patriarca had approved the hit. The report, written by Rico and agent Dennis Condon, both since retired, named four other men, including Barboza, who were involved in the plot. None of the men later convicted of the crime was named in the list.

Further documentation included a memorandum from the Boston field office to Hoover, dated a week after the murder, stating, "Informants report that . . . Vincent James Flemmi and Joseph Barboza, prominent local hoodlums, were responsible for the killing." The memo goes on to describe in detail how the murder was carried out. Hoover and his agents knew before the trial that four innocent men were being railroaded and perhaps sent to their deaths for a crime committed by one of their informants. But Barboza was considered too valuable a snitch to be sacrificed in the interest of justice. After the trial, he became the first person ever to be placed in the federal witness protection program.

Based on the emerging revelations, Limone's attorney, John Cavicchi, requested that his client's conviction be overturned and that he be granted a new trial. At a hearing near the end of December 2000, Middlesex Superior Court Judge Margaret Hinkle, clearly sympathetic to Limone's plight, took the unusual step of lifting attorney-client privilege so that Joseph J. Balliro Sr., a well-known Boston defense attorney, could divulge information he was told decades earlier about Deegan's murder. Balliro then told the court Vincent Flemmi had confessed to the crime in the 1960s before his death. The attorney had written an affidavit stating that Vincent, the brother of Stephen "The Rifleman" Flemmi, another gangster who worked in the service of the FBI, had told him that Limone and the three other convicted men had nothing to do with the crime.

Early in January 2001, Judge Hinkle vacated Limone's conviction and ordered his release from prison. Two weeks later, she threw out the conviction of Salvati who had been paroled in 1997, saying, "The conduct of certain agents of the bureau stains the legacy of the FBI." Salvati's attorney, Victor Garo, said his client had been the victim of a conspiracy. "J. Edgar Hoover and senior members of the FBI conspired to murder my client," Salvati told UPI reporter P. Mitchell Prothero. "This was not the work of rogue agents."

The congressional investigation, led by Representative Dan Burton, Republican of Indiana, chairman of the House Government Reform Committee, turned up evidence that the Boston FBI field office had allowed several informants to seize control of the city's organized crime operations and manage them under the protection of federal law enforcement officials. Mobsters James "Whitey" Bulger and Stephen Flemmi were indicted for about twenty murders which were allegedly covered up by FBI agents protecting their key informants. It was charged that Bulger and Flemmi were permitted to carry out crimes, including murder, in exchange for providing the FBI with information about rival mob families.

The committee hearings continued at least through 2002. At one point, the noted lawyer F. Lee Bailey testified that he believed the FBI had coached Barboza on how to lie on the witness stand. Bailey, who had represented Barboza briefly in 1970, said, "He told me he had quite a bit of help. I believe the testimony was furnished."

A key witness for the congressional committee was Jeremiah T. O'Sullivan, who was in charge of the New England Organized Crime Strike Force and later a US attorney in Boston in the 1970s and '80s. O'Sullivan testified that he was aware that informers were committing murders and receiving protection from the FBI, but he took no action because he feared reprisals. "With the FBI," he said, "if you go against them, they will try to get you."

One of the first casualties of the investigation was John J. Connolly Jr., a retired FBI agent who was sentenced to ten years in prison in September 2002 for racketeering and obstruction of justice. Connolly, it was charged, had essentially become a member of Whitey Bulger's infamous Winter Hill Gang in South Boston, sometimes referred to as the Irish Mafia.

Bulger was indicted for racketeering and involvement in nineteen murders. He disappeared in 1995 after Connolly tipped him off to the secret indictment. He remained at the top of the FBI's Most Wanted List until June 22, 2011, when he was captured in Santa Monica, California, by federal agents following a tip to the FBI. He had been living with his girlfriend, Catherina Greig, in a $1,165-a-month, rent-controlled apartment thee blocks from the beach. On the door was a hand-printed sign that read: DO NOT KNOCK UNDER ANY CIRCUMSTANCES. Bulger was tried in 2013 and convicted of taking part in eleven murders. In November of that month he was sentenced to two life terms. He was eighty-four years old.

Ironically, Bulger's brother, William M. "Billy" Bulger, a Democratic politician, was president of the Massachusetts Senate for eighteen years, the longest tenure in history. He also served as president of the University of Massachusetts until he was forced to resign in 2003 when he refused to testify at a congressional hearing about his communication with his brother.

Stephen Flemmi, eighty years old at the time of his arrest, pled guilty in 2003 to committing ten murders and was sentenced to forty years in prison.

Peter Limone, sixty-seven years old when he was released, shared in the largest wrongful conviction settlement in history. In 2007, he, Salvati, and the estates of Tameleo and Greco were awarded a total of $101.75 million for wrongful imprisonment.

The Ford Heights 4
Illinois

The case that became known as the Ford Heights 4 was a textbook example of corrupt practices, involving prosecutorial and police misconduct, false eyewitness identification, the perjured testimony of a jailhouse snitch, and junk science that validated an inconclusive match of both blood and hair samples. The result was the wrongful conviction of four men, all black, two of whom received death sentences; the other two were given respective terms of life and seventy-five years.

Their long night's journey through the criminal justice system began around 2:30 a.m. on May 12, 1978. A newly engaged couple,

Lawrence Lionberg and Carol Schmal, were abducted from a gas station in the virtually all-white Chicago suburb of Homewood, Illinois, where Lionberg was working the overnight shift. They were driven to an abandoned townhouse in the predominantly black section of East Chicago Heights, which later became known as Ford Heights. Schmal was raped, and she and Lionberg were shot in the back of the head. The Ford Heights 4—Dennis Williams, Verneal Jimerson, Kenneth Adams, and Willie Rainge—were arrested a few days later.

The appearance of prosecutorial bias was evident from the start, with the selection of the jury. The seventeenth potential juror called for voir dire (the questioning of potential jurors) was Leroy Posey, a pump-operator from Chicago's South Side. After answering the routine questions, Posey, who had noticed that black candidates were being regularly stricken with peremptory challenges by the prosecution, asked permission to speak. "It's obvious the state's attorneys want an all-white jury," he said. "They don't want me here." Posey was excused. The trial jury consisted of eleven whites and one black woman.

The star witness for the prosecution was Charles McCraney, who lived near the murder scene. He testified that at around three o'clock on the morning the couple disappeared he saw six to eight people—among them Williams, Rainge, and Adams—enter the abandoned townhouse. A second witness, David Jackson, who was doing time in the Cook County jail where Williams and Rainge were being held after their arrest, said he heard the two talking about how they had killed a man and "taken" sex from a woman. As neither witness was able to identify Jimerson, the charges against him were dropped but, as it turned out, only temporarily.

In some respects, the most critical "witness" in the case was a seventeen-year-old woman who saw nothing and never testified. Paula Gray, illiterate and mildly retarded, lived near the crime scene and was questioned by police shortly after the murders. Gray had quite a story to offer. She told the police and later a grand jury that she had actually witnessed the rape and murders. She said, in fact, that she provided light for the assailants in the townhouse by holding a disposable cigarette lighter while Schmal was raped seven times.

However, Gray soon recanted her statements and refused to testify at the trial. She was then charged as an accomplice, convicted, and sentenced to fifty years.

The physical evidence presented by the prosecution was as weak as the eyewitness testimony. The Type-O blood from one of the victims was the most common type and therefore an unreliable indicator, even if a match were made. Even less reliable was the examination of three hairs found in Williams's car. Unlike fingerprints, a person's hair type is not unique (except as a repository for DNA, a technology unavailable in 1978). Even under a microscope, the most certain conclusion a scientist can reach is that two hairs *could* have come from the same person. The forensic expert who testified about the hair samples said that two of the hairs found in the car were "similar" to Carol Schmal's and the third was "similar" to Lionberg's. However, the prosecutors continually substituted the word "matched" for "similar" during the balance of the trial, a designation that went unchallenged by the defense.

In 1983, Williams, who had been on death row for four years, won a new trial as a result of the ineffective assistance of counsel. Looking to buttress their case, prosecutors offered to cut a deal with Gray, and she was more than ready to accept. She agreed to revert to her original testimony that she had witnessed the crime and this time would implicate Jimerson as well as Williams. Gray insisted she had not been offered anything in exchange for her testimony. But shortly after the conclusion of the trial, some of the charges against her were dropped and, with about forty years of her sentence remaining to be served, she was released from prison on two years' probation. Both Williams and Jimerson were convicted and sentenced to death.

The Ford Heights 4 case subsequently came under the scrutiny of the Medill Journalism School investigative team, headed by Professor David Protess. They enlisted the pro bono help of Mark Ter Molen, of the Chicago law firm of Mayer, Brown & Platt. Among the team's discoveries was a file showing that five days after the crime, a witness had told police he had seen four men flee the scene of the crime. He identified all four by name, and none of the names was Williams, Jimerson, Rainge, or Adams. One of them was Arthur (Red) Robinson, who would later be identified as one of the actual killers.

As the students continued their probe, other instances of misconduct were uncovered, and the case started making its way back into the judicial machinery.

In 1995, the Illinois Supreme Court unanimously reversed Jimerson's conviction because the prosecution had allowed Gray to testify falsely about the deal she had made. Although the prosecutors never admitted striking the bargain, the judges noted that in reaching their decision they "are not required to suspend common sense." Jimerson was released on bond.

In 1996, DNA tests showed that none of the Ford Heights 4 was involved in the murders. The DNA provided a match with Robinson, who confessed and named his three accomplices. One had since died of a drug overdose; another was serving time on a murder charge. He and the remaining two were convicted and sentenced to life.

Jimerson, Williams, Rainge, and Adams were exonerated and set free. Jimerson had spent eleven years on death row; the others were each imprisoned for eighteen years. Three of the attorneys who represented them have since had their licenses to practice law revoked or suspended for other reasons. The Ford Heights 4 were awarded $36 million by Cook County to settle civil rights claims. It was the largest civil-rights settlement in US history. Williams died on March 20, 2003, of undisclosed causes. He was forty-six years old.

Earl Charles
Georgia

Earl Charles was sentenced to death on the perjured testimony of a corrupt cop. He was freed because of the dedicated precision of an honest cop and the unflagging efforts of a mother who believed that ultimately the truth would prevail.

Charles was convicted of shooting to death a Savannah, Georgia, furniture store owner and his son during a robbery late one October afternoon in 1974. Max Rosenstein and his wife, Myra, both in their seventies, along with their son, Fred, and the bookkeeper, Bessie Corcelius, were the only ones in the store when two young black men entered. After pretending to make a purchase, one of the men brandished a pistol and announced a stickup. The Rosensteins resisted. Max attempted to scoop up money from the cash register and get it into a safe and was shot in the head. Myra was hit in the face with a tape dispenser and fell to the floor bleeding. Fred was shot when he went to her aid. Bessie Corcelius hid under a desk and was still there when the men fled with the money.

The two survivors, Myra and Bessie, spent hours looking at police mug shots but were unable to identify the killers. Among the mug shots they rejected was a five-year-old photo of Earl Charles. Now twenty-one years old, Charles had been convicted of burglary and shoplifting while in his teens and had spent fourteen months in custody. A few days later, police showed the women a more recent photo of Charles, but they still did not recognize him. In yet another attempt to get an identification, Detective F.W. Wade visited Bessie at her home with another batch of photos. When she was unable to point anyone out, Wade told her it was not important because he was ready to make an arrest. On November 15, Charles was picked up in New Port Richey, Florida. A month later, he was extradited and returned to Savannah where he was charged with the double murder.

Charles had left Georgia in early September, more than a month before the crime was committed. Together with his neighbor Michael Williams and Williams's girlfriend, Charles had driven to Tampa, Florida, looking for work. He and Williams took jobs at a gasoline service station. The station manager, Robert Zachery, was wary about leaving his new hired hands to man the station unsupervised, and he asked his friend, Deputy Sheriff Lemon Harvey, to look in on them from time to time. Harvey agreed and dutifully kept notes on his visits to the station. Barely two weeks after the men had begun work, the station was robbed of about $1,000. Zachery was uncomfortable with the story they told of the holdup, and he fired them both. Charles soon found a job as a handyman for a company that managed apartment buildings, but more trouble was just around the corner.

On November 15, Charles and Williams were driving north from Tampa with two other acquaintances, Raymond Ash and James Nixon. They stopped for lunch in New Port Richey. Once inside the restaurant, Nixon went back outside, saying he wanted to retrieve something from the car. The other three finished lunch before he returned. When they went to the parking lot, they found Nixon being held at gunpoint by the owner of a nearby store who said she had caught him taking money from the till.

All four men were taken to the police station, and when their names were fed into the computer, it was discovered that Charles and Williams were wanted in Georgia for murder, armed robbery, aggravated assault, and fleeing across state lines to avoid prosecution. Myra Rosenstein and Bessie Corcelius came to Florida, in the company of Detective Wade, to identify the suspects at an extradition hearing on December 19. Both picked Charles out of a police lineup and identified him as the gunman, though Mrs. Rosenstein acknowledged that Charles looked different from the man who shot her husband. He was nonetheless returned to Georgia for prosecution; the state said it would seek the death penalty.

Testifying against Charles, in addition to Mrs. Rosenstein and Mrs. Corcelius, were Detective Wade and James Nixon. Nixon, who had been arrested on a robbery charge, said that while he and Charles were in jail, Charles bragged to him about shooting "a man and a little boy" in a Savannah furniture store. The "little boy" apparently was forty-two-year-old Fred Rosenstein, who Nixon doubtless had heard described as the elder Rosenstein's son. Wade testified that when he interrogated Zachery, the service station owner, he was told that Charles had not been at work on the day of the murders.

The case for the defense appeared to give Charles an unimpeachable alibi. Zachery, who had fired Charles, voluntarily drove to Savannah at his own expense to testify that Charles was working at the station on the day of the murders. His story was documented by time cards and payment vouchers, but was ignored by the jury. They found Charles guilty. The trial judge, who later acknowledged doubts about the defendant's guilt, sentenced him to die in the electric chair.

At this point, Charles needed an advocate who believed in his innocence and who was prepared to work tirelessly in his behalf, and he had one. It was his mother, Flossie Mae. Mrs. Charles understood that the one man who knew for a fact that her son was innocent was Robert Zachery. She called the service station owner repeatedly, soliciting his help. Zachery, who had returned home after his testimony, was astonished that Charles had been found guilty, but could think of nothing else to do. His friend Lemon Harvey, the deputy sheriff, came to his rescue. Harvey had checked up on Charles and Williams regularly when they were working at the station and had kept a detailed diary of his daily rounds. He checked the entries and discovered that he had seen the two men at work on the day of the murders. He notified Zachery who called Mrs. Charles who called Earl's attorney. Harvey was interviewed by lawyers for both the defense and the prosecution. The case against Charles began to unravel.

Nixon recanted his testimony, saying Wade had coached him and promised him he would be released in exchange for testifying, but Wade had not kept his end of the deal. Wade was further implicated for having withheld exculpatory evidence and coaching eyewitnesses. It also seemed certain that he had perjured himself at the trial. The district attorney said he would not oppose a motion for a new trial and, if granted, he would not retry the case. The judge responded by vacating the conviction, and Charles was released after spending more than three years in prison awaiting execution.

The following year, with the help of the Southern Poverty Law Center, Charles filed suit against the city of Savannah and Detective Wade. The suit claimed false imprisonment and malicious arrest. It specifically alleged that Wade had knowingly tainted the eyewitness identifications, manipulated Nixon into committing perjury, withheld exculpatory evidence, and committed perjury. In October 1983, four years after the suit was filed and three years after it was thrown out of federal district court, the Fifth Circuit Court of Appeals reversed the lower court. The claim against the city was denied, but Wade was assessed $417,000 in damages. Since Wade had few assets that could be offered in payment, the city agreed to pay $75,000 in his behalf, and all litigation was dropped.

Though Charles was vindicated, the ten-year ordeal took its toll. He felt that people still doubted his innocence. "It's a scar that's been placed on me," he told a newspaper reporter, "and I have to live with it." But, as it turned out, not for very long. In March 1991, the *Atlanta Constitution* reported that Earl Charles had "walked into the path of an oncoming car" in Cobb County, Georgia. It was an apparent suicide.

Jerry Banks
Georgia

"Southern justice in capital murder trials is more like a random flip of the coin than a delicate balancing of the scales. Who will live and who will die is decided not just by the nature of the crime committed but by the skills of the defense lawyer appointed by the court. And in the nation's Death Belt, that lawyer too often is ill-trained, unprepared and grossly underpaid."

That quote opened a special report on the quality of defense attorneys in capital cases, published in the *National Law Journal* in 1990, and referenced by Michael L. Radelet, Hugo Adam Bedau, and Constance E. Putnam in their 1992 book *In Spite of Innocence.*

The case of Jerry Banks illustrated the travesty of Southern justice, while eerily reprising the devastation that the state of Georgia visited upon Earl Charles. Banks was twice convicted and condemned to die for a double murder that occurred just weeks after the crime for which Charles was convicted. Like Charles, Banks was arrested on scant evidence, railroaded by corrupt police practices, and denied justice at every turn. He eventually was exonerated and awarded a ludicrously nominal sum by way of compensation for five years spent on death row. Also like Charles, Banks, a black man who lived at the edge of poverty, finally resolved matters by taking his own life.

Banks was rabbit hunting in a wooded area south of Atlanta in early November 1974 when he came upon two bodies partially covered by a red bedspread. Banks hurried down to the road, flagged down a motorist, and told him to call the police. The police discovered that the victims, both white, were Marvin W. King, a thirty-eight-year-old high school band instructor, and Melanie Ann Hartsfield, a former student of King's. Each had been hit with two shotgun blasts, one in the back and one in the head. Two red shotgun shells were found nearby. Banks, who had been hunting with a shotgun, said he had not fired his weapon that day. Police twice tested his gun and believed they had found a match. About a month later, a third shell was found near the crime site, and Banks was arrested and charged with murder. The legal machinery moved swiftly. Less than two months after his arrest, Banks was convicted and sentenced to death.

Banks had little money, but he put together enough to retain a local attorney, Hudson John Myers. Myers said he was hired for what amounted to "a mess of collard greens." He performed as if collard greens were too high a fee. He failed to call key witnesses who could have corroborated Banks's account of where he was at the time the crime was committed and others who had spotted more likely suspects in the area shortly before the murders. Equally important, Myers had failed to find the motorist who called the police at Banks's request. Banks was convicted on an entirely improbable scenario, highlighted by the fact that the state never suggested a motive for the crime. The jury was thus obliged to consider that Banks had killed two people for no apparent reason, then asked someone to notify police of the crime, waited for them to arrive, and eagerly handed over the murder weapon.

Not long after the trial, the so-called "mystery caller," Andrew Eberhardt, called the trial judge and told him that he had identified himself when he reported the crime and that he had been questioned by the police. In September 1975, the Georgia Supreme Court reversed the conviction because information regarding the motorist was withheld from the defense. It did Banks no immediate good. Myers presented even less of a case at the retrial than he did the first time. Eberhardt was the only witness called, and his testimony was not nearly enough to convince the jury. Banks again was convicted on two counts of murder and returned to death row.

Ironically, evidence that would eventually contribute to Banks's acquittal was used to justify the death penalty. Banks had a single-barrel shotgun which had to be reloaded after each shot, a maneuver that would have taken at least five seconds. That should have raised doubts in the minds of the jury since witnesses who heard the shots said they came in rapid succession. Instead, it was turned to the advantage of the prosecution. The jury was told that the delay in reloading three times intensified the anxiety experienced by whoever was the second victim. In the words of the Georgia statute, this made the second slaying "outrageously and wantonly vile, horrible, and inhuman" and justified imposing the ultimate sanction.

Banks's life was saved by a chance meeting with a public defender at the Henry County Jail. Alex Crumbley was visiting with some of his clients, Banks's fellow inmates, when Banks asked for a small favor. He had not heard from his lawyer in a long time, and Banks wondered whether Crumbley could inquire whether Myers was still on the case. He was not. Crumbley soon learned that Myers was not on anyone's case. He was in the process of being disbarred because of his incompetent representation of other clients. In the process of his inquiries, Crumbley had become convinced of Banks's innocence and was working his case pro bono. But in 1978, he was appointed a judge and could no longer represent Banks. Determined to press on, Crumbley enlisted a legal team that consisted of A.J. "Buddy" Welch Jr., Stephen P. Harrison, and Crumbley's younger brother, Wade, who had recently graduated from Georgia Law School.

Their first initiative resulted in failure. Both the superior court and the Georgia Supreme Court denied a request for a new trial based on ineffective assistance of counsel. Undeterred, Banks's new legal cadre pushed forward with their investigation. They found no fewer than nine witnesses who had not been called whose testimony would have served the defendant's cause. Seven people, including Paul Collier, the police chief of Stockbridge, had heard four shots in rapid succession that could not have been fired from Banks's twelve-gauge, single-barrel shotgun. Together with the mayor of Stockbridge, Collier later visited the murder site and found two green shotgun casings that did not match Banks's weapon. In addition, two witnesses said they had seen a white man brandishing a shotgun near the scene of the crime minutes after the shots were fired.

Despite the imposing array of new evidence, the trial judge denied a request for a new trial. This time, however, the superior court reversed and ordered a third trial for Banks. Six months passed while the prosecution prepared its case. But Welch, Harrison, and Crumbley made a new discovery that turned the proceedings around. They learned that the shell casings originally found at the scene had almost certainly been planted.

Philip S. Howard, the lead investigator in the case, was found to have a less than enviable record as a police officer. Howard, in fact, had a history of falsifying evidence. He had resigned from one police force and been fired from another, was convicted of forgery and, most tellingly, had "tampered with and manipulated evidence involving [shotgun] shells" in another case. Now it appeared he had done it again in an effort to convict Banks. Howard said he had found the shell casings matching Banks's gun the day before it was taken for test firings. However, credible new evidence, including the statement of a former county commissioner, indicated that the gun was tested before the shells were found. The likelihood grew that Howard had taken the test shells and planted them in the woods. Confronted with these findings, the district attorney conceded that the shotgun shells, the only evidence tying Banks to the crime, "lack[ed] sufficient legal credibility to be believed." All charges against him were dropped.

Three days before Christmas 1980, Banks returned home to his wife and three children. But his homecoming was not all one might have hoped for. He found that five years of separation were difficult to breach. He and his wife had grown apart, and she wanted a divorce and custody of the children. Three days before the divorce was to become final, on

March 29, 1981, Banks shot his wife with a .38-caliber pistol, then shot himself in the chest. He died instantly. His wife died of the gunshot wounds six weeks later.

The Banks children sued the Harris County sheriff's department for $12 million. They were awarded $150,000. The *Atlanta Constitution* called the settlement "blood money." The editorial continued: "No amount of money could ever really make up for what the system—all of us included—did to Jerry Banks and his family. But $150,000 doesn't even begin to address the level of damages, the lasting pain. In fact, it comes closer to being an insult."

Clarence Lee Brandley
Texas

Race often plays a part in wrongful arrests and convictions, particularly in the South, but rarely is it as blatant a factor as it was in the case of Clarence Lee Brandley. A custodian at Conroe High School in Conroe, Texas, Brandley was sentenced to death for raping and strangling the sixteen-year-old manager of the visiting Bellville High volleyball team on August 23, 1980. There was virtually no evidence linking Brandley to the crime, but his being black seemed to be reason enough to convict him.

The victim, Cheryl Fergeson, was found dead after the game in a loft above the school auditorium. Fergeson, who was white, would have entered her junior year in the fall. The two custodians who had found the body, Brandley and Henry (Icky) Peace, were questioned and fingerprinted. They gave blood and hair samples. They both passed lie-detector tests. But none of that seemed to matter. The investigation had been shaped on the day of the murder. According to Peace, the officer conducting the interrogation had said, "One of you two is going to hang for this." Then he turned to Brandley and added, "Since you're the nigger, you're elected."

With the new school year about to begin and parents threatening to keep their children home unless the killer was caught, the authorities knew they needed a quick arrest. The list of suspects was short. Three other custodians—Gary Acreman, Sam Martinez, and John Sessum— provided alibis for one another. There seemed to be no place else to go, and Brandley, after all, had already been elected. Texas Ranger Wesley Styles, who was put in charge of the investigation, arrested him on a charge of capital murder.

The state had little to offer by way of proof except for the statements of the other custodians, all of whom were white, which at very best obliquely placed Brandley near the crime scene that afternoon. Acreman, Martinez, and Sessum related stories so similar in detail that the defense claimed they had been coached by the police. In any event, it was difficult to deny that they each had a stake in the outcome. In individual statements, they said they had seen Cheryl enter a girls' restroom near the gym and, a short time later, Brandley approached with an armful of toilet paper. They said they warned Brandley that a girl was in the facility, and he said he was going to the boys' restroom. They did not see him again for about forty-five minutes until the search for the missing girl began. In his statement, Peace also turned the focus of suspicion toward Brandley. He said that when he told Brandley he had not found the girl in the loft, Brandley went with him to search more thoroughly. When they found the body, Peace said Brandley calmly checked for a pulse and then notified the authorities. In addition, all four said that only Brandley had keys to the auditorium.

Just five days after the crime was committed, Brandley found himself testifying before an all-white grand jury. His version of events differed slightly from those presented by his fellow custodians. He admitted disappearing for about thirty minutes, not forty-five, but said he was smoking a cigarette and listening to the radio. He also testified that there were others who had master keys that could be used to open the auditorium. All the same, the grand jury returned an indictment, and Brandley went on trial in December 1980, again before an all-white jury.

What little physical evidence existed seemed to favor the defendant. A fresh blood spot had been found on the victim's blouse that was of a type different from both hers and Brandley's. Sperm recovered from Cheryl's body had been destroyed, presumably before it was tested. The remnants of the prosecution's case that remained proved to be conclusive enough for eleven jurors. The twelfth, William Srack, was unconvinced, and Srack held his ground despite being assailed by the other jurors as a "nigger lover" during deliberations. When the trial was over, Srack was the target of threats and harassing phone calls, some of which were monitored by the police. But the jury was hung and a retrial was scheduled for February 1981.

At the second trial, yet again heard by an all-white jury, an original prosecution witness was dropped and a new one was added. John Sessum apparently was no longer willing to echo the story told by his three colleagues. He was threatened with a charge of perjury but stood fast. The state's new witness was a junior at the school, Danny Taylor, who had worked with the custodial staff briefly during the summer. Taylor testified that one day, as they watched a group of white female students pass by, Brandley had commented, "If I got one of them alone, ain't no tellin' what I might do."

In an attempt to add some meat to the bones of its case, the state called the Harris County medical examiner who verified that a belt belonging to Brandley was consistent with the injuries inflicted by the instrument used to strangle the victim. In his closing argument, the district attorney offered the information that Brandley had a second job at a funeral home and suggested that he might be a necrophiliac and had raped Cheryl after she was dead. The defense objected on the grounds that the remark was inflammatory but was overruled. This time there was no holdout. The jury returned a verdict of guilty and recommended death as the penalty. The judge obliged.

Eleven months later, as they were preparing his appeal, Brandley's attorneys discovered that a good bit of evidence the state had used at trial had mysteriously disappeared while in the custody of the prosecution. A total of 166 of the 309 exhibits that had been introduced could no longer be found. These included hairs taken from Cheryl's body that matched neither Brandley's nor her own. Also missing were photos of

Brandley taken on the day of the crime that showed he was not wearing the belt that was suggested to be the murder weapon.

The Texas Court of Criminal Appeals was unimpressed. It affirmed the conviction and death sentence. "No reasonable hypothesis is presented by the evidence to even *suggest* that someone other than [Brandley] committed the crime," the court ruled. Brandley's execution date was set for January 17, 1986. However, the defense succeeded in getting a delay. A petition for a writ of habeas corpus, claiming that the lost evidence had deprived Brandley of a fair trial, was granted, and a hearing was scheduled for the summer. The six-month delay saved Brandley's life, for his luck was about to change.

A young woman by the name of Brenda Medina, who lived in the neighboring town of Cut and Shoot, Texas, saw the case being discussed on a television broadcast. She told a neighbor she had not heard about the case before, and added that her former boyfriend, James Dexter Robinson, had told her in 1980 that he had committed such a crime. The neighbor urged her to tell a lawyer, and the lawyer told her to take her story to the district attorney. The DA concluded that Medina was unreliable, and thus he was under no obligation to share the information with Brandley's lawyers. The private attorney did not agree. He notified the defense, and an evidentiary hearing was ordered, with District Court Judge Ernest A. Coker presiding.

John Sessum, the custodian who had not testified at the second trial, now took the stand and recanted his earlier testimony. He also implicated Gary Acreman. He said he had seen Acreman follow Cheryl up a staircase and then heard her scream, "No" and "Don't." Later that day, he said, Acreman had warned him there would be trouble if he said anything about the incident. Nonetheless, Sessum chose to inform Texas Ranger Styles. It was a poor choice. Styles told him they already had their man and threatened him with arrest if he did not support Acreman's story. With Acreman now beginning to look like a suspect, his father-in-law, Edward Payne, did not help his son-in-law's position. He testified that Acreman had told him where the victim's clothes were hidden on the night of the murder, which was two days before they were found.

When Medina took the stand, she stated flatly that Robinson had confessed to the murder. A former custodian at Conroe High who had been fired about a month earlier, Robinson told her he was leaving town for a while because he had killed a girl and hidden her body. Medina said she did not believe him and thought nothing more about it until Brandley's case came to her attention years later. Robinson also appeared at the hearing. He testified that he had invented the story he told Medina because she was pregnant and was hassling him, and he wanted to frighten her into leaving him alone. Despite what appeared to be overwhelming new evidence in his favor, Brandley's request for a new trial was denied. On December 22, 1986, the Texas Court of Criminal Appeals upheld that decision. In February, a new execution date was set—March 26, 1987.

But by that time, the case had drawn wide national attention. Civil rights activists had raised $80,000 to finance further legal action. A protest demonstration in Conroe drew more than one thousand marchers. A "Free Clarence Brandley" coalition was formed. Amnesty International entered the fray. James McCloskey, of Centurion Ministries in Princeton, NJ, agreed to take the case. A former seminary student before he became an attorney, McCloskey had made a career of seeking to win freedom for innocent prisoners.

Working with a private investigator, McCloskey was able to get Acreman to give an updated version of the events on videotape. Acreman said that Robinson alone had abducted and killed Cheryl. He said he saw Robinson drop her clothes in the dumpster where they were found. Acreman later recanted his videotaped statement, but by that time events were moving in Brandley's direction. Two new witnesses surfaced who said they heard Acreman say that Brandley did not kill the girl. He said he knew who the killer was but would never tell. Only six days before the scheduled execution, Judge Coker ordered a stay.

In September 1987, a new evidentiary hearing was held. Presiding was Special State District Judge Perry Pickett, seventy-one years old and with a time-honored reputation for being scrupulously fair. The key witnesses, including Acreman, Robinson, and Styles, offered testimony that seemed to discredit one another rather than implicate Brandley.

Robinson and Acreman emerged as serious suspects. Styles was depicted as a bullying racist. On October 9, Judge Pickett concluded the hearing with a statement that rang with indignation about the manner in which the case was conducted. He said:

"The litany of events graphically described by the witnesses, some of it chilling and shocking, leads me to the conclusion [that] the pervasive shadow of darkness has obscured the light of fundamental decency and human rights." He continued with an indictment of how the prosecution was conducted, declaring that the state had "wholly ignored any evidence or lead to evidence that might prove inconsistent with their premature conclusion that Brandley had committed the murder. The conclusion is inescapable that the investigation was conducted not to solve the crime, but to convict Brandley." The judge recommended that the Texas Court of Criminal Appeals grant Brandley a new trial. Then he went a step further. "The testimony . . . unequivocally establishes," he said, "that Gary Acreman and James Dexter Robinson are prime suspects and probably were responsible for the death of Cheryl Dee Fergeson."

The court sat on the case for fourteen months while Brandley languished in prison. On December 13, 1989, a sharply divided court accepted Judge Pickett's recommendation and ordered a retrial. The prosecution, in its relentless insistence on Brandley's guilt, announced it would appeal to the US Supreme Court. Free on bail after spending nine years on death row, Brandley waited another ten months for a final disposition of his case. On October 1, the Supreme Court denied the state's request for certiorari, which would have mandated further review of the case, and Brandley's ten-year ordeal was finally over. No disciplinary action was ever taken against the officials who played a role in his conviction.

Michael Graham and Albert Burrell
Louisiana

Decades ago, before substantial reforms were made, the name Angola had the same forbidding ring of finality that Alcatraz and Sing Sing had generations earlier. Officially named Louisiana State Penitentiary, Angola was known in the world of crime and penology as one of the toughest, dead-end destinations in the country. Its death-row cells, measuring six-by-nine feet, more closely resembled the cages used to house animals at a zoo, except those cages were generally a bit more spacious. It was in such cells that Michael Graham and Albert Burrell spent twenty-three hours a day every day for thirteen years for a crime they did not commit after a trial in which the state presented no credible evidence.

Graham and Burrell were charged with shooting to death an elderly couple, William and Callie Frost, in their home in Union Parish, Louisiana, on August 31, 1986. The only evidence against them was the testimony of two witnesses, neither of whom could put the suspects anywhere near the scene at the time of the crime. The first, Burrell's ex-wife, Janet, triggered the investigation with a call to Sheriff Larry Averitt. She told the officer that she had met with Burrell on a deserted road the night of the murder and found a wallet on the car seat. It contained William Frost's identification documents but no money. Burrell then took out his own wallet, she said, and counted out twenty-seven $100 bills and told her he had killed the Frosts. The second witness was a jailhouse snitch named Wayne Brantley who said he heard both Burrell and Graham confess to the murders while they were being held. There was no other evidence of any kind. Yet Burrell and Graham were convicted in separate trials and each was sent to Angola's death house.

With death in the electric chair drawing nearer and revelations continuing to surface nationally that many death-row inhabitants did not belong there, the cases of Burrell and Graham attracted the attention of a number of criminal attorneys. Nick Trenticosta, a New Orleans lawyer, took on Burrell's appeal free of charge and added to the defense team Chuck Lloyd, an attorney from Burrell's home town of Minneapolis. The burden of seeking to clear Graham was assumed pro bono by Michele Fournet.

Working independently, the two lawyers learned fairly soon that the state had had no case worth presenting. Burrell, who was mentally retarded and unable to read or write, was clearly incapable of assisting in his own defense and should not have been forced to stand trial. They also discovered that the testimony of the state's two witnesses was worthless.

Burrell's wife admitted that she had made up the story, hoping that if Burrell were arrested she could gain sole custody of their son. She signed an affidavit stating, "What I told the police was not true." The testimony of the jailhouse snitch, Olan Wayne Brantley, was found to be no more reliable. Brantley, it was learned, had a reputation for falsely implicating others in crimes they knew nothing about. In at least two previous cases, he testified that he had overheard the suspects confess. A law-enforcement official acknowledged that Brantley was known as Lyin' Wayne. Brantley's behavior could be better understood in light of the fact that he had a history of mental illness. Although it was never revealed to the defense, he had admitted at his own trial that he had spent time in several mental hospitals where he was treated for manic depression. He also said he had written more bad checks than he could keep track of. On top of it all, Brantley had made a plea deal on unrelated charges he was facing, and that bit of information had not been passed on to the defense.

In March 2000, District Judge Cynthia Woodard threw out the convictions and sentences and ordered a new trial. Judge Woodard cited the incidents of prosecutorial misconduct and also noted that Dan Grady, one of the prosecutors, had said the case against Burrell and Graham was "so weak that [it] should never have been brought to the grand jury." Prosecutors for the attorney general's office, which assumed control of the case when the Union Parish district attorney voluntarily withdrew, said they found a "total lack of credible evidence" connecting the men with the crimes.

On December 27, 2000, the state attorney general's office filed documents with the state district court in Union Parish dismissing all charges against the men. In making the announcement, Pam Laborde said, "We have no physical evidence in this case, and that has been the problem from the start." The attorney general reopened the investigation of the shootings, noting there was a "very real possibility that someone else committed the murders."

After the charges against Burrell and Graham were dropped, a DNA test showed that blood taken from the doorjamb of the Frosts' home belonged to the victims. There was still no physical evidence that put Burrell or Graham at the scene. The trial attorneys appointed to represent Burrell were later disbarred for other reasons and sent to federal prison. The former sheriff of Union Parish also received a prison term on charges that he stole from his office. According to Michele Fornet, Graham's lawyer, the kind of prosecutorial misconduct found in the case was not unusual. "It is a problem inherent in the criminal justice system," she said.

When they were released from prison, Burrell and Graham were each given a denim jacket several sizes too large and the standard ten-dollar check the state tenders for transportation. Burrell was picked up by his stepsister in a pickup truck and taken to her small ranch in East Texas. Graham, who worked as a roofer before going to prison, headed for his mother's home in Roanoke, Virginia. His ticket home on a Greyhound bus was paid for by his attorney. It cost $127. As for the ten dollars the state gave him, Graham told a reporter for *The New York Times* that he thought about framing it, but decided to put it to better use. When the bus made a stop in Atlanta, he cashed it and gave it to a panhandler.

Joaquin Martinez
Florida

The case of Joaquin Martinez was no ordinary legal proceeding. It attracted the attention of the Pope, the King of Spain, and the Spanish government. Martinez, a Spanish national, was convicted in 1997 of murdering a young couple—Douglas Lawson and his girlfriend, Sherrie McCoy-Ward—in their home in Clair Mel, just east of Tampa, Florida. When he was sentenced to death, Martinez became a cause célèbre in the Spanish media in Miami and in Spain, which does not have the death penalty. The convicted man's mother, Sara Martinez, met with King Juan Carlos and asked him to intervene. Spanish Prime Minister Jose Maria Aznar spoke out in Martinez's behalf. Pope John

Paul II appealed for his life to be spared. Hundreds of thousands of dollars were raised to pay for his defense on appeal and, as it turned out, for a new trial.

Lawson had been shot several times with a 9mm pistol. McCoy-Ward was shot and stabbed more than twenty times as she ran to the front door trying to escape. There was little that linked Martinez to the crime except that he and Lawson had once worked together at a warehouse. It was Martinez's ex-wife, Sloane, who implicated him.

When police searched the crime scene, they found a phone list that included a pager number for someone named Joe. They called the number several times and left messages. Finally, Sloane returned the call and explained to police that she had Martinez's pager. She said that she had suspicions that her ex-husband might have committed the murders. Cooperating with the authorities, Sloane secretly recorded a conversation with Martinez at her home, during which he was said to have made "several remarks that could be interpreted as incriminating." The tape of the conversation, which was barely audible, was allowed in as evidence. Martinez's girlfriend testified that he had gone out on the night of the murders and returned with a swollen lip and scraped knuckles, looking as though he had been in a fight. With no clear-cut motive for the crime, the prosecution contended that Martinez had gone to the victims' house to buy marijuana. It was not much of a motive, and the prosecution's entire case seemed to rest on the testimony of a woman the defense portrayed as a vengeful ex-wife and on a tape that was at best suggestive.

Nonetheless, Martinez was convicted and in the end might have been executed were it not for the misstatement of one of the state's witnesses. Under direct examination, a police detective told the jury he thought the defendant was guilty. The prosecutor repeated the statement in his closing argument. Because of the improper statements, the Florida Supreme Court overturned the conviction and sentence and ordered a new trial.

The state's case was even weaker the second time around. A critical blow to the prosecution came when Circuit Court Judge J. Rogers

Padgett ruled the taped conversation between Martinez and his ex-wife was inaudible and therefore could not be introduced as evidence. Furthermore, the transcript of the tape, which had been used for clarification during the first trial, was excluded when it was revealed that it had been prepared by Lawson's father, who was the evidence manager for the Hillsborough County Sheriff's Office. The pool of witnesses also had shrunk during the four years since the first trial. One witness had died, another now refused to cooperate, and the prosecution's star, Sloane Martinez, had changed her story to the point where it was of little use to the state.

It took the jury just two hours to acquit Martinez. The verdict was broadcast live in Spain. The Spanish Prime Minister welcomed the news, saying, "I'm very happy that this Spaniard was declared not guilty. I've always been against the death penalty and I always will be."

Juan Roberto Melendez
Florida

Juan Roberto Melendez, born in Brooklyn and raised in Puerto Rico, was sent to Florida's death row in 1984 for the murder of a beauty school owner who was found shot to death in his Auburndale, Florida school on September 13, 1983. His appeals were denied and the sentence upheld, but Melendez continued to protest his innocence, and in 1988 he secured the services of an important ally. His case was taken by the Capital Collateral Representative (CCR), a public defender for those who have been sentenced to death in the northern region of Florida. CCR intervenes after the death sentence and conviction have been affirmed on direct appeal.

According to Rosa Greenbaum, who assumed responsibility for the Melendez case in 2000, "The next stage is referred to as post-conviction and, unlike direct-appeal attorneys, we are allowed to bring up non-record violations such as the withholding of exculpatory evidence and newly discovered evidence." Greenbaum found such evidence to be in no short supply, and much of it had been withheld by the state. She also discovered that the testimony of the prosecution's two key witnesses lacked any vestige of credibility.

The beauty school owner, Delbert Baker, had been shot three times, his throat had been cut, and the expensive gold jewelry he was wearing had been taken. Early in 1984, a man by the name of David Falcon contacted Florida law-enforcement officials and said he knew who killed Baker. Melendez's defense team gave the following account of the events that ensued, as reported by Bill Berkowitz on the Working for Change website:

"Falcon aspired to become a confidential informant for local law enforcement officials and he also held a personal grudge against Juan [Melendez]. Falcon claimed Juan had confessed to the killing, but he did not know basic details, such as where the crime had occurred. Falcon also implicated . . . John Berrien [who] was picked up and, after being threatened with the death penalty, told multiple stories riddled with inconsistencies and inaccuracies. Berrien finally wove a tale that was acceptable to authorities, saying he had driven Juan to the beauty school around the time of the killing.

"According to Berrien, Juan had been armed with a .38-caliber firearm that day and later described jewelry he'd taken in the robbery. Berrien also claimed [that] his cousin, George Berrien, had gone into the school with Juan that day. No weapon or jewelry was ever recovered. No physical evidence was found in Berrien's car, in which Juan and George had allegedly made their escape from the blood-deluged crime scene. George Berrien denied his cousin's story, testified on behalf of Juan's defense, and this supposed co-perpetrator was never even charged. John Berrien was sentenced to two years of house arrest as an accessory to first-degree murder after the fact."

Falcon and Berrien were the key witnesses for the state when Melendez went on trial in September 1984. Melendez's only defense was that there was no physical evidence linking him to the crime and a girlfriend who testified that she was with him at the time. The jury chose to believe the two prosecution witnesses. Melendez was convicted and sentenced to death.

Some critical evidence in Melendez's favor surfaced about a month before the trial, but the defense was unable to use it. Another man, Vernon James, had confessed to being implicated in the murder, and a tape-recorded confession was made in the presence of Melendez's investigator and attorney. In his statement, James admitted "he had been at the beauty school when Baker was murdered by two other men and . . . that Melendez had not been anywhere near the scene of the crime." Despite the existence of the tape, James invoked his Fifth Amendment right against self-incrimination when he was called to the witness stand. The taped statement then was considered to be hearsay evidence and was never shown to the judge or jury. It was, however, turned up by Rosa Greenbaum, and it became the cornerstone of her appeal that finally led to Melendez's conviction being reversed.

Greenbaum contacted the trial defense investigator, Cody Smith, and the defense attorney, Roger Alcott. They eventually found the transcript of the tape. State Attorney Hardy Pickard said he had been in possession of the transcript since the original trial. The defense also produced a dozen witnesses at two separate hearings who testified that James had made incriminating statements to them regarding his involvement in the murder and had indicated again and again that the wrong man was convicted of the crime.

Circuit Court Judge Barbara Fleischer, who heard the appeal, also found that John Berrien's trial testimony repeatedly contradicted the sworn statement he had given to the prosecutor during an interview and that the prosecutor had failed to disclose the out-of-court statement to either the defense or the jury. In addition, the judge determined that the state had misled the jury when it said Falcon had nothing to gain by testifying. In fact, charges that Falcon had broken into a residence had been dropped in exchange for his testimony.

In overturning the conviction, Judge Fleischer noted that the evidence that was withheld supported the defense's theory that another man committed the murder. She said that if the state wanted to keep Melendez in prison it must try him again and pointed out that the new evidence "seriously damaged" the state's case. Indeed it did. Berrien had lost all credibility, and Falcon and James had both died during the seventeen years Melendez spent on death row. The state agreed to drop the charges, and Melendez was finally released.

In summing up, Rosa Greenbaum said: "The important thing to remember is that this outcome does not show that the system works, as death penalty supporters might claim. If not for a courageous judge, witnesses who selflessly showed up and told the truth, the simple dumb luck of locating the taped confession of Vernon James after all these years, and the surprising fact that James told lots of people what he'd done, this story would likely have a very different ending."

Kerry Cook
Texas

The name Kerry Cook does not appear on any of the lists of innocent people released from death row, although he clearly belongs near the top of the register. Cook served almost twenty years on death row, wrongfully convicted of murder, but he was not officially exonerated until two years after he pleaded no contest in a deal that restored his freedom.

In 1978, Cook, who was twenty-two years old and living in Tyler, Texas, was arrested for the murder of Linda Jo Edwards, an acquaintance who lived in the same apartment complex. Edwards was a college student and was having an affair with her married professor. Cook had been invited into her apartment once and had left a fingerprint on a sliding glass door.

Three months after Cook had met with her, police stormed the club in which he worked as a bartender and arrested him, despite the weight of evidence that implicated the victim's much older, married boyfriend. Investigators theorized that, since the well-known nightspot had a largely gay clientele, Cook was a "degenerate homosexual" who hated women and had brutalized the body of the victim. At his trial, a fingerprint expert testified that he could date Cook's fingerprint to be twelve hours old when the body was discovered, placing him in the apartment at the time of the murder. The testimony went unchallenged although it is scientifically impossible to date a fingerprint. The only other evidence offered by the prosecution was the testimony of an eyewitness who said she had seen Cook in Edwards's apartment and that of a jail inmate, Eddie "Shyster" Jackson, who said he heard Cook confess. Cook was found guilty and sentenced to death.

In 1988, the US Supreme Court ordered the Texas court to review its decision just eleven days short of Cook's execution date. His conviction was overturned in 1991, and his retrial a year later ended in a hung jury. In 1993, a state district judge ruled that prosecutors had engaged in systematic misconduct, suppressing key evidence, and in 1994 Cook was tried a third time. This time he was convicted and again sentenced to death. But the system continued to grind away.

On November 6, 1996, the Texas Court of Criminal Appeals reversed the conviction, saying that "prosecutorial and police misconduct has tainted this entire matter from the outset." The court also ruled that key testimony from the 1994 trial could not be used in any further prosecution. A fourth trial was scheduled for February 1999. However, concerned about the possibility of yet another wrongful conviction, Cook accepted a deal. He pleaded no contest to a reduced murder charge, was sentenced to time served and released.

It was later learned that the eyewitness had originally identified Edwards's professor as the man she saw in the apartment, but she then changed her testimony and named Cook. Jackson, the jailhouse informant, recanted his testimony entirely. The fingerprint expert admitted it was impossible to date a fingerprint and said he had been coerced into testifying as he did by the district attorney's office. Most importantly, DNA tests conducted two years after Cook's release showed that the semen found on the victim matched the professor's, not Cook's.

Since his release, Cook has married and became the father of a son. The boy is named Kerry Justice. "After twenty-three years," Cook says, "Justice has finally arrived."

PART II

Eyewitness Error
& False Accusation

THE PLAYFULLY CYNICAL injunction that you should believe nothing you hear and only half of what you see has its purchase on truth in the criminal justice system. False eyewitness testimony is considered the principal cause of wrongful convictions in United States courts.

There are, of course, several types of eyewitness error, from simple cases of mistaken identification to perjured testimony or some other form of official misconduct. It is difficult to counter mistaken identification offered in good faith by a witness who actually saw the accused. But even when the sole intent of the witness is to abet the judicial process, eyewitness accounts have been found to be generally unreliable. The original identification is often made under unfavorable conditions: the witness was likely to be a good distance away from the accused who was possibly shrouded in darkness; the glimpse of the suspect was more often than not a fleeting one, perhaps no more than a second or two; and observations made in extreme circumstances, when adrenaline is running high, tend to be untrustworthy. When a defendant is convicted solely on the basis of such testimony, the possibility of error is exceptionally high.

While mistaken eyewitness testimony, even if offered honestly, freely, and with good intent, can nonetheless send innocent people to prison, testimony that is perjured or compelled can appear to a jury to be even more convincing, for it is likely to have been crafted carefully and well-rehearsed. The eyewitness or first-hand evidence offered by criminal informants in exchange for considerations such as reduction of sentence or the imposition of lesser charges is always, at best, questionable. Jailhouse snitches in search of privilege, co-defendants hoping to slip the noose themselves, or suspects looking to point the finger in other directions are all hazardous to the prospect of justice being done in a court of law. Equally hazardous is testimony prompted by agents of the prosecution—police or attorneys—eager to nail down a conviction by squeezing a witness to alter, if not fabricate, the story they tell the jury.

The Center on Wrongful Convictions recently studied eighty-six cases in which defendants sentenced to death were exonerated on claims of actual innocence (rather than on the basis of judicial error or circumstances involving prosecutorial or police misconduct) since the US Supreme Court's 1972 decision restoring capital punishment. Eyewitness testimony played a part in forty-six convictions and was the only evidence against thirty-three defendants. In thirty-two cases, only one eyewitness testified. The eyewitnesses were strangers to nineteen defendants and in nine other cases were acquainted with the defendant but not accomplices. Fifteen of the eyewitnesses were in some way accomplices of the accused, and they all had incentives to testify, ranging from full immunity to leniency in sentencing. In five cases, a non-accomplice witness received consideration from the prosecution in a pending case. In four other instances, the false testimony appeared to have been motivated by a grudge, and in another the eyewitness and the defendant formed two sides of a love triangle.

The vulnerability of eyewitness testimony became the focus of national attention in 1998 when Anthony Porter was freed from Illinois' death row following an investigation into his case by Lawrence C. Marshall and David Protess, both law professors at Northwestern University Law

School, and a cadre of journalism students at the university's Medill School of Journalism. Further investigations led to eight other innocent men on death row being released, and a nationwide drumbeat began calling into question the merits of a system of capital punishment that condemns innocent people to death. If a class of journalism students led by two law professors was so readily able to uncover the wrongful convictions and death sentences meted out to nine men, how many others awaiting execution might also be innocent? Indeed, Anthony Porter was just fifty hours away from being put to death. For how many others did time run out?

Anthony Porter
Illinois

The funeral arrangements had been made and Anthony Porter was counting down the hours of life he had left. He was scheduled to die in an Illinois death house on September 23, 1998. The stay of execution came two days earlier, but another five months would pass before he was released. He had spent more than fifteen years on death row.

The trouble began for Porter when two teenagers—Marilyn Green, nineteen, and Jerry Hilliard, eighteen—were shot to death in the bleachers overlooking a swimming pool on the South Side of Chicago late on an August night in 1982. William Taylor, who had been swimming in the pool at the time, was among those interviewed by police immediately after the shooting. Taylor first told them he had not seen who did the shooting, but at the station house he said he recalled seeing Porter running right after he heard the shots. Another seventeen hours of questioning elicited the statement that he actually had seen Porter shoot the pair.

Porter, who was known to belong to a South Side street gang, was a likely enough suspect. There were others, perhaps even more likely. The mother of the female victim, Ofra Green, told the police she suspected a man by the name of Alstory Simon, who had been feuding with Hilliard over drug money. Mrs. Green also said she had seen Simon and his wife, Inez Jackson, with the victims not long before they were killed. Questioned by police, the couple said they had not been in the park that night. A few days later, they moved to Milwaukee.

On no evidence other than Taylor's eyewitness account, Porter was charged with the double murder. His family opted to retain a private attorney rather than employ a public defender, believing it would give Porter a better chance of acquittal. It was a decision that might have cost Porter dearly. The lawyer, Akim Gursel, was to be paid $10,000 for his services. However, he never received the full payment and Gursel later said he cut short his investigation of the case due to lack of funds.

The trial, which began in September 1983, did not go well for the defendant. Gursel fell asleep at the defense table at least once, and the judge had to wake him up. The defense called only two alibi witnesses and a photographer who had taken aerial shots of the park in which the shooting took place. The jury deliberated for nine hours and returned a verdict of guilty.

With a possible death sentence on the table, Gursel waived Porter's right to have the jury decide the sentence and left it to the judge. Sentencing hearings in Illinois are carried out in three phases. During the first phase it is determined whether the convicted man is eligible for the death penalty; the second is devoted to a consideration of mitigating circumstances; and the third is for sentencing. After phase one, in which the judge decided Porter was eligible for execution, Gursel informed the judge, Robert L. Sklodowski, that one of the jurors attended the same church as Marilyn Green's mother. The juror had failed to disclose that bit of information during voir dire, and, armed with this revelation, Gursel now moved for a mistrial. As the jury had not yet been dismissed, Sklodowski questioned the juror about her relationship with the victim's mother and why she had not made it known to the court. The juror told the judge that she did not realize she knew Ofra Green until the trial was under way, but that it made no difference to her. That satisfied the judge, and he denied the motion for a retrial. The next day, Sklodowski found nothing to mitigate his final judgment and sentenced Porter to death.

Gursel appealed the verdict to the Illinois Supreme Court on the grounds that Porter had been denied a fair trial before an impartial jury. In February 1986, the court denied the appeal by a vote of four-to-three. The majority opinion noted that the juror in question did not realize she knew the victim's mother until after the trial began and therefore it was not likely that their relationship was very close. In separate dissenting opinions, one judge maintained there was no basis for the majority's speculating on the closeness of the relationship. The second dissent found that the judge's questioning of the juror had been leading and too brief to assess the relationship between the two women.

Porter carried his case to the US Supreme Court where he petitioned for a writ of certiorari which would have ordered the state court to submit the case to the higher court for review. The petition was denied, with dissents from Justices Thurgood Marshall and William Brennan who wrote that the state court had erred in requiring the defendant to bear the burden of showing actual prejudice when the probability of bias appeared to be substantial.

Porter then filed a post-conviction petition claiming he had not had the benefit of effective counsel since Gursel failed to locate and summon four witnesses who could have suggested that Alstory Simon and Inez Johnson actually committed the murders, thereby raising reasonable doubt about Porter's guilt. When his request for relief was turned down, Porter petitioned for a federal writ of habeas corpus which would have referred his case for review by a federal court. The US District Court denied the request, and that decision was affirmed by the US Court of Appeals for the Seventh Circuit.

Porter's case had been grinding through the judicial machinery for twelve years, but it now appeared he had reached the end of the line. When the Court of Appeals handed down its decision, on March 23, 1998, his execution was set for December 23. The nine-month time period proved to be salvation for Porter.

A volunteer Chicago lawyer, Daniel R. Sanders, entered the case and had Porter's IQ tested. It was measured at 51, which by all standards meant Porter was mentally retarded. Execution of the mentally retarded was legal in Illinois at the time, still several years before the US Supreme Court ruled it unconstitutional. Nevertheless, with the execution date fast approaching, Larry Marshall and three other pro bono attorneys filed a last-minute petition with the state supreme court, contending that Porter was incapable of comprehending the nature of his punishment and therefore should not be put to death. Two days before he was scheduled to die, the court granted a stay of execution and ordered the Cook County Circuit Court to hold a competency hearing to determine whether Porter was capable of understanding the consequence of his fate.

At this point, Protess and his students, along with Paul Ciolino, a private investigator, began their investigation. The first break came in December when William Taylor, whose eyewitness testimony had doomed Porter, recanted and told Ciolino and one of the students that he had not seen him commit the crime. He said in an affidavit that police had pressured him to name Porter as the shooter. On January 29, 1999, Inez Jackson, now separated from her husband, gave him up. She told Protress, Ciolino, and two students that she was present when Alstory Simon shot Green and Hilliard. Four days later, Simon gave Ciolino a videotaped confession in which he claimed to have killed Hilliard in self-defense during a disagreement over drug money. He said the shooting of Green had been accidental.

Porter was released from prison on a recognizance bond on February 5, and he was cleared of all charges a month later. In September 1999, Alstory Simon pleaded guilty to two counts of second-degree murder. He was sentenced to thirty-seven and a half years in prison.

Porter's exoneration was the first of at least nine that resulted from investigations by Protess and his student team. The effects of their efforts have already been massive, and the likelihood is that they have just begun to be felt. In January 2000, one year after Porter walked free, Governor George Ryan imposed a moratorium on all executions. In October 2002, capital punishment was put on trial in Illinois. Clemency hearings, coordinated by the Center for Wrongful Convictions, were ordered for 142 of the 158 prisoners on death row.

Experts on witness identification, false confessions, and other causes of wrongful conviction were flown in from California, New Mexico, and Texas. Some three hundred lawyers prepared briefs to be presented. A few months later, Governor Ryan would make headlines by emptying Illinois's death row.

Executing the mentally retarded had already been taken off the table by a US Supreme Court decision in the spring of 2002 in which the majority noted that a shift in public attitude over the past decade or more had rendered executions of the retarded cruel and unusual punishment. Prompted by events in Illinois, other states have begun to examine the manner in which they apply capital punishment and the likelihood that it results in the execution of innocent people. It is not possible to estimate how many have been unjustly sent to their death. But the probabilities obviously increase as the total number of executions rises.

Rudolph Holton
Florida

The flimsy nature of eyewitness testimony was plainly visible in the case of Rudolph Holton. Holton was convicted of murder and sentenced to death based almost entirely on the identification of two eyewitnesses, both of whom later recanted their testimony and were convicted of perjury.

The victim was Katrina Ann Graddy, a seventeen-year-old drug addict and prostitute who was raped, strangled, then set on fire in an abandoned crack house in the Central Park Village housing project in Tampa, Florida in June 1987. A neighbor told police he saw thirty-three-year-old Holton enter the house with a girl at 11 p.m. on the night of the murder. When they searched the premises, police found a pack of cigarettes containing Holton's fingerprints. Holton, no stranger to the police, seemed a viable suspect. He was a known drug addict with a $1,000-a-day habit and a record of more than two dozen arrests and thirteen convictions for theft and burglary. However, he had no record of violent behavior.

When detectives first interviewed him, he lied about being in the drug house. When they told him about the fingerprints, he said they could not have been his. In both instances, he was lying, but it was hardly enough to warrant his conviction for murder. Scores of drug users, including Holton, used the house and placing him at the scene was largely irrelevant. It was the flawed testimony of witnesses that sent him to death row for sixteen years. Carrie Nelson, a resident of the drug house said she saw Nelson at the scene on the night of the crime. She said she knew Holton because he had robbed her four times. Another witness, Johnny Lee Newsome, also put Holton at the scene. Yet a third, Flemmie Birkins, an inmate at Hillsborough jail who had known Holton from the streets, testified that he admitted having committed the crime. On June 30, 1987, a jury convicted Holton of murder and he was sentenced to death. The only physical evidence introduced by the prosecution was several pubic hairs found in the victim's mouth which *could have been* Holton's.

Gradually, all the evidence against Holton began to unravel. DNA testing showed that the hairs could not have been his. Elease Moore, a friend of Nelson's, said she had invented her story in order to get even with Holton for the robberies. Newsome, who was on probation, acknowledged that he did not see Holton that night. He said he lied as an accommodation to the police to keep them from investigating him further.

As for Birkins, he also admitted that he had invented his story. "I was scared," he said. "I thought the police would get me for something I was doing. I told [the detective] what he wanted to hear. I used it to my advantage." Police records that were found later corroborated Birkins's recantation. They showed that at precisely the same hour Birkins claimed Holton was confessing to him at the jail, he was being interviewed by detectives at the Tampa Police Department. Birkins, it turned out, had reason enough to fabricate his story. Although prosecutors told the jury he was given nothing in exchange for his testimony while he awaited trial on charges of burglary and grand theft, subsequent events suggested otherwise. After the prosecutor asked the judge for leniency, Birkins was given probation when he could have received a life sentence as a habitual offender. The defense was never told of the deal.

With the evidence against Holton all but shredded, a Florida judge granted him a new trial in 2001. But the state was of no mind to retry the case. Holton was released on January 4, 2003 after spending sixteen years on death row. He was awarded $100 for his inconvenience. Birkins and Newsome both pleaded guilty to perjury. Birkins was sentenced to thirteen years in prison and Newsome to a fourteen-year term.

Post-prison life did not seem to suit Holton well. Shortly after his release he married a woman he had met just a few months earlier. A year later, he pleaded guilty to aggravated battery for striking the woman with a golf club and to misdemeanor assault for a confrontation with a cousin of his. He was sentenced to two years in prison. It got worse. In 2006, Holton was convicted of attempted murder and domestic battery for choking his wife. This time his sentence was twenty years.

John Thompson
Louisiana

Right from the start, it was a bumpy road for John Thompson. It began with a false accusation, moved ahead with identification error, and proceeded through a quagmire of prosecutorial misconduct that found its way to the United States Supreme Court. Yet, against all probability, his story had a happy ending.

The improbable tale began shortly after midnight on December 6, 1984, when Raymond Liuzza was shot several times in the course of a robbery just around the corner from his apartment in New Orleans. Liuzza was still alive and conscious when the police arrived. Before being rushed to a hospital, where he died soon after arrival, he identified the man who robbed and shot him as an African American male. Two days later, acting on a tip from a man named Richard Perkins, police arrested Thompson, a twenty-two-year-old father of two, and Kevin Freeman, an acquaintance of his. The New Orleans *Times-Picayune* published photos of the two men and they soon received a call from a family saying that Thompson looked like the man who had hijacked their car and robbed them several months earlier. On that identification alone, the police charged Thompson with both the carjacking and the murder. Compounding matters, Freeman came forth and told police that he was with Thompson when they robbed and shot Liuzza but that it was Liuzza who pulled the trigger. Freeman agreed to testify against Thompson in the murder trial if prosecutors charged him only as an accessory. He was eventually tried, convicted, and sentenced to five years in prison.

New Orleans District Attorney Harry Connick Sr. decided to try Thompson on the carjacking charge first, reasoning that a prior felony conviction would help his case in the murder trial. Based almost entirely on the testimony of the three carjacking victims, Thompson was convicted and sentenced to forty-nine years. In the murder trial, which began right on the heels of the hijacking conviction, the prosecution showed that Thompson had at one time been in possession of both the murder weapon and a ring that had been taken from Liuzza's finger. As Connick had calculated, Thompson declined to take the stand in his own defense because that would have enabled the prosecution to bring his previous conviction to the attention of the jury. He therefore forfeited the opportunity to explain that Freeman had sold him the gun and the ring. Freeman, in turn, now became the prosecution's chief witness. He testified that he and Thompson had acted together in the robbery of Liuzza but that it was Thompson who had shot him. Perkins, who had called in the original tip, also was a witness for the prosecution, testifying that he had heard Thompson make incriminating remarks. For the defense, several eyewitnesses claimed they had seen only one man running from the scene of the crime. But that made little impression on the jury. They voted with the prosecution. Thompson was found guilty and was sentenced to be executed in May 1985.

Over the next fourteen years, Thompson's attorneys filed a succession of appeals, but all were denied. By 1999, the appeal process was exhausted and an execution date was set for May. But, with just thirty days remaining, things finally turned in Thompson's favor. An investigator discovered that there was a blood stain, apparently from the robber, on the clothing of one of the carjacking victims. This piece of evidence had never been brought to the attention of the defense. Worse yet, the prosecutors had rushed to have the blood tested, but when it was found to be different from Thompson's, they chose to conceal it entirely. With this new bit of information in hand, defense attorneys obtained an affidavit from a former district attorney stating that a prosecutor in the case had admitted to intentionally suppressing the blood evidence. Thompson's attorney also discovered that Perkins had received $15,000 from the Liuzza family as a reward for identifying Thompson as the killer. Given the new evidence, the trial judge granted a stay of execution and dismissed the carjacking conviction but denied Thompson's motion for a new trial on the murder charge. He did, however, reduce his death sentence to life in prison without parole.

Two years later, the outlook grew even brighter for Thompson. In July 2002, the Louisiana Fourth Circuit Court of Appeals overturned his murder conviction and remanded the case for retrial. The court ruled that Thompson was "denied his right to testify in his own behalf based upon the improper actions of the State in the other case." The court further noted that it was "the State's intentional hiding of exculpatory evidence in the armed robbery case that led to [Thompson's] improper conviction in that case and his subsequent decision not to testify in the instant case because of the improper conviction."

At the second trial, Thompson took the stand and told the jury that he had not fired the fatal shots and that he had purchased the murder weapon from Freeman after Liuzza had been killed. The defense called several new witnesses who said they had seen only one man fleeing the scene of the murder. They also testified that the man did not look like Thompson, but he did resemble Freeman. Freeman was not around to challenge their stories. He had been killed in a shootout with a security guard while in prison. In May 2003, a jury acquitted Thompson after only thirty-five minutes of deliberation. He was freed the same day after serving eighteen years in prison, fourteen of them on death row. Upon his release, he was given ten dollars and a bus ticket.

Thompson sued the district attorney's office, headed by Harry Connick Sr., and in 2008 he was awarded $14 million—one for each year spent on death row—by a federal court jury. The jury found that Thompson's years behind bars "were caused by Connick's deliberate failure to train his prosecutors on their obligations to turn over exculpatory evidence." The DA's office appealed the decision and the case was orally argued before the US Supreme Court in *Connick v. Thompson*. On March 29, 2011, the court, voting 5-4 along ideological lines, overturned the award. Writing for the majority, Justice Clarence Thomas said that the misconduct in the case was not the result of a deliberate policy of systematic indifference by the New Orleans district attorney's office. Justice Ruth Bader Ginsburg disagreed. In her dissent, read from the bench, she noted that Connick's office had in fact committed a pattern of violations, failing to disclose exculpatory blood-type evidence, audio tapes of witness testimony, a deathbed confession about the destruction of evidence by the prosecuting attorney Gerry Deegan, and eyewitness identification of the killer that did not match Thompson. In the end, Thompson received $330,000 in state compensation. Justice Ginsburg was not alone in her view. According to the Innocence Project of New Orleans, Connick's office has withheld evidence favorable to the defense in at least nine death-row cases. Four of the cases were overturned because of the misconduct.

The happy epilogue to Thompson's story was chronicled by CNN in its series of *Death Row Stories*. When he was released, Thompson was on the cusp of middle age, with no education beyond the ninth grade. He had never used a cellphone or a computer and he knew it would take a while for him to equip himself to function in a world that was dramatically different from the one he left nearly two decades earlier. He also understood that there were thousands of others who faced the same challenge.

"Men come home and the system has nothing in place to help them put their lives back together," he said. "They need to be reprogrammed because the survival tactics they learned in prison don't work in the outside world."

Thompson decided to do something about it. With the aid of his appellate attorneys, Michael Banks and Gordon Cooney, he started an organization called *Resurrection After Exoneration*, an education and outreach program that helps exonerated and formerly incarcerated inmates rebuild their lives. The organization also teaches participants how to tell their story so they can participate in community outreach efforts. He considers these essential to building empathy and understanding of the needs of inmates returning to society. "Like it or not," he says, these people are going to be in the community; it's society's responsibility to help give them a fighting chance."

Commentary: Fixing the System

"The criminal justice system is broken" has become the mantra of the judicial system and politicians of all persuasions. In all states, large and small, north and south, right-wing and left, there appears to be universal agreement that the system needs fixing. Then why, one might ask, is so little being done? The answer magnifies the difficulty of finding solutions: there is significant disagreement on what exactly needs to be fixed and in which direction lies the road to repair. Few candidates for office, regardless of what they really believe, are concerned that a hard-nosed law-and-order platform will cost them any votes. They appear to be more troubled by the possibility of a guilty man being turned loose than an innocent man being convicted. No serious candidate is eager to challenge the tough-on-crime legions that are ready to risk the lives of the innocent rather than be tagged "bleeding heart liberals."

Yet there are some clearly defined areas in which agreement is both reasonable and safe. For example, rare is the corrections official or politician who is prepared to stake his claim on the benefits of solitary confinement. Its horrors and ineffectiveness have been well documented and, from the president on down through the ranks of the judicial hierarchy, the disposition to seal the solitary cells forever is clearly gathering force. The tightening of the process of interrogation also seems to be gaining favor among both sides of the issue. These and other such remedies— the fine-tuning of the grand-jury system, for one—might well be on the way to enactment in various states. But there are vast changes of a more sweeping nature that have come under consideration.

Faulty accusations and eyewitness testimony are by far the leading causes of errant convictions, but reform in that area would be complex and uncertain. Still, New York State has taken a few small steps in that direction. In June 2015, the State Bar Association of New York and the Innocence Project joined hands in an effort to reduce the chances that innocent people will be convicted on the basis of either false witness testimony or accusations. According to *New York Times* columnist Jim Dwyer, the proposals would require investigators to treat the testimony of witnesses and suspects as if they were just another kind of trace evidence subject to contamination.

"Witnesses," Dwyer wrote, "would be shown photos of possible suspects by an investigator who was not handling the case, with the goal of eliminating even inadvertent hints or cues about the 'right' answer from detectives who might have a suspect in mind.

"Once an identification has been made, witnesses would be immediately asked how certain they were of their choice. Witnesses often become more confident over time, so a shaky choice at a police lineup hardens into concrete certainty at trial."

Dwyer cites a review of 161 wrongful convictions which found that 57 percent of the eyewitnesses had not been certain during the initial identifications but had no hesitation when testifying much later during trials, according to Brandon L.

Garrett, a professor at the University of Virginia School of Law. Gary L. Wells, a psychologist at Iowa State University, supports that finding. He says that uncertain witnesses who are given positive feedback such as "You did great" or "He's a bad guy, we thought it might be him" also grow more confident about their choices.

Of course, such twists and turns lie primarily within the province of the states rather than the federal government. But the direction in which the views on capital punishment are moving is clear enough. In August 2015, the Connecticut Supreme Court ruled that the death penalty violated state constitutional bans on cruel and unusual punishment, the same criterion that is provided in the Eighth Amendment of the Bill of Rights. The decision made retroactive the three-year-old repeal of capital punishment in the state and spared the lives of eleven death row inmates whose convictions pre-dated the ruling against the death penalty. But state decisions often resonate at the federal level. Several US Supreme Court Justices, Stephen Breyer foremost among them, have indicated their opposition to capital punishment, and a number of cases likely to come before the court in its 2015–2016 term will test the depth of their convictions. In the meantime, an increasingly large number of inmates benefit from the changing mood of the country as well as the court. And when it comes to such matters, timing is everything.

Alan Gell
North Carolina

The timing was all wrong for twenty-year-old Alan Gell. He was tried, convicted, and sentenced to death for the murder of a man who was alive and well for at least a week after Gell was presumed to have killed him.

The story began on April 14, 1995, when Allen Ray Jenkins, a fifty-six-year-old truck driver was found dead in his home in Aulander,

North Carolina. He had been shot twice in the chest with a shotgun. Jenkins had a record of having sex with underage girls and that became the focus of the police investigation. In July, three months after the body was discovered, police interviewed two fifteen-year-old girls—Shanna Hall, who was Gell's girlfriend at the time, and Crystal Morris—both of whom were known to have gone to Jenkins's home on occasion where their age did not prevent them from drinking. The girls were interviewed several times and the stories they told often conflicted. Eventually, they settled on a confession in which they said they had been accomplices with Gell in a plot to rob Jenkins. They said they carried out their plan on April 3 and, during the course of the robbery, Gell had shot and killed Jenkins. With little more than the testimony of the two girls, Gell was charged with first-degree murder, conspiracy to commit murder, armed robbery, and conspiracy to commit armed robbery. In exchange for their testimony, Hall and Morris were allowed to plead guilty to the lesser charge of second-degree murder for which they each received a sentence of ten years in prison. Gell was sentenced to death.

Gell, whose record was hardly spotless, had been in jail since June 25, having been found guilty of breaking a house-arrest sentence he had received for stealing a truck. At the 1998 trial, in addition to the testimony of the two girls, the prosecution offered the judgment of a doctor who testified that, given the decomposition of Jenkins's body, it was likely he died around April 3. The date was critical because Gell had been either traveling or in jail for most of the first two weeks in April. April 3 was the only date on which Gell could have committed the crime. The jury found him guilty and the death sentence was imposed in Bertie County, Superior Court.

Gell's initial appeal was denied in 1999, but three years later a state superior court judge found that prosecutors had withheld evidence favorable to the accused, including the eyewitness testimony of seventeen witnesses who said they had seen Jenkins alive as late as April 10. Jenkins's brother, Sidney, as well as a neighbor, Mary Hunt, recalled seeing him on April 8. Edward and Margaret Adams reported seeing him on April 9 while out for a walk. Jenkins was seen as late as April 10 in Ahoskie by a former co-worker, a restaurant waitress, and a man who said he sold Jenkins a dozen herrings on that date. On the grounds of prosecutorial misconduct, Gell's conviction was vacated and he was retried in February 2004. In addition to the eyewitness testimony regarding the date of Jenkins's death, the defense played a tape recording of Morris saying she had to make up a story to tell to the police. Also, a doctor testified that due to the exceptionally high temperature in the house the body could have decomposed quickly and Jenkins could well have died as late as April 14. On February 18, Gell was acquitted on all charges and released.

Having spent six years behind bars, four of them on death row, Gell filed a lawsuit accusing the North Carolina State Bureau of Investigation of fabricating evidence and obstructing justice. In 2009, he accepted a settlement of $3.9 million.

The Gell case raised concerns about the manner in which the death penalty was applied in North Carolina. "If the attorney general's office had had its way, Gell would be dead now," said Rich Rose, a law professor at the University of North Carolina and an adviser to the school's Innocence Project. "This case surely shakes the confidence of the people of North Carolina both in the state's capital punishment system and in the people who administer it."

Shortly after Gell's exoneration, the North Carolina Coalition for a Moratorium was formed, a statewide group of organizations and individuals who support a temporary suspension of executions while the system of capital punishment was studied. Calling the Gell case a "travesty of justice," David Neal, a spokesman for the Moratorium, said, "This is exactly why we need to take a step back, temporarily halt all executions, and figure out what is going wrong in these cases."

The moratorium went into effect in 2007. Within the next two years, three innocent men—Jonathan Hoffman, Glen Edward Chapman, and Levon "Bo" Jones—were released from death row. Between 2007 and 2014, the murder rate in North Carolina steadily declined.

Jonathan Hoffman
North Carolina

On December 11, 2007, capital murder charges against Jonathan Hoffman were dismissed and he was set free from death row, eleven years after he was convicted of fatally shooting Danny Cook in his jewelry store in Marshville, North Carolina. Hoffman had been arrested in January 1996, on the basis of an anonymous tip. There was no physical evidence connecting him to the crime. He was sentenced to death on the testimony of several witnesses, the most persuasive being his cousin, Johnell Porter, who said Hoffman had confessed to him that he had committed the murder. A second witness was a folk healer who claimed he had sold Hoffman a special root that would keep him from being arrested. On no more convincing evidence, Hoffman, an African American, was tried and convicted by an all-white jury and sentenced to death in November, 1996. On appeal, he argued that the prosecution's selection of the jury involved racial discrimination, but the court affirmed his conviction.

Hoffman's attorneys then played their trump card. They leveled a charge of prosecutorial misconduct. At a hearing in 2004, they introduced newly discovered evidence that Porter's testimony had been bought and paid for. In exchange for his testifying against his cousin, they said, Porter had received thousands of dollars in cash and immunity from federal charges that were pending against him. All of this had been concealed from the defense.

It took little imagination to contemplate prosecutorial misbehavior on the part of Hoffman's prosecutors, Ken Honeycutt and Scott Brewer. When Honeycutt was the district attorney in Union County, he often came to court wearing a gold lapel pin shaped like a hangman's noose. Similar pins were awarded to assistant DAs who won death penalty cases. Both Honeycutt and Brewer were later criminally and civilly investigated for not revealing the deals promised to Porter.

The trial court ordered a new trial. In March 2006, while Hoffman awaited his retrial, Porter recanted his testimony. He said he invented the story because he wanted to even the score with Hoffman for stealing money from him. Nearly two years later, the district attorney dismissed all charges against him and Hoffman was released in December 2007.

Joseph B. Cheshire, V, one of Hoffman's lawyers, said, "The release of Jonathan Hoffman continues the exposure of a pattern of wrongful prosecutions and convictions in North Carolina." He went on to say that "these miscarriages of justice continue to undermine public confidence in our criminal justice system and make our citizens wonder how many other people are wrongfully imprisoned in our state."

Glen Edward Chapman
North Carolina

The "pattern of wrongful prosecutions and convictions in North Carolina" continued for a time even as the Coalition for a Moratorium morphed into the NC Coalition for Alternatives to the Death Penalty. Just four months after Hoffman was exonerated, Glen Edward Chapman was set free after spending nearly fourteen years on death row.

Chapman was convicted in 1994 of the murders of two women— Tenene Yvette Conley and Betty Jean Ramseur, both reputed prostitutes—whose bodies were discovered within a week of one another's in two abandoned houses in Hickory, North Carolina. When Chapman's sperm was found in Conley's body, he was charged with murdering both victims. He admitted having smoked crack with both of them and with having had consensual sex with Conley, but denied killing either of them. There was no other physical evidence linking him to the crimes.

The trial, which began on October 31, 1994, was a sham from start to finish, involving false accusation, perjury, prosecutorial misconduct, and inadequate defense. The state's case was lean and insubstantial. The prosecutor maintained that Chapman was the last person seen with Conley before her body was found. The house where Ramseur's body was found had been set on fire, and the prosecutor claimed Chapman had tried to burn the house down in order to destroy evidence of the crime. Two witnesses who testified that Chapman had confessed to them, later recanted, saying they had been intimidated by the police and prosecutors.

Chapman's attorneys offered little in the way of a defense. Both of them, Robert Adams and Thomas Portwood, were reputed alcoholics. Adams has been disciplined by the North Carolina State Bar and Portwood later died of an alcohol-related illness. Portwood in fact admitted to drinking heavily—as much as twelve drinks a day—during other capital trials. One client who was tried during such a drinking binge, Ronald Frye, was executed in 2001. On November 10, Chapman was convicted on two counts of first-degree murder and sentenced to death.

During post-conviction investigation, appellate lawyers found that exculpatory evidence had been concealed from the defense. In the Ramseur case, a credible confession by another person and witness testimony that identified another man as the killer in a photo lineup had been withheld. The charge that Chapman had burned down the house where Ramseur's body was found was discredited by evidence that the fire was set after the body had been removed.

The newly uncovered facts in the Conley case proved even more compelling. Witnesses testified that they had seen the victim, after prosecutors said she had been killed, in the company of a man who had a record of violent behavior towards her. In fact, evidence was introduced indicating that Conley might not have been murdered at all, but had died from an overdose of cocaine.

After six post-conviction hearings over the next four years, Superior Court Judge Robert C. Ervin issued a 186-page order granting Chapman a new trial, citing withheld evidence; lost, misplaced or destroyed documents; the use of weak, circumstantial evidence; false testimony by the lead investigator; and ineffective assistance of defense counsel. The district attorney dismissed all charges against Chapman and he was released from prison on April 2, 2008.

Upon his release, Chapman spent most of his time working in low-wage jobs and "relying on the support of his adopted hometown of Asheville, where yearly fundraisers were held in his honor. He traveled around the state speaking about his exoneration and the many flaws in the criminal justice system that led to his conviction. 'I can forgive,' Chapman says, 'but that doesn't mean I have to forget.'" He died in July 2015, at the age of forty-eight.

Levon "Bo" Jones
North Carolina

One month after Chapman was freed, murder charges against Levon "Bo" Jones were dropped and he was released from prison on May 2, 2008 after spending thirteen years on death row in North Carolina. As in Jonathan Hoffman's case, it was the false testimony of one key witness that determined the defendant's fate.

Along with two presumed accomplices—Larry Lamb and Ernest Matthews—Jones was convicted of killing Leamon Grady, a local bootlegger, who was found dead in his home in Duplin County early on the morning of February 28, 1987. He had been shot once in the head. No one was charged with the crime for several years. That changed when, in August 1990, a reward was posted for information leading to an arrest. A woman named Lovely Lorden volunteered to earn the reward. Lorden told investigators the crime had been committed by her ex-boyfriend, Levon Jones. Jones was in prison at the time, serving time on an assault charge that had been brought by none other than Lorden herself. Lorden offered a virtual menu of differing statements regarding the Grady murder, but finally settled on a chronicle that early on the morning of February 28, she rode with Jones and the other two men to Grady's house with the intent of robbing him. Lorden said she stayed in the car while the three men entered the house. Jones, she said, was carrying a pistol. She heard two gunshots, then the men returned to the car and they drove away. Jones, Lamb, and Matthews all were charged with first-degree murder on August 14 1992.

Lamb was the first to be tried. Lorden was the chief witness for the prosecution, and that was about all they had. There was no physical evidence connecting Lamb or any of the other defendants to the crime.

The murder weapon was never found. Evidence that might have been favorable to the defense never surfaced. For example, not shown to the jury was evidence that another suspect had been alone with Grady on the night of the murder, lied to the police regarding his whereabouts that night, and then left town. Lamb's attorney did not interview any witnesses or conduct any investigation of the case. He was convicted and sentenced to death. Upon being sentenced, Lamb told the court: "I will take whatever time you give me and I will go with it with pride, but [I want] to let you know you haven't solved this case by locking me up."

Jones went on trial three months later, in November 1993. The state asked for the death penalty, presumably because Jones was alleged to have fired the fatal shot. Once again, it was Lorden who carried the burden for the prosecution. Jones's attorneys, one of whom was related to the victim, appeared to be extraneous to the case. They interviewed no witnesses and filed no motions. Not surprisingly, the jury found Jones guilty and he was sentenced to death. The conviction was upheld by the North Carolina Supreme Court in 1996.

Matthews, who, like Lamb and Jones, contended he was innocent, took a lesson from the two previous cases. He pleaded no contest to second-degree murder, robbery, and conspiracy, and was sentenced to twenty years in prison.

In 2006, US District Court Judge Terrence Boyle overturned Jones's conviction because of the inefficiency of defense counsel, but Jones remained in prison awaiting a possible retrial. As it turned out, none was necessary. In December 2007, Lovely Lorden recanted the testimony she had given at trial fourteen years earlier. In an affidavit prepared by Jones's attorneys, she admitted that much of her testimony was "simply not true." She said law officers had coached her on what to say and threatened her with the possibility of prosecution if she failed to cooperate. As an added incentive, she received a $4,000 reward from the governor's office for providing clues that led to Jones's arrest. In light of the new evidence, the district attorney dropped all charges against Jones on May 2, 2008, and he was released from prison the same day.

Judge Boyle criticized Jones's defense attorneys for "constitutionally deficient" performance, noting their failure to research the credibility of Lovely Lorden. The judge continued, "Given the weakness of the prosecution's case and its heavy reliance on the testimony of Lovely Lorden, there is a reasonable probability that, but for counsel's unprofessional errors, the result of the proceeding would have been different."

Now, Lamb was the only one of the three still in prison, Matthews having been released in 2000. But the future soon took a turn in Lamb's favor. Christine Mumma, executive director of the North Carolina Center on Actual Innocence had been investigating Lamb's case since 2006 when Jones's conviction was overturned. On May 29, after the charges against Jones were dismissed, Mumma met with District Attorney G. Dewey Hudson who had received information that Grady had been killed by two other men. Hudson requested that the state reinvestigate the case. In 2010, based on Lorden's recantation and the implication of other suspects in the crime, Mumma filed a petition for a new trial on Lamb's behalf. A hearing on the petition was held in May 2013. Three months later, Superior Court Judge W. Douglas Parsons vacated Lamb's conviction. The evidence demonstrated, he said, that Lorden had "both personal and financial motives to fabricate evidence" against the defendants. He went on to say that "fundamental fairness and due process dictate that Lorden's testimony and credibility cannot sustain Lamb's convictions." The state dismissed the charges and Lamb was released on August 13, 2013.

Michael Blair
Texas

On September 4, 1993, seven-year-old Ashley Estell mysteriously disappeared, apparently kidnapped, while she and her family watched her brother play soccer at Carpenter Park in Plano, Texas. Her body was found the next day along a roadside. She had been strangled.

Michael Blair, who had a record as a sexual offender, was a likely suspect. He was brought in for questioning three days later when two evidence technicians from the Plano Police Department noticed his car in the area where the victim's body was found. They followed the car as it drove away and eventually conducted a traffic stop. Inside the car, alongside Blair, was a flyer regarding the search for the victim. Blair told the officers that he, along with dozens of other members of the community, had volunteered to assist in the search for the victim and he wanted to see the location where the body was found. The police asked Blair to accompany them to the station. Throughout a ten-hour interrogation, he denied having any involvement in the crime.

All the same, police started building their case. Three eyewitnesses told police they saw him in the park that day. They all identified Blair in a photo lineup but not before his picture had appeared in the media. Two of the witnesses said they saw Blair's photo on television before identifying him. No eyewitness ever claimed to have seen Blair together with the victim.

The search for forensic evidence turned up hairs and fibers found on Blair, the victim, and in Blair's car. Investigators also came up with a clump of hairs from Jack Carter Park, which is more than two miles from Carpenter Park where the victim was last seen. Although there was no evidence that either Blair or the victim had been in Jack Carter Park on the day of the crime, the clump of hair would become a key piece of evidence at the trial.

Blair was arrested on September 14, charged with capital murder. His case went to the jury in 1994. The main evidence against him was the testimony of eyewitnesses who said they saw Blair in the park the day the victim disappeared and the hair and fibers found on Blair and the victim. The physical evidence was, at best, questionable. An analyst from the Southwest Institute of Forensic Sciences (SWIFS) testified that the clump of hair found in Jack Carter Park contained hairs microscopically similar to both the victim's and Blair's. He also noted that the clump contained hair from other unknown individuals. The SWIFS expert noted that hairs found in Blair's car had a "strong association" with hairs from the victim but that he could not make a positive identification. An FBI expert testified that the chemical makeup of fibers from a stuffed animal in Blair's car "most resembled" fibers found on the victim's body with only "subtle differences."

Taken as a whole, the hair and fiber evidence was inconclusive, according to lawyers from the Innocence Project. A spokesman for the Project said, "Because there is not adequate empirical data on the frequency of various class characteristics in human hair, an analyst's assertion that hairs are consistent or similar is inherently prejudicial and lacks probative value." But it was good enough for the jury. After only twenty-seven minutes of deliberation, they found Blair guilty of capital murder. He was sentenced to death.

Blair was scheduled to be executed in July 1999, but his legal team, which included the Innocence Project, got him a stay until more sophisticated DNA testing could be performed on the forensic evidence. DNA testing was relatively new in those days and was painfully slow. In Blair's case it began in 2002, eight years after he was sent to death row, and continued into 2008. Every test excluded Blair as a potential contributor of the biological evidence found at the crime scene. All of the hair analysis was contradicted. In addition, human tissue found under the victim's fingernails did not match Blair's and tests conducted by the state on the victim's clothing pointed to the involvement of another man who was an early suspect at the time of the crime but was since deceased. In light of the new evidence, Collin County prosecutors asked a trial judge to vacate Blair's conviction and all charges were dropped in August 2008. Blair was removed from death row but he remains in prison. While on death row, he confessed to other crimes he had committed, pled guilty, and was given a life sentence.

One of the ironies of Blair's case is that his death sentence provided a footnote in the history of failures in the penal system. Less than a year after he was sentenced to death, then-Governor George W. Bush signed "Ashley's Laws," named for the victim in the case, which expanded punishment and mandated registration for sex offenders. Innocence Project co-director Barry Scheck said Blair's wrongful conviction and the community's rush to expand punishment in the wake of the case illustrates serious flaws in the criminal justice system.

"Troubling questions about our criminal justice system are raised any time DNA testing shows that someone on death row is innocent," Scheck said. "But in this case, the community rushed to judgment because Michael Blair had a record as a sex offender—while the apparent real perpetrator, who had no record, evaded justice. More than just an irony, this should give everyone pause about legislating or reaching court decisions based on community fear and outrage. This case starkly shows that the system makes mistakes and that those mistakes can have chilling consequences. Michael Blair was almost executed for a crime that DNA testing shows he did not commit. Even more troubling is the reality that the kind of evidence that led to Michael Blair's wrongful conviction is used in countless cases nationwide every day. Eyewitness misidentification and unreliable forensic science convicted Michael Blair, but DNA has finally shown the truth."

Yancy Douglas and Paris Powell
Oklahoma

It was a gangland-style killing, the kind that was so popular in the black-and-white noir movies of an earlier time. A hatchback automobile came cruising down a street in Oklahoma City, the door on the driver's side flung open, both the driver and the passenger opened fire, and two teenagers were shot, one fatally. The victims on that June night in 1993 were fourteen-year-old Shauna Farrow and seventeen-year-old Derrick Smith, walking home together from a party. Farrow was mortally wounded; Smith was injured but survived. Smith's survival did not auger well for Yancy Douglas and Paris Powell.

A member of the Southeast Village Crips street gang, Smith was facing charges for drug trafficking and he needed a break. When questioned by police about the identity of the shooters, Smith was equivocal at first but eventually named Douglas and Powell, both members of a rival gang. The police moved quickly. Douglas and Powell were arrested and charged with the crimes in August 1993.

The two men were tried separately, almost two years apart. Smith was the key witness in both trials, identifying Douglas and Powell as the shooters. He also said he had received no special deals from prosecutors in exchange for his testimony. Both defendants were convicted and sentenced to death, Douglas in October 1995, Powell in May 1997.

The appeal process brought no relief. But in 2001, Smith wrote an affidavit recanting his testimony. He said he had been drunk and high on the night of the shooting and was unable to identify the shooters. The police, he said, had pressured him into naming Douglas and Powell in exchange for a reduced sentence for his drug-trafficking charges. Still, it was not easy to get the convictions overturned. Various courts declined to act on the new evidence, but the Tenth Circuit Court of Appeals vacated the convictions in 2009. Prosecutors chose not to retry the case, all charges were dropped, and Douglas and Powell were released from prison after serving fourteen years.

In 2011, Powell was arrested in Oklahoma City and charged with several felony counts, including rape, kidnapping, robbery, and larceny. He represented himself at trial and was acquitted on all counts.

In 2013, the attorney who prosecuted the case was suspended for 180 days by the Oklahoma Supreme Court. The court ruled that the prosecutor had abused the subpoena process to compel witnesses to cooperate, failed to disclose evidence to the defense, and obstructed the defense's access to evidence.

Anthony Graves
Texas

Justice has come slowly, in bits and pieces, for Anthony Graves and his quest is not yet over. Graves spent sixteen years on death row and barely survived two execution dates for a horrendous crime he did not commit. The crime was the multiple murders of Bobbie Joyce Davis, her daughter, and four grandchildren in Somerville, Burleson County, Texas, in 1994. After the family had been killed, their house was set ablaze.

Five days later, Robert Earl Carter, a prison guard and the father of the youngest victim, was arrested by Texas Rangers when he attended the funeral with bandages covering a number of burns. After being told he had failed a lie detector test, Carter told the Rangers a story that would place Graves on death row despite no other evidence of consequence. He said he had driven his wife's cousin, Graves, to the Davis home at Graves's request and waited outside while the murders were committed. A few days later, Carter recanted his story, and not for the last time. He said that the Rangers had determined the crimes could not have been committed by one person alone and threatened his life if Carter did not identify his accomplice.

Graves had three alibi witnesses—two siblings and his girlfriend—who said they were with him on the night of the murders. But only his brother Arthur testified at trial. His sister and his girlfriend later would explain that they were intimidated by the district attorney, Charles Sebesta, who informed them that anything they said could be used against them and they themselves might be charged. Carter, who had already been convicted and sentenced to death for his involvement in the slayings, offered to testify on Graves's behalf. He told the DA, his assistant, and the DA's investigator that Graves was not involved in the crime. The defense was never told that Carter had changed course and recanted. There was no physical evidence tying Graves to the murders. Based almost entirely of Carter's pre-recantation testimony, Graves was convicted and sentenced to death.

In the meantime, Carter continued to advocate on Graves's behalf. He solicited the help of his high school English teacher and of the Davis family. Two weeks before he was scheduled to be executed, in 2000, he stated flatly that Graves was not involved in the crime. In his final statement before being administered a lethal injection, he said: "It was me and me alone. Anthony Graves had nothing to do with it. I lied on him in court . . . Anthony Graves don't even know anything about it." He repeated his statement minutes before his execution.

Nonetheless, it was not until 2006 that a panel of the Fifth Circuit Court of Appeals ruled that DA Sebesta had engaged in prosecutorial misconduct, suborning perjured testimony that he knowingly put before the jury and withholding testimony that could have influenced the jury in the defendant's favor. The court overturned the conviction and ordered a new trial. The new district attorney, Bill Parham, began reviewing the evidence as he stitched together a new case. He hired former Harris County Assistant District Attorney Kelly Siegler as a special prosecutor. Siegler soon concluded that it was impossible to make a case against Graves. He said:

"After months of investigation and talking to every witness who's ever been involved in this case, and people who've never been talked to before, after looking under every rock we could find, we found not one piece of credible evidence that links Anthony Graves to the commission of this capital murder. This is not a case where the evidence went south with time or witnesses passed away or we just couldn't make a case anymore. He is an innocent man."

Graves was released from prison in October 2010. According to Texas law, wrongfully convicted people are entitled to $80,000 for every year they spent in prison. In Graves's case, the amount would come to $1.45 million. But Christmas would not come early, or easily, for Graves. There was a technicality that got in the way. While Graves's conviction was overturned, the order releasing him from prison did not declare his "actual innocence," making him ineligible to receive compensation. But Graves would not relent. As he continued to press his case, an angelic presence by the name of Nicole Casarez came to his aid. Casarez was a Houston-based attorney and journalism professor at the University of St. Thomas in Houston. Working with the Innocence Project of Texas and journalism students at St. Thomas, Casarez was determined to set things right. She labored tirelessly on Graves's behalf for eight years. It took a new law, passed by the state legislature in 2011, that got Graves the award he was owed.

Graves was not the type to allow such dedication to go unrewarded. "I wanted to repay Nicole, but I knew she'd never accept money from me," Graves said. "I thought about giving her an amazing trip somewhere, but I wanted to give her something that would live on."

What Graves did was to create the Nicole B. Casarez scholarship in Law at the University of Texas Law School. But he was not through giving back. He works with the Texas Defender Service, a non-profit organization that assists death-row inmates. He also created the Anthony Graves Foundation, a mentorship and development program for at-risk youth and children adversely affected by the criminal justice system. "These children," Graves says, "become the prison pipeline. Our mission is to end this crippling ripple effect and develop the minds of our youth. The Anthony Graves Foundation gives these children a choice and a chance to live happy, productive lives, and become the powerful, new foundation of our communities."

As recently as 2014, Graves was still trying to right the wrongs of the past. In an email to the *Austin Chronicle*, he said he hopes to hold Sebesta and the Texas justice system accountable for the misconduct that led to his wrongful conviction. He said he intends to pursue every legal avenue available to achieve that goal, including filing a federal civil rights lawsuit and exploring the possibility of convening a state court-of-inquiry review which would hold Sebesta criminally liable for failure to turn over to the defense exculpatory material that would have helped to clear Graves of any wrongdoing. Graves said he was pursuing the matter "in hopes of restoring faith in our criminal justice system. No one is above the law, and everyone should be held accountable—including prosecutors who abuse their authority . . ."

Ryan Matthews
Louisiana

The fallibility of eyewitness testimony, even offered by well-intentioned citizens, needs no further demonstration than the case of Ryan Matthews. Matthews was convicted of murder and sentenced to death on the flawed identification of eyewitnesses who just got it wrong and the equally flawed mechanics of the criminal justice system.

Matthews, seventeen at the time, was charged with felony murder following the shooting death of the owner of a convenience store in Bridge City, Louisiana, not far from New Orleans. On April 7, 1997, a man wearing a ski mask and brandishing a gun entered the store and demanded money. When the owner of the store, Tommy Vanhoose, refused, the gunman shot him four times and fled. On the way out, still shooting, he removed his mask and dove through the passenger-side window of a waiting car. A witness subsequently picked up the ski mask and turned it over to the police.

His flight and escape was seen by several witnesses. One eyewitness said she was in her car at the time and saw the gunman run from the store, fire shots in her direction, and leap into the car. Shown an array of photos by the police, she tentatively identified Matthews as the perpetrator. By the time of the trial, two years later, she said she was certain Matthews was the gunman. Two other passengers in her car said they saw the assailant shed his mask as he fled the store. The driver said he had seen the gunman's face in the rearview mirror while he was being shot at and trying to block the escape of the getaway car. Several hours later, the driver identified Matthews as the shooter; the other passenger did not. The identifications were problematic at best. The witnesses all seemed to agree that the gunman was no taller than five-feet-eight; Matthews, a shade over six feet, was nonetheless picked out as the man they saw discarding his mask as he dove into the car.

Matthews and Travis Hayes, also seventeen, had been stopped by police several hours after the crime was committed because the car they were riding in fit the description of the getaway car. They were arrested and Hayes was questioned for more than six hours. Initially, he told investigators that he and Matthews were not in the area when the crime took place. But later, he changed his story and said that he was the driver of the getaway car and that it was Matthews who went into the store. He heard shots being fired and then Matthews ran out and got into the car. Matthews insisted on his innocence from the start and never wavered.

The prosecution made its case chiefly on the eyewitness identifications. The defense offered evidence that forensic testing of the mask excluded both defendants. Another forensic expert testified that the car the boys were driving when they were stopped by police could not have been the getaway car because the window on the passenger side, the one Matthews was said to have jumped through while making his escape, was inoperable and could not be rolled down.

The trial was brief, one might say abbreviated, and conducted at a pace that suggested the judge was in haste to move along to matters more pressing. On the third day, testimony was taken until 10 p.m. At that time, the judge denied a defense motion to adjourn and ordered both attorneys to make their closing statements. The jury was then sent to deliberate. At 4:20 a.m., they sent a note to the judge saying they were unable to reach a verdict. The judge ordered them to continue deliberations. Forty minutes later, at 5 a.m., they brought in a verdict of guilty. Matthews was convicted of first-degree murder and sentenced to death. Hayes was convicted of second-degree murder and sentenced to life in prison.

Defense investigators William Sothern and Clive Stafford Smith, of the Louisiana Crisis Assistance Center, were convinced of the two teenagers' innocence and continued to examine the evidence. In March 2003, four years after the convictions, the investigators got lucky. DNA testing in another murder case cleared Matthews and Hayes. The other murder had occurred a few months after Vanhoose's death just a few blocks away. A local resident, Rondell Love, confessed to the crime and was convicted. In prison, he is said to have told other inmates that he also killed Vanhoose. When Sothern and Smith learned of Love's admission, they turned their attention to his case. They found that DNA taken from the ski mask clearly pointed to Love and excluded both Matthews and Hayes. In August 2004, Matthews's conviction was overturned and he was set free. Hayes was finally released in December 2006.

PART III

False Forensics or Junk Science

A S FAR BACK as history can take us, the engines of human striving have been driven by the quest for absolute certainty. Socrates searched for truth and justice in their immutable forms. Aristotle ventured farther afield, seeking the heart of the matter in pursuits as different as drama and biology, poetry and politics. The scientific method picked up where the frontier of philosophy ended. The laboratory became the temple in which those of serious mind bent a knee to worship. Each new advance brought us closer to a truth that could not be questioned, and that, after all, was the goal. Certainty, as difficult to apprehend as the Holy Grail, would free us from error and doubt and make us secure in our belief that truth was the coin of our noblest endeavors.

It took a while before we discovered that science was a fickle accomplice. Today's truth was at best tomorrow's probability. Scientific certainty was as fragile as any other. It seemed that the more we learned, the less we could be sure of, for each new discovery put in question all that preceded it. Every Ptolemy would be succeeded by a Galileo; for every true believer, a Darwin was waiting in the wings. Truth depended, finally, on the prism through which it was viewed. When what once passed for scientific certainty is eclipsed by new findings, it is disparagingly referred to as junk science or, at trial, false forensics.

In the courtroom, the introduction of scientific evidence is replete with hazards. There is always the question of whether the jurors—and in some instances even the judge—are able to comprehend it, and the more formidable question of how seriously that theory's application is treated by the forensic community. In recent years, the testimony of handwriting analysts has been called into doubt, and even more critically, the infallibility of fingerprint identification, once considered the bedrock of absolute certainty, has become suspect.

In a 1993 case dealing with handwriting analysis, *Daubert v. Merrell Dow Pharmaceuticals*, the Supreme Court ruled that judges may exercise their own discretion in deciding whether to admit expert testimony regardless of their personal knowledge in that field. Judges in two subsequent cases took opposite views on the matter of handwriting analysis. One decided that it was not sufficiently scientific to be admissible. The other, citing a recent study, noted that the relatively new use of computer programs invested the technique with 98 percent accuracy.

Until the advent of DNA technology, fingerprints had long been considered the surest route to forensic certainty. The Chinese were said to have used thumb prints as a means of identification more than two thousand years ago, but the father of modern fingerprint technology was Sir William J. Herschel, a British government official in Bengal, India. Herschel's system, devised principally as a means of preventing impersonation, was in popular use by 1858. Sir Francis Galton founded the present system about thirty years later, and Juan Vucetich, of Argentina, applied it to criminal investigations for the first time in 1891.

The core of fingerprint analysis is the belief that no two individuals have the same set of prints. Of course that is a premise based on scientific projection. Not every set of prints has been compared with every other, but the sheer volume of instances in which the principle has held true without contradiction had wrapped fingerprint identification in a cloak of infallibility. Recently, however, it has come under closer scrutiny. In criminal investigations, the critical question is not whether two sets of prints can be exactly alike, but whether they can be similar enough to fool an analyst. There have been numerous cases in which fingerprints have been misidentified. Prints taken at a crime scene, for example, are often smudged or too indistinct to be identified with absolute certainty. The FBI's computerized fingerprint identification system is said to be more than 99 percent accurate, but when it is unable to tell the difference between two sets of prints, human analysts make the determination, and their conclusions often differ.

All the same, fingerprint analysis is still far more reliable than other forms of "junk science" evidence. Suspects have been wrongly convicted on the basis of faulty ballistics technology, inaccurate medical diagnoses, and testimony induced under hypnosis. Even DNA technology, now considered as close to infallible as one might ever hope, is subject to human error. If the test is not made with proper controls, it can lead to the conviction of the wrong man.

Anthony Ray Hinton
Alabama

Good Friday, 2015, was better than good for Anthony Ray Hinton. It was, one might say, a resurrection of sorts. It was the day that Hinton walked free after spending thirty years on Alabama's death row following a decades-long fight to prove his innocence. Hinton was convicted of the 1985 murders of two fast-food restaurant managers on the flimsiest of evidence.

The murders occurred five months apart. On February 25, 1985, John Davidson, assistant manager of a Southside Mrs. Winner's, was forced into the restaurant's cooler and shot twice in the head. Thomas Vason, an assistant manager at a Captain D's in Woodlawn, suffered the same fate in precisely the same manner. But it was a third such crime, in which the victim survived, that drew the attention of the police to Hinton. On July 26, the night manger of a Bessemer Quincy restaurant, was assaulted and identified Hinton as the perpetrator. The police searched his mother's home, where Hinton lived, and found a handgun which, they said, matched the bullets found at the scene. They concluded that it was the same gun used in the other two shootings. Hinton was promptly arrested, convicted of the two murders, and sentenced to death.

The state's case was weak, almost non-existent. There was no eyewitness testimony that placed Hinton at the scene of either crime. He was never charged with the Quincy shooting whose victim had identified him. Furthermore, Hinton had what the defense described as a "powerful alibi": a cadre of co-workers confirmed that he was at work at the time of the Quincy shootings, fifteen miles away from the crime scene. As for the forensic evidence, subsequent tests raised doubts that the weapon taken from Hinton's home had fired the bullets; it even called into question whether all the bullets were fired from the same gun. Hinton's court-appointed lawyer, Sheldon C. Perhacs, mistakenly believed that he was allowed only $1,000 to hire an expert witness. Hiring on the cheap, Perhacs retained as a ballistics expert a visually impaired civil engineer with no expertise in firearms identification who admitted he could not operate the machinery necessary to examine the evidence. At trial, jurors chuckled as the defense's "expert" struggled to answer questions under cross-examination. According to a report by Alan Blinder in *The New York Times*, a prosecutor described him as a "one-eyed charlatan."

Time moved slowly on death row and more than a decade passed before Hinton found respite. Bryan Stevenson, the executive director of the Equal Justice Initiative, intervened, providing Hinton a new defense, Stevenson filed a motion for dismissal. A panel of experts, including a former FBI official, reviewed the forensic evidence and reported that the conclusions of the Alabama authorities were suspect. But state authorities were unyielding. According to the *Times*, the Alabama attorney general said, "The experts did not prove Mr. Hinton's innocence, and the state does not doubt his guilt."

The US Supreme Court thought otherwise. In 2014, the Court ruled that Hinton's trial defense had been "constitutionally deficient," mandating a new trial and obliging prosecutors to examine the forensic evidence which they knew to be the backbone of their case. They later wrote that Hinton's conviction depended on "an absolute, conclusive determination that the bullets recovered from [the victims'] bodies were in fact fired through the barrel of the firearm taken from the defendant's home." Following a new analysis, the prosecutors found that state experts "could not conclusively determine that any of the six bullets were or were not fired through the same firearm recovered from the defendant's home."

After the Supreme Court's decision, the Alabama Court of Criminal Appeals granted Hinton a new trial. His defense attorneys asked Jefferson County Judge Laura Petro to dismiss the case. On April 1, 2015, two Alabama prosecutors—Chief Deputy County District Attorney John Bowers and Assistant District Attorney Mike Anderton—filed a motion to drop all charges against Hinton when three experts were unable to link the bullets to the gun. Petro dismissed the case and ordered Hinton freed.

Stevenson summed up Hinton's ordeal this way: "We have a system that treats you better if you're rich and guilty than if you're poor and innocent, and this case proves it." He went on to say, "Race, poverty, inadequate legal assistance, and prosecutorial indifference to innocence conspired to create a textbook example of injustice. I can't think of a case that more urgently dramatizes the need for reform than what has happened to Anthony Ray Hinton.

Robert Dunham, executive director of the Death Penalty Information Center, tied Hinton's case to the decline of public approval of capital punishment. "Cases like Anthony Ray Hinton's," he said, "give the public pause about the death penalty. From the very outset, this case exhibited many of the classic signs of innocence."

Upon his release, Hinton sounded grateful but, not surprisingly, a degree bitter. "I shouldn't have sat on death row for thirty years," he told reporters. "All they had to do was test the gun. They had every intention of executing me for something I didn't do." But it was Good Friday, and Hinton spoke also of mercy. "I've got to forgive," he said. "I lived in hell for thirty years, so I don't want to die and go the hell. So I've got to forgive. I don't have a choice."

Timothy Howard and Gary Lamar James
Ohio

Four smudged fingerprints were the only forensic evidence that the state presented in a trial that sent Timothy Howard and Gary Lamar James to prison for twenty-six years for a crime they did not commit. The crux of the matter was that none of the fingerprints belonged to either suspect, the police knew it and withheld that bit of information from the defense.

The crime at issue took place on December 21, 1976, when two armed men robbed the Ohio National Bank in Columbus. One jumped over the teller's cage and stole approximately $1,207 while the other fatally shot the seventy-four-year-old security guard, Berne Davis.

The trouble for Howard and James, childhood friends and both 23 years old, began almost immediately when two eyewitnesses picked them out of a police lineup. When the *Columbus Dispatch* printed their photos, identifying them as suspects, the two men went voluntarily to the police on December 23 to offer alibis and clear their names. Howard said he had spent the day at home with his sister, but she declined to sign a waiver of rights until she consulted her attorney. James contended he had been at the optometrist with his girlfriend less than an hour after the robbery, but he didn't have enough money to pay for his glasses. Neither alibi satisfied the police, and both men were arrested and charged with capital murder.

Howard and James were tried separately in 1977. The heart of the state's case, aside from the false forensics, was the eyewitness testimony, which was none too convincing. Most of the eyewitnesses said they had seen the photos of the two men in the newspaper following the murder. The bank's security camera was of no help, as it was not equipped with film on the day of the crime. During the trial, the prosecution, apparently aware of the weakness of its case, told the jury that Howard and James had robbed a U-Haul rental store owned by a friend of Berne Davis on the day before the bank robbery. However, a later investigation would uncover a police report indicating that the owner of the store, whose identification was the only evidence against the two men, had been unable to pick the suspects out of a photo lineup.

While eyewitnesses were less certain in their identification of Howard than of James, both men were convicted and sentenced to death in 1977. Their death sentences were commuted to life in prison a year later when the Ohio courts declared the death sentence to be unconstitutional. That same year, James's appeal to the Ohio Tenth Circuit Court of Appeals was denied. Howard's appeals to the Ohio Supreme Court were rejected in December 1978 and again in April 1982. But Howard was persistent. He continued to claim his innocence, filing requests for case documents under the Freedom of Information Act and soliciting the help of attorneys, ministers, and the media. Finally, in 1997, some twenty years after being sent to prison, his luck turned. The Centurion Ministries, a New Jersey-based non-profit organization that investigates wrongful convictions, agreed to take on both his and James's case.

Assisted by a private investigator, Centurion discovered evidence that Howard and James had been convicted as a result of police corruption, primarily on the part of Detective Thomas James. A thorough investigation revealed that the case of Howard and James was not unique. James was found to have made a practice of twisting and concealing evidence to achieve convictions, and he had been thrown off the Columbus police force for misconduct. During the course of its investigation, Centurion learned that many eyewitness reports contradicted testimony that identified Howard and James as the perpetrators. In addition, a Columbus police officer was found to have lied when he testified that fingerprints found at the scene were too smudged to be of any use. In fact, one of the prints had been analyzed and offered no match for either Howard or James. The investigator also obtained an affidavit from an FBI agent who had aided the prosecution, stating that he had doubted the guilt of the defendants since 1977, when two Cincinnati men, one of whom bore a strong resemblance to James, were arrested for robbing another Ohio National Bank.

In December 2002, the Franklin County Court of Common Pleas held a hearing to reconsider Howard's guilt in the light of the new evidence. At the same time, attorneys continued to pursue a hearing for James. Having examined the new evidence, the judge and prosecutors offered Howard a deal: If he pled no contest to manslaughter, he would be released from prison for time served. Howard disdained the offer, refusing to confess to a crime he did not commit. He chose instead to remain in prison until he was legally exonerated. A few months later, on April 16, 2003, the court overturned his conviction and he was released on bond. The Franklin County prosecutor, after filing a motion to appeal, thought otherwise and dismissed the charges against both men.

Still, Howard was not yet ready to let it go. He filed a wrongful conviction suit against the state seeking to be compensated for the time he spent in prison. The case went to trial early in 2006. The testimony of the eyewitnesses was raked over, the defense showing that most every eyewitness was, at one time or another, less than certain of their identifications. In one typical instance, Franklin County Deputy Sheriff Diana Smoot shifted her position while still on the witness stand. Smoot, who was fourteen when the bank was robbed, was entering the bank at the time Davis was shot, She had testified against Howard at the first trial and identified him as one of the suspects and she repeated that testimony at the new court proceeding. But when defense attorney James Owen cross-examined her, Smoot was no longer certain. She said she could not say that her identification was 100 percent accurate.

"Would it be fair to say," Owen asked, "that during those conversations you'd said you could not make a positive ID now, and you couldn't back then either?"

"Right," Smoot said, "I said l couldn't be definite."

Another witness, bank manager Lillian Joyce Williams, had identified James as the shooter in 1977, but could not identify his accomplice. But on the witness stand twenty-nine years later, when asked to identify the second man, she pointed at Howard. Under cross-examination, it was disclosed that she was unable to identify him in 1977.

"The question is, did you look at both of them?" the defense attorney asked. "And your answer was 'Just vaguely. I cannot tell you what the other one looked like, other than he was a black person.' And that was it. Do you recall saying that?"

"Uh, yeah," she said, "I probably would have said that."

During summation, Owen addressed the issue of the fingerprints: "The forensic evidence you got were those four latent prints which don't incriminate Timmy," he said. "Any other forensic evidence, crime scene, search unit, FBI, police? Anything? Nothing . . . Those fingerprints aren't his because he wasn't there. It's plain and simple."

Plain and simple it was. Howard was awarded $2.5 million in compensation from the state of Ohio. It was a victory that, though sweet, was short-lived. Just about one year later, he died of a massive heart attack. He was fifty-three years old. He had spent about half his life behind bars for a crime he did not commit.

James, in a separate suit, was awarded $1.5 million.

Ernest Ray Willis
Texas

Faulty forensics sent Ernest Ray Willis to death row for eighteen years, convicted of capital murder in the death of two people who were killed in a house fire in Iraan, Texas. He was charged with committing arson on the basis of a botched investigation which led the authorities and the court to conclude that the fire had been set intentionally. As it turned out, the fire was caused by an electrical failure; there was no convincing evidence that arson was involved.

The fire broke out in the early hours of June 11, 1986, in the home of Cheryl and Michael Robinson. Killed in the blaze were twenty-four-year-old Elizabeth Belue and twenty-five-year-old Gail Allison who had been up late drinking with their hosts. Willis and his cousin, Bill Willis, house guests of the Robinsons, escaped unharmed. The Robinsons, ironically, were not home when the fire erupted. They had been arrested following a violent quarrel outside the house. The four guests remained and went to sleep. When the flames engulfed the house, only the Willises made it out safely. Belue and Allison were found dead.

For reasons unknown, the sheriff investigating the case suspected the fire had been set intentionally. Arson experts corroborated his suspicion. They said they found "pour patterns" on the floor—charred marks that were presumably left by a flammable liquid, or accelerant, that had been poured inside the house and found in the carpet. Ernest Ray Willis, who was the first out of the house and who had suffered less injury than his cousin, became the state's number one suspect. Officers at the scene said Willis had been acting strangely, but there was no physical evidence pointing to him and he clearly had no motive. He was, in fact, an unlikely suspect.

Willis was staying with the Robinsons as their guest because he suffered from chronic back pain that made it difficult for him to work and they offered him a place to stay in exchange for his repairing their car. Willis told police that the fire woke him at about 4 a.m. and that he ran through the house trying to wake the others before he was forced to flee the flames. Outside, he said, he started breaking windows to allow air into the house and to create routes of escape.

Nonetheless, the police found Willis's story unconvincing. He was arrested in October and charged with capital murder. At trial, prosecutors described him as a "cold-hearted" murderer, a "monster," an "animal," and a "satanic demon." They reinforced their characterization of Willis by referring to his dazed mental state at the scene of the crime and by noting that throughout the trial he appeared confused and emotionless. The defense offered nothing to rebut the state's contentions. They did not, for example, tell the jury that Willis's distracted mental state might well have been the result of state-administered medication he was taking. Nor did they call any character witnesses, including several who could have testified that Willis had once risked his life to save a boy from drowning. He was convicted on August 4, 1987 and sentenced to death. The conviction was upheld by the Texas Court of Criminal Appeals in 1989 and, a year later, the US Supreme Court denied a petition for a writ of certiorari, which would have mandated the Court to hear an appeal of the conviction.

The road to justice and freedom was a long and winding one for Willis, and it was embarked on inadvertently. While in prison, Willis took to writing letters as a means of connecting to the outside world. One of his favored correspondents was the mother of a mentally retarded inmate who refused to communicate with his family. Willis sent her periodic updates on her son, and by way of gratitude she sent copies of his letters to the law firm of Latham & Watkins. In 1992, a team of the firm's attorneys agreed to take Willis's case on a pro bono basis.

Among their findings was that for several months before the start of the trial, the state had been giving Willis high doses of anti-psychotic drugs along with his usual pain medication without telling him, despite the fact that he had displayed no signs of psychosis. It was likely the effects of these drugs that accounted for the defendant's dazed, expressionless state at trial. Investigators also discovered a psychological evaluation that concluded that Willis would present no threat to society if released. That report, which might well have spared him the death penalty, was never turned over to the defense.

Based on the newly discovered evidence, an appellate court granted Willis's petition for habeas corpus, but it was denied by the Texas Court of Criminal Appeals in 2000. However, the new developments raised doubts regarding Willis's guilt. A new Pecos County district attorney initiated his own review of the case. He retained arson experts who determined that the previous arson specialists had reached false conclusions. There was, they said, no substantive evidence that the fire had been set intentionally. The "accelerant" that was suspected of causing the fire was in fact "flashover burning," which is consistent with an electrical fault fire. Their final conclusion was that the cause of the fire was "undetermined."

In 2004, US District Judge Royal Ferguson granted a federal writ of habeas corpus, ruling that the state had administered medically inappropriate anti-psychotic drugs without Willis's consent, that the state suppressed evidence favorable to Willis, and that Willis had received ineffective counsel at both the guilt and sentencing phases of his trial. He ordered the state to either free Willis or retry him. The state attorney general's office decided not to appeal and all charges against him were dropped. He was released from prison on October 6, 2004 with $100, ten days of medication, and the clothes on his back. As of 2012, he had received nearly $800,000 in compensation from the State of Texas.

Coincidentally, and tragically, another case of false arson, very similar to Willis's, was played out at around the same time but with far different results. Cameron Todd Willingham was convicted in 1992 of setting fire to his home in Corsicana, Texas, in which his three daughters perished. Willingham was convicted on the basis of the same false forensics that the state introduced in Willis's case, but he did not enjoy the good fortune of a private investigation. On February 17, 2004, eight months before Willis was freed, Willingham was executed by legal injection. Almost certainly, Texas executed an innocent man.

In a 2006 report, an independent five-member panel that included some of the country's leading arson experts found that neither of the fires was set intentionally; there was no arson. The panel reported that the evidence and forensic analysis in both the Willingham and Willis cases "were the same" and that "each and every one" of the forensic interpretations state experts made in both men's trials has been proven scientifically invalid. The report stated: "While any case of wrongful conviction, acknowledged or not, is worthy of review, the disparity of outcomes in these two cases warrants a closer inspection."

Barry Scheck, co-director of the Innocence Project, which is affiliated with the Cardozo School of Law in New York City, urged the Texas Forensic Science Commission to fully investigate the issue and recommend changes in the state's forensic system that could prevent wrongful convictions in the future. Even at the time of Willingham's trial, he said, the forensic methods used by prosecution experts to classify the fire as arson were known to be faulty and unreliable.

John Ballard
Florida

Florida leads the nation in overturned convictions. That can be interpreted in two ways: either the state's trial system is ineffective or its appellate system is exceptionally alert at detecting trial-court errors. In the case of John Ballard there could be little doubt which view applied. Ballard was convicted of two murders and sentenced to death in 1999 on virtually no evidence at all.

The two victims—Jennifer Jones, seventeen, and Willy Ray Patin Jr., twenty-two—were found bludgeoned to death in the duplex apartment they shared in Golden Gate, Florida, a small town in southwestern Collier County. Ballard became a suspect on the basis of a few hairs and a fingerprint of his found in the apartment. That was the only physical evidence the state had and it was hardly compelling. Ballard was a neighbor and long-time friend of the couple and visited their home often. After a two-year investigation that yielded nothing further, Ballard was arrested on two counts of murder and one of robbery although nothing appeared to be missing.

Ballard went to trial in 2003. Although the state held robbery to be the motive, the subject was never put before the jury. Nor was any attention given to Jones's past. She was a known drug addict and had been the object of gang violence more than once. Just a week before the couple was killed, another man had fired shots at their apartment but no effort was made to identify or locate the man. Also ignored were bloody fingerprints and about 100 other hair samples found at the scene, none of them belonging to Ballard. The prosecution's flimsy case was good enough for the jury; he was found guilty on all charges. Although only nine of the twelve jurors voted to apply the death sentence, the judge decided otherwise, saying, "You have not only forfeited your right to live among us, but under the laws of the State of Florida, you have forfeited your right to live at all."

The Florida Supreme Court did not agree. In 2006, it found that the evidence presented by the state was insufficient and unanimously overturned Ballard's conviction, ordering his acquittal. It was only the third time in the past thirty years that the court ordered a judgment of acquittal rather than asking for a retrial.

Curtis Edward McCarty
Oklahoma

Curtis Edward McCarty was convicted twice and sentenced to death three times based on forensic evidence that was mishandled and manipulated by an analyst who was later fired for committing forensic fraud in a number of cases. The crime in question was the 1982 murder of a police officer's daughter. Pamela Kaye Willis was found dead in her Oklahoma City home. She was nude and had been stabbed and strangled. McCarty fell under suspicion for no other reason than that he was an acquaintance of the victim.

Shortly after the murder, Oklahoma City Police chemist Joyce Gilchrist compared hairs found at the crime scene with McCarty's and determined there was no similarity. All the same, police continued to interview McCarty periodically over the next three years. Finally, in 1985, he was arrested and charged with Willis's murder. The basis for his arrest was the word of Gilchrist, who had changed her notes to indicate that the hairs found at the scene could have been McCarty's. Defense attorneys did not discover the change in her testimony until 2000 when Gilchrist was being investigated for fraud in other cases.

At McCarty's trial in 1986, Gilchrist testified that forensic tests on the hair samples showed McCarty "was in fact" at the crime scene. She also stated that McCarty's blood type matched the blood type of semen found on the victim's nude body. That was the crux of the prosecution's case. McCarty was convicted and sentenced to death.

He spent two years on death row before his conviction was overturned by the Court of Criminal Appeals due to prosecutorial misconduct and improper forensic procedures. Oklahoma District Attorney Robert H. Macy was singled out by the court, citing the case as being "replete with error" and Macy's conduct as "improper" and "unprofessional." Barry Scheck, whose Innocence Project would later take up McCarty's case, said: "This is by far one of the worst cases of law enforcement misconduct in the history of the American criminal justice system. Bob Macy has said that executing an innocent person is a risk worth taking—and he came very close to doing just that with Curtis McCarty." Macy had a history which would not belie Scheck's judgment. He had sent seventy-three people to death row during his twenty-one-year career, more than any other prosecutor in the country. Twenty of them had been executed.

McCarty was retried in 1989 with Gilchrist once again offering her flawed testimony for the state. Her testimony was the same as at the first trial and the jury returned the same verdict. McCarty was again convicted and sentenced to death. In 1995, an appellate court upheld McCarty's conviction but ordered a new sentencing trial because the judge in the second trial was deemed to have committed an error in his instructions to the jury. After hearing four days of testimony in 1996, the new jury handed down McCarty's third death sentence.

In 2000, Gilchrist was being investigated for reporting false forensic results in other cases. She was also asked to re-examine the hair evidence in McCarty's case and she agreed that it was suitable for DNA testing. But the result would never be known, for when the defense asked to see the new evidence, Gilchrist told them that the samples had been either lost or stolen. The hairs never were found. At the close of the investigation, Gilchrist was fired for the forensic fraud she had committed in several cases. Her false testimony, it was discovered, had contributed to two other wrongful convictions that were later overturned by DNA testing. She had testified in thousands of other cases during her twenty-year career, leaving one to wonder how many others were wrongfully convicted on the basis of her fraudulent forensic testimony and how many of them had been executed.

In 2002, attorneys for McCarty were able to secure DNA testing on sperm recovered from the victim's body. The tests showed no match with McCarty. A year later, McCarty's fortunes turned when the Innocence Project became involved in his case. Post-conviction attorneys Vicki Werneke and John Echols also joined the defense team. In 2005, they won a new trial after an evidentiary hearing before Judge Twyla Mason Gray. Judge Gray ruled that McCarty's conviction was tainted by Gilchrist's misconduct. At a third trial, McCarty was represented by the Innocence Project, along with attorneys Perry Hudson and Marna Franklin. In 2007, additional DNA testing nullified any connection to McCarty. Further forensic analysis showed that a bloody footprint on the victim's body could not have been McCarty's. Based on the new, exculpatory evidence and the misconduct of Gilchrist, the defense moved to dismiss the charges before a third trial was held. On May 11, 2007, Judge Gray granted the motion and McCarty was released. He had been in Oklahoma prisons and jails for twenty-two years, nineteen on death row.

Commenting on the case, Peter Neufeld, co-director of the Innocence Project, said: "For anyone who believes the death penalty is being carried out appropriately in this country, and anyone who believes that prosecutors and government witnesses can always be relied on to pursue the truth, this case is a wake-up call. Three separate times, an innocent man was sentenced to die because of the actions of an unethical prosecutor and a fraudulent analyst."

Michael Lee McCormick
Tennessee

The tale of the conviction, imprisonment, and exoneration of Michael Lee McCormick is so convoluted that it would be risible were it not so tragically pathetic. It centers, among other things, on shoddy forensics, an undercover police officer posing as a parolee, a murder that may or may not have occurred, and a litany of lies spun by the defendant that contributed to his exoneration.

The story began to unfold in the early morning hours of February 13, 1985 when the body of Jean Nichols, a twenty-three-year-old pharmacist, was found dumped in the parking lot of a shopping mall in Chattanooga, Tennessee. She had been shot twice in the head and once in the hand. Tests later showed she was highly intoxicated.

In the course of their investigation, police learned that Nichols had met a man at a restaurant the previous night, they had exchanged Valentine's Day gifts, and parted at about 11 p.m. Nichols went on to visit some night spots on Brainerd Road, a late-night entertainment strip in Chattanooga. Her body was found at two in the morning by a man foraging for recyclable cardboard in the shopping mall dumpsters. He said her body was still warm. Her car was found nearly three hours later, parked near the Brainerd Beach Club, a popular night spot among singles.

Police fingered thirty-two-year-old McCormick as a suspect when they discovered he was a friend of Nichols's brother, known as "Happy" Nichols, who lived with Jean in the home of their grandmother. The two men had met at a junior college where Happy was a student and McCormick was a media technician. It turned out to be an unholy alliance. The pair indulged regularly in drugs and they had stolen electronic equipment from the college. When Jean completed her pharmacy degree in 1984 and moved into her grandmother's home with her brother, she learned of his activities with McCormick. She demanded the stolen equipment be removed from their home and that Happy end his relationship with McCormick and straighten out his life.

At this point the story begins to grow hazy; it becomes difficult to tell truth from fiction. Police learned that McCormick, who was divorced not long ago, claimed that he called his ex-wife at 9 o'clock on the morning of February 14, some seven hours after Nichols's body had been found, and told her of the murder. He said he had been dating Nichols, that he had bought her a drink at about 9:30 the night before. He also presumably told his ex-wife that he had been questioned by police, which was verifiably untrue.

Police did in fact decide to question McCormick after a former girlfriend of his told them that he had visited her on the night of February 13. He stayed from about 9:30 until just after 11 p.m. and left in an intoxicated state. When questioned, McCormick denied that he had seen Nichols since she had returned from pharmacy school. He said that on the night in question he had met a friend at a restaurant, had some drinks, and they left, in separate vehicles, for the Brainerd Club where he stayed until 11 and then went home. He admitted calling his ex-wife but said what he told her was a fabrication intended to get her sympathy or make her jealous. At the same time, he admitted burglarizing the college and stealing electronic equipment. McCormick agreed to give samples of his hair, blood, and saliva and consented to a search of his house and car. Nothing connecting him to the crime was found, although police picked up a hair from the interior of Jean Nichols's car that analysts said was similar to McCormick's hair. Not long after he was questioned, McCormick left for a brief visit to Arizona. When he returned, he was arrested for the burglary at the college, to which he had confessed, served a short term in prison, and was released on parole.

Now, the tale becomes even murkier. Apparently convinced that McCormick was involved in the murder of Nichols, police crafted a decidedly unconventional means of making their case. In January 1987, an undercover police officer posing as a parolee introduced himself to McCormick at a parole office. They struck up a friendship and eventually decided to share an apartment. Over the next month, the officer, Eddie Cooper, staged a series of criminal activities, involving the transfer of stolen cars, in which he got McCormick to participate. In the course of their conversations, according to Cooper, McCormick told him about murderers he met in prison and Cooper mentioned he had once been offered $20,000 to kill someone in Knoxville.

On February 9, the lead detective in the Nichols murder case staged a fake arrest in a neighborhood bar where McCormick and Cooper were having a drink. McCormick, apparently unnerved, told Cooper about his burglary conviction and that he had been a suspect in the Nichols murder case. Cooper later alleged that McCormick told him he had turned down $1,000 to kill Nichols and that he knew the killer's identity. Cooper went on to say that McCormick told him the motive for the murder concerned the drug inventory at her place of work and that she had been shot three times. Cooper's incredible story continued.

On February 16, he said, he and another man exchanged a sum of cash, with McCormick looking on, implying that Cooper had hired someone else to carry out the Knoxville murder. The next day, McCormick is said to have confessed to killing Nichols while Cooper taped the conversation. Again, according to Cooper, McCormick said he killed her over an argument regarding drug money. He said he met her at the Beach Club and they left together. After killing her, he dumped her body in the parking lot, parked her car back at the Beach Club, and drove home. He said he disassembled the gun and tossed the parts in various places.

On February 18, McCormick was arrested and charged with murder. He was convicted on July 1, principally on Cooper's testimony and the similarity of the hair sample found in Nichols's car. Given the scant evidence presented by the prosecution, the defense had little to offer by way of rebuttal. The defense noted that McCormick was an alcoholic and was widely regarded as a chronic liar. His so-called confession to Cooper was an attempt to impress a fellow parolee and an effort to get some of the money from the Knoxville murder contract. The jury would have none of it. McCormick was convicted and sentenced to death.

His conviction was upheld on appeal, but in 1990, following a post-conviction hearing, his confession to Cooper was ordered suppressed. The defense attorney stressed that the prosecution relied on a recorded confession by a man who "they knew to be an alcoholic and a notorious liar." Despite the suppression of the evidence that was at the heart of his conviction, McCormick remained on death row, awaiting a new trial in 2007. By then, DNA tests had been performed on the hair sample which eliminated McCormick as a suspect. Now, there was no evidence at all that pointed to him as the killer and he was acquitted on December 3, 2007. He had spent sixteen years on Tennessee's death row.

Kennedy Brewer
Mississippi

The old legal maxim that justice deferred is justice denied has few better exemplars than Kennedy Brewer. Arrested and wrongfully convicted of the rape and murder of his girlfriend's three-year-old daughter, Brewer served seven years on Mississippi's death row before being exonerated. In addition, he languished in jail for another eight years awaiting trial.

In the early morning hours of May 3, 1992, Christine Jackson, the daughter of Brewer's girlfriend, Gloria Jackson, was abducted from her home, raped, and murdered. Two days later, the child's body was found in a creek in Noxubee County about five hundred yards from her home. On the night she was abducted, Brewer had been babysitting for Christine and her two younger siblings, both of whom were Brewer's biological children with Gloria. Brewer became an immediate suspect because he was present at the time of the crime and police said there was no sign of forced entry. Apparently unnoticed by police was a broken window near where the child slept, which might have served as a convenient point of entry for an intruder. Brewer was arrested and charged with capital murder and sexual battery. He spent the next three years in jail awaiting trial, which began in March 1995.

The prosecution speculated that Brewer had raped and killed Christine in the Jackson home, then carried her body to the creek, a short distance away, As for forensic evidence, a semen sample that was taken from the victim's body was said to be insufficient for DNA testing. It came down, then, to a number of marks on the girl's body that the medical examiner, Steven Hayne, believed to be bite marks. Hayne summoned Dr. Michael West, a forensic odonotologist, to analyze the marks. West concluded that nineteen marks found on the victim's body were "indeed and without a doubt" inflicted by Brewer's top two teeth. Somehow, he said, the bottom teeth had left no impression. West's certainty seemed somewhat remarkable since bite-mark analysis had never been considered scientifically conclusive. In fact, by the time the trial started, West had become the first member of the American Board of Forensic Odonotology to be suspended. Nonetheless, the court admitted his testimony. It was, after all, the only evidence the state had.

To counter West's testimony, the defense called upon Dr. Richard Souviron, a licensed dentist and founding member of the American Board of Forensic Odonotology, who testified that the marks were not human bite marks but insect bites that were the result of the body having been left in the water for days. Souviron insisted that it was nearly impossible to leave bite marks with only the top two teeth. Despite the prosecution's presenting virtually no credible evidence, Brewer was convicted on March 24, 1995, and sentenced to death.

In 2001, while he was on death row, advanced DNA testing was conducted on semen recovered from the girl's body in 1992. The tests excluded Brewer as the source of the semen and indicated an unknown male profile. The following year, Brewer's conviction was vacated, but the district attorney, who had prosecuted the case at trial, said he intended to retry the case and again seek the death penalty. Brewer was moved from death row to pre-trial detention in the county jail where he remained for five years while the prosecutor failed to move the case to trial. Finally, in the summer of 2007, the Innocence Project stepped in and, aided by Andre de Gruy of the Office of Capital Defense Counsel in Mississippi, secured Brewer's release from jail and prepared to represent him at a new trial. At about the same time, due to conflicts of interest in the Noxubee County district attorney's office, Ben Creekmore, the district attorney of Oxford, Mississippi, was appointed special prosecutor in the Brewer case. Creekmore decided not to seek the death penalty and agreed to allow bail to be set. Brewer was released in August 2007 while awaiting a new trial.

Meanwhile, the Innocence Project continued to investigate the case and asked the Mississippi attorney general's office to intervene. During the investigation, further DNA testing implicated another man, fifty-one-year-old Justin Albert Johnson, whose DNA provided a match. One of the original suspects, Johnson lived with his parents, just a few houses down from the victim's home. Although he was the only suspect with a history of committing sexual assaults against women and young girls, his possible guilt was ignored when investigators focused on Brewer as the prime suspect.

Under questioning, Johnson confessed to the murder of Christine Jackson and to a similar crime—the murder of Courtney Smith in September 1990, also in Noxubee County—and told investigators he had acted alone in each case. The two crimes were almost identical. Courtney Smith, also three years old, was raped, murdered, and left in a pond near her home. The ex-boyfriend of the child's mother, Levon Brooks, was arrested and convicted, largely on the basis of bite-mark analysis performed by West who, once again, was brought into the case by Hayne, the medical examiner. The same sheriff's officer investigated both crimes, and the same district attorney prosecuted both cases. On each occasion they overlooked evidence that pointed to Johnson and homed in on innocent men.

"If local law enforcement had properly investigated these crimes, they would have stayed focused on Albert Johnson from the beginning," said Vanessa Potkin, staff attorney for the Innocence Project. "In fact, if Albert Johnson had been apprehended for the first crime, the second one would never have happened—and the three-year-old victim would be approaching her eighteenth birthday."

On February 15, 2008, charges against Brewer were dropped and he was exonerated. On the same day, the Innocence Project, along with the Mississippi Innocence Project co-counsel, won Brooks's release from prison; he was exonerated in March 2008 based chiefly on Johnson's confession, as DNA testing could not be conducted in his case.

Legal assistance in the two cases was provided by the firm of Skadden, Arps, Slate, Meagher & Flom LLP and Affiliates; Andre de Gruy of the Office of Capital Defense Counsel of Mississippi; and Robert B. McDuff.

The state of Mississippi paid Brewer $500,000 in compensation. In 2009, Brewer filed a civil lawsuit against West and Hayne for $18 million. The suit was still pending in the fall of 2015.

Paul House
Tennessee

The Innocence Project, abetted by the improbable intervention of the US Supreme Court, also played a pivotal role in winning freedom for Paul House after he spent twenty-two years on death row for a murder of which he was innocent. In the summer of 1985, the bloodied body of the victim, Carolyn Muncey, was found under some brush on the bank of a creek near her home in rural Luttrell, Tennessee. She had been raped and beaten and was wearing only a nightgown and a house coat.

Shortly before the crime, House had moved into his mother's home, not far from the scene. Being new to the community and with a criminal record, he became the police's prime and, in fact, only suspect. The authorities wasted no time in moving forward. The state's case was at best circumstantial. Two prosecution witnesses testified that they had seen House wiping his hands on the night of the crime near where the body had been found. A pair of jeans belonging to House was found to have blood on them, and a forensic expert said at trial that the ABO blood type matched House's. The blood type also was said to match the semen found on Muncey's underwear. In February 1986, House was convicted of first-degree murder and sentenced to death.

Even as House's attorney began the process of appeal, evidence began to accumulate suggesting that House was innocent. Several potential witnesses came forward with information that implicated Muncey's husband. A number of neighbors said that Mr. Muncey was habitually abusive. Two women claimed they heard him confess to the crime at a party one night. A third woman said she saw him hitting his wife at a neighborhood dance. A fourth said he had asked her to provide an alibi for him on the night Muncey was killed.

In addition to the eyewitness evidence, new forensic data also was introduced. Further analysis of the blood found on House's jeans indicated that it was probably not deposited on the night of the murder. A former Tennessee State Medical Examiner said he believed the blood sample showed enzyme decay which was consistent with blood taken at the victim's autopsy and transported in vials without preservative or refrigeration. The decay, he further testified, would not likely be found in blood that came in direct contact with House's pants while the victim was alive. Additional data suggested that blood collected at Muncey's autopsy had spilled on House's jeans after they were collected as evidence. The blood vials were not sealed and were transported by two law enforcement officers to the FBI lab, about ten hours away. The blood was believed to have spoiled during the trip due to heat exposure. Also, FBI records showed that a significant amount of blood from the autopsy vials was missing when the officers arrived at the lab.

Yet more exculpatory evidence surfaced in the nineties, after House had spent more than a decade in prison. Advanced DNA testing revealed that the semen taken from Muncey's nightgown and underwear belonged to her husband, not House. The new results contradicted the trial testimony offered by an FBI expert who had told the jury that only House's blood group antigens could have been the source of the semen stains.

House's appeals, asking that his conviction be overturned on the basis of the new evidence, were rejected by several courts. In 2005, the case came before the U.S, Supreme Court, which rarely hears cases such as House's. The Innocence Project filed an amicus curiae, or friend-of-the-court, brief on his behalf. On June 12, 2006, the Court ruled that no "reasonable juror" would have convicted House had the new evidence been available at the time. His case was remanded to the district court in Tennessee for a full review.

District Court Judge Henry Mattice Jr. overturned House's conviction and ordered the state to either release him from custody or retry him within 180 days. The state's appeal was rejected. Bail, initially set at $500,000, was reduced to $100,000. An anonymous benefactor posted the 10 percent bond and House, by that time confined to a wheelchair with chronic multiple sclerosis, was released from the Lois M. DeBerry Special Needs Facility on July 2, 2008. All charges against him were dropped the following year.

Gussie Vann
Tennessee

The crime for which Gussie Vann was sent to death row was as repellant as a crime can be. It involved the rape and murder of his own daughter, eight-year-old Necia. Shortly before midnight on July 30, 1992, Gussie's wife, Bernice, called 911 and reported that her daughter had apparently fallen in her bedroom with a rope around her neck and was not breathing.

When paramedics arrived at the Vanns' mobile home near Riceville, Tennessee, they found Bernice weeping outside. Gussie, forty-two, was inside holding Necia, who was wearing only her underpants, and attempting to revive her by performing CPR. Gussie, who was nude, told the paramedics that he had gone out a bit earlier to purchase cigarettes and candy. When he returned, he said, he had undressed to take a shower when his wife found Necia and called to him. The girl, who had been medically diagnosed as a dwarf, was pronounced dead on arrival at the hospital.

When doctors examined her, they found bruises on her neck, a slight tear in the opening of her vagina, and no muscle tone in her anus, indicating, they said, multiple episodes of anal penetration. The official diagnosis was that Necia had been strangled. Questioned by police, Vann said that he, his wife, and their four children had been watching a movie and eating popcorn earlier in the evening. He suggested the girl might have choked on the popcorn. He said she had never given any indication of wanting to commit suicide. Two weeks later, based on the physical condition of the body, both Gussie and Bernice, twenty-eight, were charged with capital murder, rape, and incest.

While the cases were pending, a twelve-year-old niece of Gussie's came forward and alleged that he had raped her twice in 1991. Gussie was charged with two counts of aggravated rape; Bernice was charged as an accomplice for helping get the girl into his bedroom. Gussie went on trial first on the rape charge and denied the allegations. He was convicted in January 1994, based primarily on his niece's testimony. Additional support for conviction came from his wife, who entered into a plea agreement with prosecutors, offering to testify against Gussie in return for leniency in her own sentencing. Bernice, whose IQ of 62 was borderline retarded, took the stand and told the jury that her husband had forced her to watch the rape. Gussie was sentenced to fifty years in prison.

The murder charges against the Vanns were severed. Gussie went on trial first in McMinn County Circuit Court in 1994. The entire case against him was based entirely on forensic evidence, much of which was later found to be invalid. At trial, police testified that they found a strip of a bedsheet tied to a knob on a dresser drawer in a knot they believed to be too tight to have been tied by a young child. A torn strip that appeared to match the first one was found in another bedroom. A search of the mobile home produced a rope tied in a noose, a pornographic videotape, pornographic magazines, and unopened packages of condoms. A DNA analysis of the clothing Necia wore on the day she died yielded no evidence of blood, semen, or saliva that matched Vann's.

Ronald Toolsie, a state medical examiner, testified that a depression in the girl's neck was consistent with strangulation and the rope found in the home. He also said he found evidence of repeated sexual abuse, including anal penetration, although the girl's hymen was intact. The most recent instance of sexual abuse was believed to have occurred around the time of her death. Toolsie also noted that nothing resembling popcorn was found in her stomach. Gussie was found guilty of felony murder and two counts of incest.

At his sentencing hearing, he denied killing or sexually abusing his daughter. He recounted for the jury the sad details of his early life as one of fifteen children of a tenant farmer. He began working on the farm at the age of ten and left school after the third grade with an IQ measured in the second grade at 69. He later worked as a truck driver and suffered serious head injuries when he was beaten during an attempted hijacking in 1989. He began taking pain medication, became addicted, and fell victim to recurrent seizures; he was hospitalized following a nervous breakdown. The jury was unmoved. Gussie was sentenced to death.

In July 1995, in an effort to resolve both cases brought against her, Bernice pled guilty to aggravated child abuse, facilitation of aggravated rape and accessory after the fact. She was sentenced to twenty-five years in prison, served the full sentence, and died after a brief period on parole.

Gussie's conviction and sentence were upheld by the Tennessee Supreme Court in September 1998. An amended post-conviction petition was filed in May 2003 by the Tennessee Office of the Post-

Conviction Defender. An evidentiary hearing was not begun until four years later. For Gussie, it proved to be well worth the wait. The Knox County medical examiner, Darinka Mileusic-Polchan, testified that based on her review of the autopsy report, Necia had died an accidental death. She said that Toolsie's determination of death by strangulation was incorrect. She went on to say that there was no evidence of anal penetration. Toolsie and the emergency room physician who examined the girl's body had mistaken a normal physical reaction after death— the loosening of muscle tone in the anus—for sexual abuse. Another defense expert, Dr. William McCormick, agreed with the medical examiner's conclusions.

The defense proceeded to offer a scenario that could have accounted for Necia's death. Evidence was offered showing that the torn bed sheet had been tied to a knob on the top drawer of the dresser so it could be used to pull open the drawer. It was therefore possible that the girl, shortened by dwarfism, might have been standing of the edge of the bottom drawer to reach something on top of the dresser when she slipped and fell. The sheet, the defense suggested, might then have entangled around her neck, asphyxiating her.

In June 2008, McMinn County Senior Judge Donald P. Harris set aside Gussie's conviction, declaring that he had received an inadequate defense. His trial lawyers, the judge said, had failed to seek the views of medical experts who could have countered the evidence produced by the state. In effect, Judge Harris noted, Gussie's defense attorney had conceded that Necia had been raped, an issue that was disputed and critical to Gussie's conviction. Further medical evidence presented at the hearing noted that because Necia suffered from dwarfism, she lacked a part of the anatomy that connects the head to the spinal column, leaving her head unstable.

The judge's findings were definitive. The "most damaging" piece of medical testimony—that the girl had been vaginally and anally raped just before death—was, he said, "nothing more than inconclusive post-mortem anatomical findings." He went on to describe the failings of Gussie's trial attorneys as "not only prejudicial, but disastrous" and led to Gussie's conviction on the basis of "inaccurate, exaggerated and speculative testimony."

Initial plans for a retrial were dropped and the prosecution dismissed the charges on September 29, 2011. Vann remains in prison, however, serving the fifty-year sentence on the 1994 rape conviction.

Commentary: DNA

The counter to false forensics is the use of DNA evidence, introduced in the sixties but refined and perfected over the next few decades. In a legal system frayed by error and uncertainty, the advent of forensic DNA testing is often referred to as a magic bullet. DNA technology can provide scientific proof, beyond all doubt, of a suspect's guilt or innocence. It has been revolutionizing the criminal justice system in much the same way that the discovery of fingerprinting did more than a century ago. Although a fingerprint is nearly as unique as a DNA sample, fingerprints are more easily concealed. DNA is contained in blood, semen, saliva, hair follicles, and skin cells, all of which are more difficult to remove from a crime scene.

First identified as the molecule of heredity, DNA has been part of the scientific tableau for the past half century. It was used initially to resolve a few paternity and immigration cases. A British geneticist at the University of Leicester, Alec Jeffreys, who pioneered in its application, estimated that the odds against two people, other than identical twins, sharing the same DNA profile are billions to one.

It was not for several decades that advances in technology made it possible to analyze and match samples quickly and cheaply enough for DNA fingerprinting to be used in the justice system. That happened for the first time in England in 1986. It was introduced in American courts a year later by a biochemist named Edward Blake, but it did not make its way into popular use until the mid-nineties. Since then, hundreds of wrongly convicted people have been exonerated by DNA evidence, at least a dozen of them freed from death row. It is estimated that DNA fingerprinting has resulted in as many as 25 percent of suspects charged with crimes being released from custody before going to trial.

Perhaps the principal effect of DNA testing is that it has brought to light the glaring inefficiencies of a system that convicts innocent people by the hundreds and sentences a substantial number of them to death. It is no longer possible to believe with any assurance that if a person is convicted he is probably guilty, that if he is sent to his death he no doubt deserves to die. That has all changed now. The reasoning is elementary: If DNA has established with scientific certainty that dozens of innocent people have been sentenced to death, can one harbor the belief that similar mistakes were not made in cases where DNA evidence was unavailable? Now, one who supports capital punishment is obliged to live with the uneasy suspicion that innocent people are being sent to their death.

Curiously, the case that spawned the revolution in attitude toward the criminal justice system was not a capital case. The first DNA exoneration in the United States involved a rape that never took place. The conviction was the product of perjured testimony, prosecutorial misconduct, and defense strategies that backfired. The wrongly convicted man spent the better part of twelve years in prison, but the price he paid was not entirely forfeited. It opened the door to freedom for countless others who had fallen prey to the system.

Gary Dotson
Illinois

Gary Dotson was the victim of a hoax. He was convicted of raping a young woman who was never in fact assaulted in a trial that rested almost exclusively on the false testimony of a police forensic scientist.

Ironically, it was old-fashioned blood typing that was used to convict him, and breakthrough DNA blood testing that finally set him free.

The web of events in which Dotson became trapped began on the night of July 9, 1977. A police patrol officer noticed a young woman standing alongside a road near a shopping mall in Homewood, Illinois, a suburb of Chicago. It was late at night and she looked disheveled and appeared to be distressed. The officer asked if she was all right. The woman identified herself as Cathleen Crowell. She was sixteen years old and worked as a cashier and cook in a fast-food chain restaurant in the mall. Then she related the following tale:

After leaving work, she was walking across the mall parking lot when a car with three young men in it pulled up alongside her. Two of the men grabbed her and threw her into the rear seat. One of the men climbed into the back seat with her, tore her clothes off, raped her, and scratched several letters onto her midsection with a broken beer bottle.

The officer took her to a hospital where a rape examination revealed what appeared to be a seminal stain on her panties. Several pubic hairs and a vaginal smear were taken as evidence. A drawing was made of the marks on her abdomen. The letters were illegible and appeared to be shaped in an unusual crosshatched pattern.

Three days later, Crowell's parents took her to the police station where she worked with a sketch artist to develop a likeness of her assailant. She described him as a young, white male with stringy shoulder-length hair. She did not mention his having any facial hair. When police showed her a mug book she identified Gary Dotson, a twenty-two-year-old high school dropout who had had minor brushes with the law in the past. The police arrested Dotson at his nearby home in a working-class suburb where he lived with his mother and sister. Although Dotson wore a full mustache which could not have been grown in the five days since the alleged attack, Crowell nonetheless picked him out in a police lineup.

Dotson went on trial for rape in May 1979. There were two chief witnesses for the prosecution. Crowell, who appeared to be a model student at her local high school where she studied Russian and was a member of the junior varsity swimming team, identified Dotson with total conviction, saying, "There is no mistaking that face." The other key witness was Timothy Dixon, a state police forensic scientist who had been assigned to the case. It was Dixon's testimony regarding blood types that probably clinched the case against Dotson, adding scientific near-certainty to Crowell's eyewitness identification. The problem was that Crowell was lying and Dixon was offering information that was at best incomplete, at worst intentionally misleading.

Dixon told the court that type-B blood antigens had been found in the stain in Crowell's panties and that Dotson was a B-type secretor, placing him in a 10 percent minority in the white male population. Of course 10 percent of the white male population would still provide a substantial number of other suspects, but even those percentages were misleading. Type-O blood contains the same antigens as type-B, and taken together they account for two-thirds of the white male population. Furthermore, Crowell herself had B-type blood so it could have been her own secretions that produced the stain. The prosecuting attorney, Raymond Garza, also appeared intent on deceiving the jury. In his summation he stated that several pubic hairs taken from the victim matched Dotson's, although at that time it was technically impossible to make that determination. He also described Crowell as a sixteen-year-old virgin, which she was not.

Dotson's defense, based on eyewitness misidentification, rested entirely on the alibi provided by four of his friends who testified they were with him at the time Crowell claimed to have been raped. The prosecutor called them liars, and the jury apparently agreed. They found Dotson guilty; he was sentenced to twenty-five-to-fifty years. His appeal was denied three years later and to all appearances the case was concluded. In fact, it would follow a long and circuitous route that led finally to Dotson's exoneration.

The first turn came in 1985 when Crowell became stricken by conscience. She had married a high school classmate, David Webb, three years earlier. They had moved to New Hampshire and joined the Pilgrim Baptist Church, and Cathleen, now known as Cathleen Crowell

Webb, confessed to her pastor, the Reverend Carl Nannini. She told him that she had fabricated the story eight years earlier because she was concerned she might have become pregnant during a sexual encounter the previous day with her boyfriend, David Bierne. The rape story was intended as a cover-up in the event her fears were realized. She said she inflicted the superficial wounds on her body and tore her clothing to lend credence to her story.

Pastor Nannini retained an attorney, John McLario, who contacted the Cook County State's Attorney's Office. When the prosecutors appeared uninterested, he notified a Chicago television station which broke the story on March 22, 1985. Warren Lupel, a commercial attorney, agreed to represent Dotson as a favor to a client who knew Dotson's mother. Lupel petitioned the court to set aside the conviction, and the trial judge, Richard Samuels, ordered Dotson's release on $100,000 bond on April 4, pending a hearing the following week. Dotson, who had already spent six years in prison, had reason to be optimistic even beyond Webb's recanting. A new report, prepared by the chief forensic serologist of the Illinois State Police, seemed to corroborate her confession. It acknowledged that Dixon's blood-type testimony was flawed and that the semen could have come from O-type secretors, among which was David Bierne. But Dotson's run of luck did not last long. It ended at the hearing on April 11.

Unaccustomed as he was to criminal proceedings, Warren Lupel committed a tactical error when he called a defense witness who had not testified at the previous trial. The witness was Dotson's closest friend, Bill Julian, who was one of the four friends who provided his alibi. Earlier, the other witnesses had stated that one of the girls had been driving the car on the night in question. Now, Julian said he was the driver. When the discrepancy was noted, the other witnesses agreed that they originally had lied about the driver because Julian was driving with a suspended license. Although the explanation was plausible enough and the driver's identity did not go to the heart of the matter, the credibility of the defense seemed to be shaken. Judge Samuels, unmoved by the new forensic evidence and Webb's recantation, declared that the woman's trial testimony seemed more credible than her revised story. He revoked the bond and sent Dotson back to prison, but his odyssey through the criminal justice system was far from over.

With public sentiment clearly running in Dotson's favor, Governor James R. Thompson granted Lupel's petition for clemency. The three-day hearing attracted media representatives from far and near, and Dotson's and Webb's testimony was carried live on local television stations. Dotson was, in effect, given a split decision. His clemency petition was denied by the Governor, but Thompson commuted his sentence to time served. Dotson was released on parole.

Freedom did not necessarily nourish Dotson's life style. He had taken to drinking beer regularly and in large quantities. It was not unusual for him to have a six-pack for breakfast and to continue drinking through the day. He had not found work and had no steady means of support. He signed several book and movie contracts but never followed through on any of them. Webb, in an apparent act of penance, gave Dotson $17,500 which she had received as an advance from a publisher of religious books. It would not take Dotson long to dispose of it. One of his most devoted drinking companions was a twenty-one-year-old bartender named Camille Dardanes, who had befriended him during his hearings. Now, with a hefty stake in hand, he and Dardanes went off to Las Vegas and married. On their return to Illinois, they bought two cars and rented and furnished an apartment. Two months later they were broke. Evicted from their apartment, they moved in with Dotson's mother. Camille found work as a waitress, but Gary remained unemployed.

In January 1987, Camille gave birth to a daughter. Gary tried to turn the corner by joining Alcoholics Anonymous, but his attempt at rehabilitation didn't last long. The drinking resumed and the fabric of their lives began to unravel. On a Sunday evening in August, driving home from a day in the park, Gary and Camille quarreled and Gary slapped her. He then took their eight-month old daughter and bolted from the car. Camille chased after them, and flagged down a cruising police car. She told the officers that her husband was a convicted felon and had taken their baby. She said he had struck her, and she wanted to press charges. From that point on, things began to spin out of control. Gary was arrested, charged with domestic battery, and held without bond since the offense might have violated the terms of his parole.

During the proceedings that followed, Gary found a new advocate. Civia Tamarkin, a journalist who wrote for *People* magazine, had interviewed Gary for an article and was convinced he was innocent of the rape charge. Now, she found him a new attorney, one who was steeped in criminal law and well acquainted with the workings of the legal machinery in and around Chicago. He was Thomas M. Breen, a former assistant state's attorney in Cook County, and he set to work immediately. Camille, despite her initial wish to press charges, decided she would not cooperate with the prosecution, and the domestic battery case against Gary was dropped. He was not yet in the clear, however.

Dotson indeed was found to be in violation of parole, and the Illinois Department of Corrections invoked a "parole hold" on him, requiring he be held in custody pending a hearing before the Illinois Prisoner Review Board. Although the hearing appeared to go well, the board repealed his parole and reinstated his original sentence. Dotson now faced an additional sixteen years of prison time.

Breen was not happy with the turn of events. He did not think Dotson's parole should have been revoked for a domestic spat in which his wife no longer wished to press charges. Even his parole officer, Phillip Magee, seemed to agree. In his report to the review board he said: "His [Dotson's] violation neither indicated criminal orientation, nor does he appear to otherwise represent a serious threat to public safety." Breen was further irritated because the review board never notified him directly of its decision; he learned of it from a reporter who was covering the case. Now, desperately seeking a pivot that might turn things in Dotson's favor, the attorney found one where one might least have expected it.

In the October 26, 1987 issue of *Newsweek* magazine, Breen came across an article entitled "Leaving Holmes in the Dust." The writer, Sharon Begley, reported that DNA technology would make it possible to connect a suspect to a crime and, conversely, could exonerate a suspect who was innocent. Investigating further, Breen learned that DNA had not yet been used in a criminal case. Since Dotson's conviction now rested almost entirely on blood evidence, Breen saw the new scientific technique as made-to-order. He filed a motion with Judge Richard J. Fitzgerald of the Criminal Division of the Cook County Circuit Court, asking that DNA testing be used in the Dotson case. The assistant state's attorney, J. Scott Arthur, offered no objection. Governor Thompson also approved and asked Alec Jeffreys, the British geneticist and pioneer in DNA fingerprinting, to conduct the test.

With DNA technology still in its infancy, Jeffreys was initially unable to obtain a conclusive result. The sample had degraded over the years and the evidence had become stale. Governor Thompson, who seemed determined to bring the case to a conclusion, decided to take the testing a step further. Edward Blake, a biochemist and forensic scientist in California, had been pushing DNA techniques to their limits. Thompson ordered that Webb's panties be sent to Blake along with fresh blood samples from both Dotson and David Bierne.

On August 15, 1988, Blake informed Thompson, the prosecutors, and Breen that the test had positively excluded Dotson and identified Bierne as the source of the semen. A day later, Breen asked the governor to grant Dotson unconditional clemency on the grounds of actual innocence. But Thompson was hesitant. He said he would not act on the clemency petition until he received a recommendation from the Prisoner Review Board. In the meantime, Dotson was housed involuntarily in a residential center for alcohol and substance abuse. Nine months passed without any action being taken, and Breen filed a new petition for post-conviction relief. On August 14, almost a year after results of DNA testing eliminated Dotson as a suspect, Judge Fitzgerald granted the motion. The Cook County State's Attorney's Office immediately announced that the charges against Dotson would be dropped.

The first case of DNA exoneration in the United States was now in the books, and the lid was pried open on a new era in the American penal system. Five years later, in 1993, DNA was used for the first time to free a man who had served time on death row.

Kirk Bloodsworth
Maryland

Kirk Bloodsworth was the first man to be cleared as a result of DNA evidence after being sentenced to death. He walked free in 1993 after spending nearly ten years in a Maryland prison. The crime of which he was convicted was a particularly gory one.

On July 25, 1984, nine-year-old Dawn Venice Hamilton went to play outside her cousins' apartment near Golden Ring Mall in the Rosedale section of Maryland, just outside of Baltimore. When she failed to return, her aunt called the police. A few hours later, she was found dead in a nearby wooded area. She had been beaten with a rock, sexually assaulted, and strangled. A sneaker had made an impression on her neck, and a stick was inserted in her vagina. Her underwear was found hanging from a tree. A chunk of cinder block, believed to be the murder weapon, was found near her head. Two boys who had been fishing in the vicinity told police they had seen Dawn enter the woods with a man who had blond curly hair. Three other residents of the apartment complex also claimed to have seen a blond, curly-haired man in the area on the day of the crime. A composite sketch was drawn up and given to newspapers and television stations.

Kirk Bloodsworth, a twenty-three-year-old ex-Marine, worked at the Golden Ring Mall, but he was off on the day of the murder. He and his wife had been having marital problems, and he had followed her from their Cambridge, Maryland home to the Middle River area of Baltimore County in an effort to patch things up. A week later, he decided the marriage could not be saved, and he left without telling her. His wife called the police to file a missing person's report. The name rang a bell. Not much earlier, they had received an anonymous call saying the composite sketch resembled a man named Kirk.

When Bloodsworth returned to Cambridge a few days later, he was questioned by the police. One of the boys who had been fishing said Bloodsworth looked like the man he had seen, even though his hair was red rather than blond. Bloodsworth told the police that he had left Cambridge because his marriage was troubled and he wanted the comfort of being with friends. He said he had notified his mother-in-law that he was leaving and did not understand why his wife had filed a missing persons report. He also noted that while the suspect was described as about six-feet-five, thin, and blond, he was only about six feet tall, rather burly, and had bright red hair. He said he had never seen Dawn Hamilton. Nonetheless, Bloodsworth, who had no previous record, was arrested and charged with sexual assault, rape, and first-degree murder.

There was no physical evidence linking him to the crime. The FBI, which was involved in the investigation, had the girl's panties examined and determined there was nothing there that would either help or hurt the state's case. The sole basis for his arrest was the identification by five eyewitnesses, none of whom had ever seen him in the presence of the girl. The trial turned on degrees of credibility. It was the word of the state's witnesses which placed him near the crime scene against the testimony of the defendant's friends who said they were with him at the time of the murder. The jury believed the prosecution's witnesses. Bloodsworth was found guilty and sentenced to death.

In 1986, Bloodsworth's attorney filed an appeal contending that the police had had other suspects, including one who more closely resembled the composite sketch, and another man who had helped search for the missing girl and had found her underpants hanging from the tree. It was information, the defense maintained, that should have been revealed during the trial. The Maryland Court of Appeals agreed. Bloodsworth's conviction was overturned in July 1986 because the police had withheld evidence. He was tried again in April 1987 and again was convicted. This time he was sentenced to two consecutive life terms instead of death.

After having spent two and a half years isolated on death row, Bloodsworth was imprisoned with the general population. It was a mixed blessing. Though life on death row was depressing and bleak, Bloodsworth found that living among the general run of prisoners could be even tougher, since child molesters were disdained by even the toughest of convicts.

Bloodsworth continued to press his appeals with a new, court-appointed attorney, Robert E. Morin. He passed the time writing poetry and reading books by the hundreds. One of the books, *The Blooding*, by Joseph Wambaugh, a former Los Angeles cop, described how British police used DNA to solve murders in the Yorkshire area. He discussed the matter with Morin. Dawn's panties had contained a semen stain smaller than a dime. Morin recalled that the FBI had already tested the panties and could gather no useful evidence from the stain. But that was more than five years ago, and DNA technology had been advancing quickly.

In April 1992, Morin sent the victim's panties and shorts, as well as the stick that had been inserted in her vagina, to Edward Blake in California. Blake, who had intervened on Dotson's behalf, was by now recognized as the father of forensic DNA testing in the United States. He headed the only private lab, Forensic Science Associates (FSA), which was then conducting DNA tests for criminal justice purposes. The samples were still fresh. The evidence had been locked up and preserved. The stain had been air-dried, and DNA can remain in dried samples of body fluids for years. Morin paid the ten-thousand-dollar testing fee, as Bloodsworth's family had exhausted their life savings financing his defense. It took a year for the results to be returned. On May 17, 1993, the lab issued its report. It concluded that Bloodsworth's blood samples did not match any of the evidence it had tested. However, the lab also requested a fresh sample of Bloodswoth's blood for retesting to resolve questions about proper labeling on the original sample. On June 3, FSA issued a second report stating that its original findings were replicated: Bloodsworth could not be responsible for the stain on the victim's underwear. A few weeks later, the FBI conducted its own test of the evidence and came to the same conclusion.

Three months later, on June 28, 1993, Bloodsworth walked free. After another three months, Maryland Governor William Donald Schaefer issued a full pardon. The state paid Bloodsworth $300,000 for lost income, based on the estimate that he would have earned approximately $30,000 a year from the time of his arrest to his release. Bloodsworth was the first man sentenced to death who was cleared as a result of DNA evidence.

Rolando Cruz and Alejandro Hernandez
Illinois

Not everyone was immediately convinced of the infallibility of DNA testing. The most serious doubters often were police and prosecutors, and that did not bode well for suspects in their jurisdictions. Two such suspects—Rolando Cruz and Alejandro Hernandez—spent ten years, much of it on death row, in an Illinois prison while four police officers and three former prosecutors played fast and loose with the criminal justice system. They were unimpressed that DNA evidence had excluded the pair from having been involved in the crime with which they were charged.

The crime was a heinous one. It was the kidnapping, rape, and murder of a ten-year-old girl, Jeanine Nicarico, in DuPage County, Illinois in 1983. The police questioned Hernandez, who was borderline mentally retarded and inclined toward fantasy, based on a tip from an anonymous caller. Hernandez, who was nineteen years old, told them that he and some of his friends, including Cruz, who was twenty, knew something about the crime. They apparently were enticed by a $10,000 reward that had been offered for information leading to an arrest. Police officers told Hernanderz and Cruz they would be considered heroes in the community if they helped solve the murder. Neither was able to provide any information that was not already public knowledge. However, police said that when Cruz was questioned he offered details of the crime that he told them came to him in a vision. No record was made of those statements, and Cruz later denied making them.

In January 1984, the district attorney announced that his office had insufficient evidence to bring charges against any suspect. The community, which was outraged by the brutality of the crime, was becoming impatient. Six weeks later, Cruz and Hernandez were charged with raping and murdering the young girl. The lead detective in the case, who had insisted all along that the two suspects were not the murderers, resigned in protest, saying that the state was proceeding against innocent men.

Nevertheless, Cruz and Hernandez were tried and convicted on perjured government testimony and questionable courtroom decisions. Cruz's alleged dream visions were admitted into evidence on the basis of the testimony of sheriff's detectives although there was no written or visual record of Cruz having made the statements. In Hernandez's case, an officer who claimed that the defendant had incriminated himself during interrogation, admitted he had not documented those remarks until almost four years after the questioning. Other officers said they never took notes or maintained that their notes had been lost or destroyed. Cruz and Hernandez were sentenced to death.

Shortly after the trial, a repeat sex offender and convicted murderer, Brian Dugan, confessed that he alone had committed the crime. He also admitted to five other crimes—two rape-murders and three rapes. His confession included many details of the crime which only the perpetrator could know. A number of his other crimes were similar in nature to the one for which Cruz and Hernandez were sitting on death row, and several witnesses established conclusively that Dugan had committed the crimes by himself.

In 1988, the Illinois Supreme Court overturned the convictions and death sentences on the grounds that the defendants should have had separate trials. Two years later, Cruz and Hernandez were each retried, and again they were convicted. Their second trials were as tainted as their first. Dugan's confession was never offered in evidence because it was concealed from the defense team. It would not be disclosed for more than four years. A former cellmate of Cruz's who, in exchange for a four-month reduction in his sentence, had testified in the original trial that Cruz had admitted committing the murder, refused to testify at the second trial, stating that his story had been invented. Robert Turner, another death row inmate with Cruz, testified against him. He said Cruz had confessed to committing the murder with Hernandez and Dugan. However, two other death row inmates told the court that Turner had said he was going to set up Cruz using law books that described the crime. The prosecution told the jury that Turner had been offered nothing in return for his testimony, but nine months later one of the prosecutors spoke on his behalf at a resentencing hearing.

In 1990, a volunteer legal team headed by Lawrence C. Marshall, who was affiliated with the Center on Wrongful Convictions, agreed to represent Cruz on appeal. A divided Illinois Supreme Court granted Cruz another new trial because evidence regarding Dugan's confession had been excluded by the trial judge. In the meantime, the role of DNA technology as used in the Bloodsworth case came to the attention of the defense, and a test was ordered. The results were conclusive: Cruz and Hernandez were excluded as possible rapists of Jeanine Nicarico. The sample matched Dugan's DNA, but, despite all evidence of their innocence, the state insisted on pressing the case against Cruz and Hernandez. The prosecutor, in the face of what now was regarded as scientific certainty, declared, "The DNA results . . . do not in any way negate Cruz's involvement in the Nicarico crime." The state decided to proceed with a third trial.

In 1992, Assistant Attorney General Mary Brigid Kenney wrote a memorandum identifying numerous errors made in the prosecution of Cruz and urged that they be acknowledged to the court. The memo concluded: "I cannot, in good conscience, allow my name to appear on a brief asking . . . to affirm his conviction." State Attorney General Roland Burris responded by removing Kenney from the case, and she responded by resigning. In her resignation letter, she wrote: "I was being asked to help execute an innocent man. Unfortunately, you [the attorney general] have seen fit to ignore the evidence in this case."

For the new trials, the team of four defense attorneys, which included Marshall, opted for a bench trial, which made the judge, rather than a jury, the finder of fact. Marshall found that interviews with jurors from the previous trials indicated that many of them had been "caught up in the emotion that surrounds a crime of this kind." During Cruz's trial, a police officer admitted having lied under oath. He said he had fabricated Cruz's initial statement about seeing the crime scene in a vision. After hearing all the prosecution's evidence, the judge directed a verdict of not guilty. Still, prosecutors seemed intent upon retrying Hernandez, whose conviction had also been overturned, but they dropped the charges on the eve of the trial. Cruz was set free in November 1995; Hernandez a month later.

Shortly after the two were released, a special prosecutor was appointed to investigate whether police and prosecutors had violated the law in pursuing their case against Hernandez and Cruz. A grand jury later indicted four sheriff's deputies and three former prosecutors, a group that became known as the DuPage 7, on charges of perjury and official misconduct. Although they were acquitted of the charges, DuPage County later agreed to pay $3.5 million to settle civil rights claims filed in federal court by Cruz, Hernandez, and Stephen Buckley, a third defendant who had been implicated. The district attorney who prosecuted Cruz later became attorney general of Illinois. Another prosecutor in the case became a judge. Brian Dugan remained imprisoned for a number of other rapes and murders, but he was not charged with the murder of Jeanine Nicarico.

Ray Krone
Arizona

When Ray Krone walked out of Arizona State Prison at Yuma on April 8, 2002, he became the one-hundredth innocent person convicted of capital murder to be released from custody since 1973, according to the Death Penalty Information Center. Krone was freed by DNA evidence after being convicted twice and spending ten years in prison, including three on death row. His was the twelfth DNA exoneration in the United States since 1993.

Krone was convicted of first-degree murder and kidnapping in the stabbing death of Kim Ancona, a thirty-six-year-old Phoenix cocktail waitress whose body was found in a local lounge on December 29, 1991. In an apparent frenzy to make an arrest, Phoenix police charged Krone with the crime two days later. He was assigned an attorney by the state. The evidence against him was circumstantial, and he was convicted chiefly on the basis of expert testimony that bite marks found on the victim's breast matched Krone's distinctive dental pattern. During his trial, the press labeled him the "snaggletooth killer." The trial lasted about a week, and the jury returned a verdict of guilty after deliberating for two hours. The judge sentenced him to death.

Krone's parents, Carolyn and Jim Leming, retained a private attorney, Christopher J. Plourd, and in June 1995 the Arizona Supreme Court overturned the conviction and granted Krone a new trial at which DNA evidence would be introduced. Aware that the state's case hinged almost completely on what the prosecutor called Krone's "unique dentition," Krone's lawyer used his opening remarks to contend that the bite marks were not the defendant's and that saliva found on the victim provided a DNA pattern that excluded Krone. However, the DNA test was not entirely conclusive, and the jury again found Krone guilty.

But Maricopa County Superior Court Judge James McDougall was unconvinced. Saying he had a list of troubling questions about the case and serious doubts about the "clear identity of the killer," he sentenced Krone to twenty-five years to life on the murder charge and an additional twenty-one years for kidnapping. Although he was moved off death row, the prospect of spending the rest of his life in prison for a crime he did not commit was of little comfort to Krone. He said he gave up hope when the jurors ignored what he thought to be overwhelming evidence and testimony in his favor. "[T]hat pretty much ruled out all the faith I had in truth and justice," he said later. Thirty-nine years old when he was sentenced for the second time, he would be seventy-five before he became eligible for release.

Once again, DNA technology came to the rescue. Alan Simpson, a member of Krone's defense team, had a new DNA test performed in 2002 on saliva found on the victim's tank top. The results not only cleared Krone as a possibility, but they were found to be a perfect match for Kenneth Phillips, who was serving time in the same prison for an unrelated sex crime and who had lived about six hundred yards from the bar where Ancona was killed. In addition, a dental expert said that Phillips could not be eliminated as the person who left the bite mark on the victim's breast. Krone was released four days after a police lab confirmed the DNA match with Phillips.

The futility of working within an inexact system that too often condemns innocent men was reflected in a statement made by Rick Romley, a Maricopa County prosecuting attorney. "What do we say to him?" Romley asked. "An injustice was done and we will try to do better. And we're sorry."

PART IV

Snitch Testimony

IN THE ARGOT of the criminal justice system, they are called jailhouse snitches; in more formal terms, they are known as incentivized witnesses. But there is nothing ambiguous about their function: They offer courtroom testimony for the prosecution in exchange for an incentive, usually the dropping of a criminal charge or its reduction to a lesser charge. If the witness is already incarcerated, he is likely to have his sentence reduced or his parole accelerated. The hazards of such a system hardly need explaining. How much trust can be invested in the testimony of a convict promised early release if he is ready to say what the authorities tell him to say? Yet dozens of innocent people have been sent to prison, many of them to death row, on the weight of bartered testimony that, in effect, has been bought by police or prosecutors. Law enforcement agents insist that well-placed informants are an integral part of the process, that the surest way to justice is to squeeze one suspect or prison inmate to provide the incriminating evidence needed to convict another. It is by no means a technique of recent invention. Its roots are set deep in the practice of Anglo-American law.

In eighteenth century England, the use of "crown witnesses" was accepted as a central tool in the criminal justice system. It was a straight-forward arrangement known both to prosecution and defense and therefore entirely without subterfuge. Informants for the state escaped prosecution and received for their services a stipend referred to as "blood money." It was an arrangement that not only countenanced perjury but encouraged it, proving along the way that there was little honor among thieves. Of course a crown witness of renown might well have suspected that a day would come when he would fall victim to a witness no more credible than he was. That is what happened to Charles Cane.

Cane had offered the testimony that delivered two men to the hangman in 1755. The following year, he found himself in the prisoner's dock confronted by another witness for the crown and suffered the same inglorious end. The perceptive clergyman that ministered to him noted that it was no surprise to Cane. He had, the clergyman said, expected "nothing less than hanging to be his fate at last, but not of the evil day's coming so soon."

More than two centuries later, the United States proved that it conceded nothing to the motherland when it came to producing "professional" informants. Leslie Vernon White had established a reputation as the best in the business and in 1989 was featured on a segment of the television program *Sixty Minutes*. White's story was first chronicled by *Los Angeles Times* reporter Ted Rohrlich. A career criminal, White fabricated confessions in at least a dozen cases. He would pick up details about crimes from news sources and get information via the prison telephone. He noted that his was a competitive business, with many informants seeking an edge in collecting information that would make their stories credible. They even celebrated their calling with slogans such as "Don't go to the pen, send a friend" and "If you can't do the time, just drop a dime."

Two reporters for the *Chicago Tribune*—Ken Armstrong and Steve Mills—studied the role that snitches and other incentivized witnesses played in the cases of ninety-seven people who were released from death rows throughout the United States between 1976 and 1999. Their findings were analyzed in a research report by Rob Warden for the Center on Wrongful Convictions.

The study found that prosecutors used incentivized witnesses in 39 percent of the ninety-seven cases. The thirty-eight people wrongfully convicted on the basis of that testimony served a total of 291 years in prison before they were released, an average of nearly eight years each. Sixteen of the thirty-eight defendants were convicted on the testimony of jailhouse snitches, almost all of whom said they had heard the defendants confess. Other informants, some of them suspects in the same case, testified against the remaining twenty-two. In eighteen cases, informants with incentives were the sole basis for conviction, and police or prosecutorial misconduct contributed to more than one third of those cases. Of the thirty-eight states that practiced capital punishment at that time, seventeen had wrongful convictions based at least in part on incentivized testimony. Recantation by the informants was the reason for exoneration in almost half the cases.

It is not possible to estimate how many innocent people might have been sent to death row or, worse, executed, as a result of such fabricated testimony. It is nearly certain, however, that at least one innocent man was put to death solely on the basis of the incentivized testimony of two witnesses.

Sonia Jacobs and Jesse Tafero
Florida

Justice came too late for Jesse Tafero. He and Sonia "Sunny" Jacobs, his common law wife, were sentenced to death in Florida for the murder of two highway patrolmen in 1976. They were convicted largely on the testimony of a third accomplice who, to all appearances, was the actual killer. Jacobs's conviction was overturned in 1992 on a writ of habeas corpus when it was discovered that the prosecution witnesses had lied. Tafero, who was convicted on the same evidence, would likely have been released as well. But by then he had been dead two years, executed in brutal fashion in the electric chair.

Early on the morning of February 20, 1976, state highway patrol trooper Philip Black and a visiting Canadian constable named Donald

Irwin, approached a green Camaro parked at a rest stop on Interstate 95 in Broward County. Asleep in the car were Jacobs, Tafero, and Walter Rhodes, an ex-con whom Tafero had met while both were serving prison terms. The patrolmen thought they saw a gun on the floor of the car. They woke the occupants and asked Tafero and Rhodes to get out. At some point after that, both police officers were shot dead. Jacobs, Tafero, and Rhodes fled the scene in the police car, but soon ditched it and resumed their flight in a stolen car. Shortly after, they were caught at a police road block and arrested.

Ballistics tests indicated that both policemen were shot with the same gun. Tests also showed that Rhodes definitely had fired a gun, since he was the only one who tested positive for gunpowder residue. Tafero, it was determined, might have fired a gun or simply handled a gun after it was fired. Tafero told police that Rhodes had shot the policemen and then handed him the gun so that Rhodes could drive the getaway car. Rhodes was in fact behind the wheel when the car was stopped at the roadblock. However, Rhodes named Tafero as the shooter and agreed to take a polygraph test. Police said he passed the test but withheld the results from the state. Yet it was on the basis of the lie-detector test that the prosecutor justified a plea bargain for Rhodes, who agreed to testify against Tafero and Jacobs and to plead guilty to second-degree murder in return for a life sentence.

Tafero and Jacobs were tried separately but were convicted on the same basic evidence. In addition to Rhodes's testimony, jailhouse informants said that Tafero and Jacobs had confessed to them. There also was testimony from two eyewitnesses. One said he saw a man in brown, which was what Tafero was wearing, spread-eagled and leaning over the hood of the police car when the shots were fired. Another said he saw a man wearing blue, Rhodes, move from the front of the car to the rear just before the shooting. However, neither witness was able to identify the shooter on sight. Both Jacobs and Tafero were found guilty. The jury recommended a term of life imprisonment for Jacobs and a death sentence for Tafero. The judge overruled the jury and sentenced Jacobs to die as well.

In 1981, the Florida Supreme Court commuted Jacobs's sentence to life in prison after her lawyers learned that the polygraph test was inconclusive and indicated that Rhodes might have been lying. The following year, Rhodes recanted, saying he—not Tafero or Jacobs—had fired the gun. He later recanted on his recantation, then recanted again and altered his story repeatedly over the years.

Tafero's conviction was affirmed in 1981. Various motions and appeals in state courts were denied in 1983, 1984, 1987, 1988, and 1990. The Eleventh Circuit Court of Appeals, a federal court, reviewed the case in 1986 and 1989 and confirmed the conviction each time. The appeal process finally ran out for Tafero; so did time. In May 1990, he was executed in horrifying fashion. During the execution, Tafero's head seemed to catch fire with flames and smoke shooting through the top. The electric current was interrupted and resumed three times. Witnesses said that Tafero continued to breathe and move after the first interruption. His brutally slow, painful death prompted many to consider whether continued use of the electric chair might violate the Eighth Amendment's injunction against cruel and unusual punishment.

As for Jacobs, who grievously mourned Tafero's death, her prospects were growing somewhat brighter. A childhood friend of hers, filmmaker Micki Dickoff, had taken an interest in her case. Scanning court transcripts, affidavits, and old newspaper clippings, Dickoff found errors in the state's case. It was learned that Rhodes had failed the polygraph test, and withholding the results from the defense was a violation of the defendants' constitutional rights. A federal appeals court determined that only Rhodes could have fired the gun. The testimony of the state's witnesses was found to be false. The prosecution had suppressed the statement of a prison guard that corroborated Rhodes's recantation of his initial testimony. Dickoff assembled a color-coded brief and presented it to the Eleventh Circuit Court of Appeals. The court overturned Jacobs's conviction on a writ of habeas corpus.

Rather than risk the likelihood of an acquittal on retrial, the Broward State Attorney's Office offered Jacobs a deal. If she would enter a plea in which she did not admit guilt but agreed not to bring a civil suit, she would be released immediately. Jacobs, twenty-nine years old when she was sent to prison, now forty-five and the mother of two grown children, accepted the offer. She walked free on October 9, 1992. Since the tainted evidence that resulted in Jacobs's release was virtually identical to that which sent Tafero to his death, it is a near-certainty that he too would have been freed and that an innocent man had been executed.

Joseph Amrine
Missouri

The question of executing an innocent person on the basis of a legal technicality was at the heart of the case against Joseph Amrine. His was also a classic study of the danger inherent in the use of snitch testimony.

Amrine was sentenced to death for the murder of Gary "Fox" Barber, a fellow inmate at the Potosi Correctional Center in Cole County, Missouri, where Amrine was serving a prison term for robbery, burglary, and forgery. Barber was stabbed to death with an ice pick on October 18, 1985, in the prison's recreation room. There were about fifty inmates and two correctional officers in the room at the time, but there was no consensus on what actually occurred.

The suspect of first choice was Terry Russell, another inmate. John Noble, a corrections officer who was there at the time, said he saw Russell and Barber engaging in "horseplay" and Barber chasing Russell until he collapsed. He did not, however, witness the fatal confrontation. Another inmate said Russell and Barber had been in a fight the previous week.

When Russell was brought in for questioning, he said Amrine had admitted to him that he killed Barber as revenge for a story making the rounds that Barber had taken advantage of him sexually. Russell said he did not see the murder because he had left the room to get an aspirin for a headache. When he returned, he said, the room was sealed but he saw officers loading Barber onto a stretcher. In exchange for his testimony, Russell received protective custody and a commendation to the parole board.

Amrine insisted he knew nothing of the murder. He said he was playing cards at the time and six other inmates supported his claim. The state was unable to muster any physical evidence that would link Amrine to the scene of the crime. Only Russell's questionable testimony implicated Amrine—until two additional witnesses were summoned forth. To all appearances, the authorities persuaded two other inmates to join Russell in pointing the finger at Amrine. One of them was questioned as many as thirty times by investigators to make sure he got his story straight. Both were granted reduced criminal charges and protective custody in exchange for their testimony.

Amrine's public defender did little to counter the state's charges. He met with Amrine and other witnesses for no more than forty-five minutes prior to going to trial. He failed to interview two witnesses who later said they were playing cards with Amrine at the time of the crime, one of whom claimed to have seen Russell stab Barber. He never told the jury that Russell had been the initial suspect in the case. He did not make it clear that Officer Noble, the only non-inmate present at the time of the crime, offered an account that substantially differed from Russell's and who was the only witness who would not profit from his testimony. Defense counsel did no better when it came to physical evidence. He offered no objection when the prosecution submitted as evidence dried blood found on Amrine's shirt that a state serologist had said was not fresh enough to determine the age or type of the blood. On October 30, 1986, Amrine, who is black, was convicted by an all-white jury and sentenced to death.

At a post-conviction hearing a year later, Russell and Randall Ferguson, another of Amrine's three accusers, recanted their testimony and admitted to lying on the witness stand. With recantations from two of his three accusers, Amrine filed a petition for habeas corpus in the US District Court of the Western District of Missouri. Judge Fernando Gaitan Jr. denied the appeal, insisting that the testimony of the third eyewitness, Jerry Poe, still implicated Amrine. Some ten years later, in 1997, Poe did recant and the US Court of Appeals for the Eighth Circuit remanded the case to Judge Gaitan. Now, the good judge found that Poe's recantation was unreliable and since that was the only "new" evidence submitted, he denied Amrine's appeal, never considering the question of guilt or innocence. Not long after, all three accusers admitted in letters, videotaped depositions, and signed affidavits that the authorities had induced them to lie with threats of violence from other inmates and promises of favored treatment in exchange for their cooperation. The overall result was that over the course of more than a decade, Amrine's four appeals and an application for pardon to Missouri Governor Bob Holden were all denied.

In November 2001, the Missouri attorney general asked the State Supreme Court to set an execution date. However, a documentary about Amrine's case had attracted a good deal of public attention, and the justices decided to hold off on setting a date, pending further investigation. The gift of time served Amrine well. With his appellate counsel, Sean O'Brien and Kent Gipson, working on his behalf, Amrine appealed to the Supreme Court of Missouri. Assistant Attorney General Frank Jung argued that the Supreme Court had no jurisdiction in the case because there was no constitutional violation during his first trial. Jung chose to ignore all evidence pointing to Amrine's innocence. In fact, he went so far as to urge the court to execute Amrine even if it found him to be innocent.

It was a narrow, perhaps narrow-minded, view of justice which held that the law must be applied in its most literal terms regardless of consequence. If a convicted man could not show that he was a victim of judicial or prosecutorial error during the course of his trial, proof of his actual innocence was irrelevant. It was a theory that made a mockery of the concept of justice, in fact nullifying the purpose for which it was intended. The law, in effect, came to depend on a robotic calculus that rendered thought and reason little more than abstractions.

Four of the seven justices disagreed with the attorney general's judicial theory. They overturned Amrine's conviction. In their decision, they established "actual innocence" as a Missouri standard which allows the court to overturn sentences upon its "loss of confidence" in a capital case even if there are no technical errors. Writing for the majority, Judge

Richard B. Teitelman stated that Amrine had proven that a "manifest injustice" would occur without habeas relief even though the conviction was the product of an otherwise fair trial. "It is difficult to imagine," he said, "a more manifestly unjust and unconstitutional result than permitting the execution of an innocent person."

The court ordered the state to either release Amrine or give him a new trial. Bill Tacket, the local prosecutor, filed new murder charges against Amrine, but withdrew them a month later, saying that there was absolutely no evidence to implicate him in the crime. On July 28, 2003, Amrine was released after spending twenty-six years in prison, seventeen of them on death row.

Laurence Adams
Massachusetts

Laurence Adams spent thirty years in a Boston prison, convicted solely on the testimony of three members of the same family, two of whom were facing criminal charges at the time. Adams and Harry Ambers, a co-defendant, were arrested in 1972 for robbing and bludgeoning to death a transit worker on a Massachusetts subway platform.

Wyatt Moore and his sister Susie both testified that while they were all together one evening in their mother's home, Adams confessed to having committed the crime. There was no forensic evidence or any eyewitnesses to support the charges made by the Moore family. Adams's entire family testified that he was at home with them at the time of the crime. Nonetheless, Adams, nineteen years old and an African American, was pronounced guilty of first-degree murder by an all-white, all-male jury in 1974. Both he and Ambers were sentenced to death, but they served only a year on death row. Their sentences were commuted to life in prison in 1975 when the Massachusetts Supreme Judicial Court ruled that the state's death penalty statute was unconstitutional and capital punishment was abolished in the Commonwealth of Massachusetts.

Adams lost an appeal based on ineffective representation by his defense counsel, but in 1993 a court ruling afforded access to state records that previously had been unavailable. An attorney appointed to investigate Adams's case found evidence of gross police and prosecutorial misconduct as well as ineffective legal defense. According to previously suppressed records, the state's star witness, Wyatt Moore, and his sister Susie both had criminal charges against them dropped or reduced in exchange for their testimony against Adams. Wyatt, in fact, was in prison on the date he claimed to have been in his mother's home hearing Adams confess to the crime. To compound the shallowness of his testimony, his cellmate at the time was Warren Ambers, who had been a suspect in the murder, along with his brother, Harry. Adams's attorney also uncovered police records in which Harry Ambers admitted to committing the crime in concert with his brother, Warren. As for Adams's defense, it was discovered that at the time of his trial his counsel also represented Warren Ambers on unrelated charges. The dual representation created a conflict of interest, as he was unable to identify one of his clients, Warren Ambers, as a suspect in the case of another, Laurence Adams. Shortly after the new evidence was discovered, and shortly before her death, Susie Moore recanted her testimony against Adams.

In April 2004, Chief Suffolk Superior Court Judge Robert A. Mulligan overturned the 1974 murder conviction, citing a series of violations of Adams's rights, including the withholding of evidence. Adams, who earned a bachelor's degree in sociology while in prison, was released on May 20, 2004, precisely thirty years after his conviction. "He's had remarkable patience," said his attorney, John J. Barter, who spent nine months trying to prove his client's innocence. "It's not a matter of him being there but not being culpable," he said. "He wasn't there."

Dan L. Bright
Louisiana

It took the testimony of only one eyewitness—a felon on parole—to convict Dan L. Bright of felony murder and get him sentenced to death. It took a redacted FBI file, obtained through the Freedom of Information Act, to get him exonerated eight years later.

The events that triggered his unlikely odyssey through the criminal justice system began, entirely in his absence, on Super Sunday 1995. It had been a good day for a fellow named Murray Barnes. He had won $1,000 in a Super Bowl betting pool in a New Orleans bar. He had watched the game with his cousin and a friend, and all three had done a good bit of drinking well into the night. They left after midnight. As Barnes walked to his truck, two men approached, shot him three times, and then fled. Barnes ran back into the bar but it was too late. He died of internal bleeding shortly afterwards.

When police arrived at the scene, Barnes's cousin, Freddie Thompson, described the shooter as a light-skinned African American wearing a hooded sweatshirt. Several weeks later, an anonymous caller told police that Dan L. Bright had been involved in the shooting and a warrant was issued for his arrest. Bright was not entirely unknown to the police. He had a record of small-time criminal activity, and he appeared to be a viable suspect. His mother did not know her son was in trouble until she saw him featured on television as one of America's Most Wanted. Although Bright insisted he had nothing to do with the crime, he followed his mother's urging and turned himself in.

Bright was charged with felony murder. The prosecution maintained that he had attempted to rob Barnes of his Super Bowl winnings before shooting him, thus providing the aggravating factor that warranted a charge of capital murder. There was no forensic evidence connecting Bright to the crime, and Thompson, the only eyewitness, testified that he had been drinking heavily that day. By contrast, two defense witnesses testified that Bright was with them in another location at the time of the crime. That testimony was the best of what Bright received by way of a defense. His attorney, later described by the jury foreperson as "bumbling, unprepared, and perhaps drunk," failed to counter the state's case at every turn. He did not, for example, point out that Bright, who is left-handed, had a cast on his left arm, which would have made it difficult for him to handle a gun. The attorney met with Bright only once before the trial. In later hearings, it was learned that he said his only aim was to "earn his fee" by getting a life sentence rather than the death penalty. By his own standard, he did not earn his fee. Following a one-hour trial and less than two hours of deliberation, the jury found Bright guilty and sentenced him to death.

The death sentence was soon after reduced to life without parole when his new attorney pointed out that the prosecution could not establish any attempt to rob the victim, nullifying the capital murder charge. While the court agreed to drop the charge to second-degree murder, it rejected defense claims that the testimony of the eyewitness was unreliable and that Bright's original defense was inadequate. During the course of the appeals process, the defense became convinced of Bright's innocence and determined that it would seek post-conviction relief.

The move that turned the case in Bright's favor was the inspiration to look into any files the FBI had kept on Bright. His attorneys found there indeed was such a file and that the document had been heavily redacted. Of critical significance was a line that read: "The source further advised that Daniel Bright, AKA 'Poonie' is in jail for a murder committed by [name redacted]." Invoking the Freedom of Information Act, they got a federal district court to force the FBI to release the un-redacted version of the document. The name that was withheld turned out to be Tracey Davis. The defense attorneys also uncovered information the prosecution had suppressed concerning the criminal history of Freddie Thompson, including the fact that he was a convicted felon in violation of parole when he testified against Bright.

Despite the new evidence, the Orleans Parish Criminal District Court denied Bright's petition for post-conviction relief on June 10, 2003. A year later, however, the Louisiana Supreme Court vacated Bright's conviction and sentence and remanded the case for a new trial because the prosecution had suppressed exculpatory evidence. The court held that the specific facts of Thompson's criminal record and the fact that he was still on parole when he testified against Bright raised questions about the veracity of his trial testimony. It said: "This conviction, based on the facts of this case which include a failure to disclose what the state now says is significant impeachment evidence, is not worthy of confidence and thus must be reversed." On June 14, 2004, the district attorney dropped all charges and Bright was released.

Bright settled a federal wrongful conviction lawsuit for $77,000. He received $208,000 in compensation from the state of Louisiana.

Derrick Jamison
Ohio

"There is a double standard when it comes to justice in our judicial system, especially with wrongful conviction," says Derrick Jamison. "If you are a minority or a low-income citizen, the pursuit of justice can be elusive. But if you are rich, it happens overnight." Jamison was speaking from first-hand experience. An African American, he spent nearly twenty years on Ohio's death row for a murder and robbery of which he was innocent.

The police had little to go on when bartender Gary Mitchell was robbed and beaten to death in the Central Bar in downtown Cincinnati. Several witnesses said they saw two men fleeing the scene on that night in August 1984, but their description of the perpetrators was vague. When Derrick Jamison was arrested for robbing a Cincinnati restaurant on October 12, he seemed to bear a resemblance to the description of one of the men but not close enough for police to charge him with murdering the bartender.

Three months later, a man named Charles Howell was arrested on a charge of sexual assault. While in custody, Howell confessed to being an accomplice in the Central Bar robbery and murder, and he named Jamison as the primary killer. He offered to testify against Jamison in exchange for a lighter sentence in the sexual assault case. He was convicted of aggravated robbery and sentenced to ten years in prison.

Jamison was indicted for murder in March. In addition to Howell's questionable testimony, the state produced a shoe print from the scene of the crime that was similar the shoes Jamison was wearing when he was arrested for the restaurant holdup. In October, the jury found him guilty and he was sentenced to death. Jamison filed appeals with the

Ohio Court of Appeals, First Appellate Circuit, in 1988 and 1992, but both were denied.

A few years later, a new attorney found exculpatory evidence that had been withheld from the defense. In police interviews, several witnesses offered descriptions of the two men fleeing the crime scene that differed vastly from those that originally had raised the suspicions of the police. Describing the two men running from the scene, one was said to be about five-foot-six and carrying a brass pipe, presumably the murder weapon, the other about six feet tall. Howell was about an even six-feet and Jamison six-foot-four. Thus, Howell's claim that Jamison had acted as his accomplice now appeared shaky. By way of further contradiction, Howell never mentioned a brass pipe being used in the attack. He had said Jamison had punched Mitchell and kicked him repeatedly in the head.

On May 20, 2000, fifteen years after his conviction, Jamison's attorney filed a habeas corpus petition with the US District Court for the Southern District of Ohio. The Court granted the writ on the grounds that the suppression of exculpatory evidence had denied Jamison a fair trial. The district attorney chose not to retry the case, and on February 28, 2005, the Ohio Court of Common Pleas dismissed the charges against Jamison. He was removed from death row and released from prison on October 25, 2005.

Recalling the day of his release, Jamison said: "In the twenty years I experienced 'dead man walking' I never had anything to smile about. But on that day, I felt the smile come from within my heart. The sun shone down on me that day."

Michael Toney
Texas

It was what police call a cold case, all but forgotten. More than a decade had passed since a bomb detonated in a Lake Worth, Texas, home in 1985, killing three people. There appeared to be no suspects and the case lay fallow until 1995 when, in the wake of the Oklahoma City bombing, the Department of Alcohol, Tobacco and Firearms reopened the case as part of a program to investigate all unsolved domestic bombings.

The incident took place on November 28, 1985. A family returning home to their trailer found a briefcase at the front door. They brought it inside, and when fifteen-year-old Angela Blount opened it, a bomb exploded. The girl was killed, along with her father, Joe Blount, and a cousin, Michael Columbus. There seemed to be no reason for anyone to plant the bomb at the Blount residence. A man who lived across the street and was believed to be involved in the sale of illegal weapons, said he thought the bomb might have been meant for him.

When the case was revived, initial queries led nowhere. But in 1997, an inmate in the Parker County jail told police that a fellow inmate, Michael Toney, told him he had planted the bomb. Toney, who was in prison on a burglary charge, proclaimed his innocence, but, apparently in their haste to solve a case of domestic bombing, police charged him with capital murder. Shortly before the trial began, the jailhouse informant recanted his story. He said he had concocted the story with Toney, thinking that his volunteering to aid the authorities in their search might gain him favor, possibly even an early release from his sentence. They did not think Toney would be charged and tried simply on the basis of his testimony.

There was no physical evidence connecting Toney to the crime, but prosecutors managed to find two new witnesses to testify against him at trial: his ex-wife, Kim; and a former friend, Chris Meeks. When first questioned by police, Kim said she knew nothing about the bombing, but she later recalled that she, Toney, and Meeks had been near the Blounts' trailer park on the evening of the murders. Furthermore, she said Toney had entered the trailer park carrying a briefcase she had seen was packed with bombs a few days earlier. When he left the trailer, she said, he no longer had the briefcase. Meeks, who also had originally denied any knowledge of the case, now told police a similar story. Toney was convicted on May 20, 1999 and sentenced to death.

Toney's appeal and petition for habeas corpus were both denied. However, on a second petition, the defense produced evidence that the prosecution had withheld fourteen documents that contradicted the testimony of the witnesses against Toney and suggested that police had fed them the incriminating information. The Texas Court of Criminal Appeals overturned the conviction on December 17, 2008 because the prosecution had withheld exculpatory evidence. The Tarrant County district attorney's office then withdrew from the case. The attorney general's office, which was specially appointed to assume control, dismissed the indictment against Toney and he was released from prison on September 2, 2009.

However, Toney had little time to enjoy his freedom. A month later, on October 3, he was killed when the truck he was driving veered off the road and overturned, throwing him from the vehicle.

Reginald Griffin
Missouri

The time-worn adage that there is no honor among thieves requires little more in the way of evidence than the case of Reginald Griffin who was sentenced to death for the 1983 murder of a fellow inmate at the Missouri Training Center for Men in Moberly. A bevy of inmates implicated Griffin, recanted their testimony, pointed their fingers elsewhere, and made deals with prison authorities, offering their testimony in exchange for favors, either real or hoped for.

The crime in question took place on July 12, 1983, following a prison-yard quarrel among inmates over a television set. James Bausley, the owner of the set, was stabbed to death and a sharpened screwdriver was confiscated from an inmate named Jeffrey Smith as he was leaving the area where Bausley was stabbed. Smith was placed in administrative segregation and convicted of unlawful possession of a weapon. A homemade knife was found about twenty feet from Bausley's body.

During the investigation of the murder, two inmates, Paul Curtis and Wyvonne Mozee, told authorities they saw Griffin, who was serving a twenty-year sentence for armed assault in 1981, stab Bausley. They also said that two other inmates, Doyle Franks and Arbary Jackson, aided Griffin. Griffin, Franks, and Jackson were all charged with capital murder in 1987 and tried separately.

Griffin went on trial in Randolph County Circuit Court in January 1988. The prosecution's case rested almost entirely on the testimony of Curtis and Mozee. Curtis testified that he saw Griffin, together with Franks and Jackson, arguing with Bausley over the television set and that Griffin hit Bausley in the back and stabbed him in the chest with a twelve-inch homemade knife whose handle was fashioned from a yellow rag. He said Griffin threw the knife onto the roof of the prison gymnasium and fled the scene. Mozee died before the trial began, but the transcript of his preliminary hearing was read to the jury. His statements were much the same as Curtis's. Curtis admitted that his testimony was given in exchange for the prosecution's promise to help him on unrelated theft charges and to notify the parole board of his cooperation. Curtis's story was confirmed by subsequent events. By the time the trial started, he had been paroled and the state had paid his rent for one month after his release.

As for forensic evidence, the prosecution offered a thirteen-inch knife with a yellow cloth wrapped around the handle that had been found near the site of the stabbing. A medical examiner testified that the knife could have caused Bausley's wounds. Although preliminary tests for the presence of human blood were positive, subsequent testing found there was no human blood on the knife.

For the defense, two inmates—David Steele and Eddie Johnson—testified that Mozee had told them he had made a deal with prison authorities to testify against Griffin in return for an early release and he had agreed to say "whatever they wanted just as part of the deal." Johnson said Mozee told him that he had not seen the stabbing. Another defense witness, Leonard Rogers, testified that he had seen someone running from Bausley's body, and it was not Griffin.

Griffin was convicted of capital murder in January 1988 and sentenced to death. Franks was convicted of second-degree murder and sentenced to life in prison, to be served consecutively to a life sentence he was already serving. Jackson was acquitted.

After spending five years on death row, Griffin's death sentence was vacated in 1993 because it was found that, at the sentencing phase of his trial, the criminal record of another man named Reginald Griffin had been submitted to the jury in error. Griffin was re-sentenced to life without the possibility of parole.

Across the next decade, Griffin lost a number of direct appeals, but Franks eventually came forth and stated that Griffin had nothing to do with Bausley's murder. In fact, as early as 1989, one year after Griffin's conviction, Franks had said that Jeffrey Smith was the one who stabbed Bausley and that a guard caught Smith with a knife or a screwdriver shortly afterward.

In 2005, Griffin filed a state petition for a writ of habeas corpus, invoking the 1963 Brady Rule, which requires the prosecution to disclose evidence favorable to the defense. An evidentiary hearing was held in 2007 which ultimately cleared Griffin and resulted in his release. At the hearing, Curtis admitted that he did not see the stabbing; he was in a vocational auto mechanics class at the time in a different part of the prison. He said he learned about the killing from Franks while in administrative segregation for an unrelated fighting incident. Franks, who was in an adjoining cell, boasted about committing the murder, Curtis said. He explained that he lied because he was facing transfer to Jefferson City, the highest security state prison at the time, and he feared for his safety in a tougher environment. He made a deal with the authorities to implicate Griffin in exchange for parole.

For his part, Jackson, who had already been acquitted, testified that Griffin was not in the prison yard at the time of the murder. He said he saw Bausley, Franks, and Smith arguing about who owned the television set and that the dispute seemed about to turn violent. He said that he tried to break it up but that he left when Franks and Smith produced sharp-edged weapons.

The defense staked its claim on the grounds that the prosecution had failed to disclose that a knife had been confiscated from Smith immediately after Bausley was stabbed.

Despite all the new exculpatory evidence, Griffin's motion for a new trial was denied. However, in August 2011, the Missouri Supreme Court, en banc (before a full court rather than just a quorum), granted the writ of habeas corpus and vacated the conviction. In an unusually detailed, often caustic, description of how the state violated Griffin's rights, the Court wrote:

"The State suppressed the fact that prison guards confiscated a sharpened screwdriver from inmate Smith just minutes after Bausley was stabbed. . . Smith was placed in administrative segregation for possessing the sharpened screwdriver, and the State successfully prosecuted Smith for possessing the screwdriver. The State was obviously aware of the evidence yet did not disclose it to Griffin.

"Griffin has established prejudice. The present state of the evidence in this case shows that there are at least five substantial post-trial developments that raise serious doubts regarding the factual accuracy of Griffin's conviction.

"There is no physical evidence connecting Griffin to the weapon found in the gymnasium. There is no physical evidence demonstrating any contact between Griffin and Bausley. Instead, Griffin's continued incarceration for Bausley's murder is premised on the recanted testimony of inmate Curtis and the impeached testimony of deceased inmate Mozee. Overlaying the entire case is the revelation that the State failed to disclose evidence that tended to implicate Smith, impeach Curtis and Mozee, and bolster the trial testimony of inmate Rogers, who maintained that the inmate fleeing the crime scene was not Griffin.

"In light of these circumstances, Griffin's conviction is no longer 'worthy of confidence.' Because Griffin has shown that the nondisclosure of the Smith evidence was prejudicial to Brady purposes, he has established the 'prejudice' necessary to overcome the procedural bar to granting him habeas corpus relief. Accordingly, Griffin's conviction for the murder of James Bausley is vacated."

The Court ordered the fifty-year-old Griffin's release within sixty days unless the state decided to retry him. However, with one of the prosecution's eyewitnesses now on record that he did not witness the murder, the credibility of the other eyewitness impeached by new evidence that he did not witness the crime, and a confession by Franks that he did commit the murder, the state had no evidence on which to proceed. In December 2012, Griffin was released on bond pending a retrial. On October 25, 2013, the prosecution dismissed the charges.

Nicholas Yarris
Pennsylvania

Nicholas Yarris was convicted of rape and murder largely on the testimony of a jailhouse informant, but in a sense he inadvertently implicated himself. His unlikely escapade began in late December 1981 with a routine stop by police for a traffic violation on a Pennsylvania roadway. A violent confrontation ensued in which Yarris was said to have attacked the officer. He finally was subdued and charged with attempted murder of a police officer. While in custody and being questioned, Yarris played a long shot in an effort to win favor with the police. He named an acquaintance of his as the man who raped and murdered a young woman just four days earlier in a brutal attack that had the police scurrying for leads to the perpetrator.

On December 16, a young sales associate from the Tri-State mall in Pennsylvania was abducted in her car when she completed her day's work. When she was late returning home, her husband notified the police. Her yellow Chrysler Cordoba was soon found abandoned on a roadway in Chichester, Pennsylvania. Her body, covered with newly fallen snow, was found the following day in a church parking lot about half a mile from her car. She was still clothed, but her thick winter clothing had been cut open to give her attacker access. She had been beaten, stabbed, and raped, and it was later determined that she had bled to death from multiple stab wounds in her chest. Biological materials, including sperm samples and fingernail scrapings, were collected from the victim's body. A pair of gloves, presumably belonging to the killer, was also found in the victim's car.

The problem for Yarris was that when the man he identified as the woman's assailant was ruled out by police, Yarris himself became the prime suspect. Conventional serological tests (as opposed to DNA) indicated that he could not be excluded as the source. To make matters worse, a jailhouse informant came forth to tell police that Yarris was their man. In addition, several of the victim's co-workers volunteered that they had seen him harassing the victim before she entered her car. It was enough. Yarris was convicted in 1982 and sentenced to death.

A long struggle followed during which Yarris, insisting he was innocent, pressed for DNA testing of the evidence found at the crime scene. In 1989, he became one of Pennsylvania's first death row inmates to demand post-conviction DNA testing to establish his innocence. At the time, DNA testing involved a prolonged procedure, and Yarris waited on death row as the testing of the various pieces of evidence continued through the 1990s. None of the tests were conclusive. Yarris's luck finally turned in 2003 when a medical examiner, Dr. Edward Blake, conducted a final round of testing. It showed that the gloves found in the car and the spermatozoa taken from the victim's underpants belonged to the same person, and it was not Nicholas Yarris.

Based on the new findings, the court vacated Yarris's conviction, and he became the 140th person in the United States to be exonerated by post-conviction DNA testing, the 13th from death row where he had spent twenty-one years.

James Richardson
Florida

Had it all started just a few years later, events might have played out differently for James Richardson. But it was 1968, the whole country seemed to be on fire, the South was seething with a century's worth of racial hostility, and small backwater towns like Arcadia, Florida, were still dishing out their own version of southern justice. A black, poverty-ridden fruit-picker like James Richardson was easy prey when a quick arrest was needed for a horrendous crime. And the crime of which Richardson was accused was as horrendous as one could imagine. He was charged, convicted, and sentenced to death for murdering all of his seven children.

Arcadia, the seat of DeSoto County, is located in a remote pocket of Southwest Florida between Sarasota and Fort Myers, about thirty-five miles inland from the Gulf of Mexico. The lush citrus groves fueled a large part of the local economy. James and his wife, Annie Mae, worked in those fields, picking oranges, earning twenty-five cents for each box they filled. Both were illiterate; James had an IQ of about seventy-five—not quite mentally retarded but low enough to be classified a "slow learner." All the same, he was well liked in the community and reputed to be a devoted father. It was all the more shocking, therefore, when he was arrested on October 31, 1967, and charged with murdering his children.

The Richardson children, aged one to seven, had been poisoned five days earlier, their food laced with parathion, a highly toxic agricultural pesticide. Arcadia's police chief, Richard Barnard, and DeSoto County Sheriff Frank Cline shared responsibility for the investigation. They searched the house and a small shed in the backyard and found nothing suspicious. Cline noticed a metallic scent which he knew to be parathion, but none was found on the premises. However, the following day, police received an anonymous phone call saying that a sack of parathion had been found in the shed behind the house. Cline knew his search had been thorough. "It wasn't there yesterday," he told the press. But it was there now, casting the first shadow of suspicion on Richardson. At the same time, word began drifting through town that Richardson had recently purchased a $14,000 life insurance policy for the children. The police now had what they believed to be motive, means, and opportunity. Richardson was promptly charged with murder. Annie Mae also was arrested and charged with child neglect.

The prosecution should have sensed that something was wrong with its case at the coroner's inquest. One of those testifying was Bessie Reese, the Richardson's next-door neighbor who had been watching the children the day they were poisoned. It was Reese who served the children lunch that day and, according to another neighbor, Charlie

Smith, it was Reese who suggested they search the shed for the poison. Another witness, Gerald Purvis, an insurance salesman, testified he tried to sell Richardson life insurance for his children, but Richardson said he couldn't afford it and no sale was made. The assistant prosecutor, John "Red" Treadwell nonetheless persuaded the coroner's jury that Richardson might have believed that a policy had been purchased. The jury returned with an indictment: the Richardson children had been murdered with premeditation.

John Spencer Robinson, a thirty-year-old civil rights activist from Daytona Beach, became interested in the case as he watched it unfold on local television. Richardson said he liked the similarity in the sound of their names and chose Robinson to represent him from a list of names offered to him by the head of the Arcadia NAACP. It was, in some respects, an unfortunate decision. Although Robinson was convinced of Richardson's innocence and totally committed to his cause, he was principally a family law attorney and had never tried a murder case. He and his partner, Richard Whitson, took the case at no charge.

At the outset, circumstances looked promising to Robinson. Bail was set at $7,500, incredibly low for a case involving seven murders. A few days later, an anonymous benefactor posted the bail, and Richardson was released. In addition, the child-neglect charges against Annie Mae were dropped. It appeared to the defense that the prosecution knew it had no case. They expected all charges would be vacated at a hearing to be held on March 25, 1968. However, they soon discovered the prosecutors had a new card to play; in fact they had two cards. Their names were Ernell Washington and James Weaver, and they were ready to tell a jury that Richardson had confessed to them when they were together in the Arcadia jail. It was the first hard evidence the state had, and the judge found it to be convincing. Bail was revoked and Richardson was returned to jail. The trial was set for the end of May.

The entire legal proceeding moved quickly. The jury, all white, was selected on the first day. The following day, Weaver took the stand and told his "confession" story. Washington was not able to appear in court. After testifying at the March hearing, he was released from prison and a few weeks later was shot to death in a local bar. But the state sent in a replacement from its bench. James Cunningham, a former inmate, testified that he too had heard Richardson confess. On the third day, the state rested. The defense tried to impeach Washington's testimony, showing that he had been given probation on his attempted-murder charge in exchange for his testimony. A few other character witnesses were called, but it meant little. It took the jury just ninety minutes to return a verdict of first-degree murder. Since there was no recommendation of mercy, the judge imposed the mandatory sentence—death in the electric chair.

Not long after Richardson was sent away, Mark Lane, a New York attorney, came to Arcadia. Lane had achieved national renown in the sixties as the author of a book advancing a conspiracy theory for the assassination of President Kennedy. He was intrigued by the case and had begun doing research for a book entitled *Arcadia*, which would be published two years later. As he interviewed some of the central characters, he became increasingly convinced of Richardson's innocence. He also began to have doubts about the role played by Bessie Reese. He learned, for example, that Reese had been convicted of killing her second husband in 1955 and had served four years of a twenty-year sentence before being paroled. He also discovered that her first husband had died under curious circumstances and that some suspected the cause of death was food poisoning. Charlie Smith told Lane it was Reese who had found the bag of parathion in the shed, as he had testified at Richardson's trial. Finally, Lane learned that Reese had a grudge against Richardson. Her third husband had left her for Richardson's cousin, and she blamed Richardson and threatened to "get" him.

On April 21, 1971, a year after Lane's book was published, the appeals court unanimously affirmed Richardson's conviction and sentence. But the specter of execution would soon be lifted. On June 30, 1972, the US Supreme Court handed down its decision in *Furman v. Georgia*, nullifying more than six hundred death sentences throughout the country. As the seventies passed, Robinson withdrew as Richardson's attorney and was replaced by Lane and Florida co-counsel Ellis Rubin.

In 1988, Lane returned to Arcadia for a public rally in support of Richardson and obtained possession of the state's nearly 1,000-page file of the Richardson case, which apparently had been pilfered years earlier from the office of ADA Treadwell. The file contained numerous bits of information Lane thought was suppressed evidence. Encouraged by his findings, Lane visited Bessie Reese at a nursing home where she was spending her last years, suffering from Alzheimer's disease. Two aides at the home told Lane that Reese had confessed many times that she had poisoned the children.

The case was beginning to break open now. Lane turned the mildewed Richardson file over to Governor Bob Martinez and petitioned the governor for his immediate release. He also petitioned the state supreme court for a new trial. Unexpected help came from a young woman, Virginia Dennis, who was an eight-year-old friend of the Richardson children at the time of the crime. Virginia said she had eaten breakfast with them on the day they died, but neither she nor they had gotten ill. That meant the poison had to be added to their food at lunch, after both James and Annie Mae had left for work.

Martinez ordered a new investigation and turned the case over to one of the state's top prosecutors, Dade County District Attorney Janet Reno, who later served as US attorney general in the Clinton administration. Two months later, on April 11, 1989, Reno filed her report. It contained a litany of prosecutorial misconduct and perjured testimony—information withheld from the defense; witnesses, including Sheriff Frank Cline, who had lied under oath; a jailhouse snitch who had recanted. At a hearing on April 25, retired Circuit Court Judge Clifton Kelly, who had been recalled to service to hear the case, said he did not believe Richardson had been given a fair trial. "The enormity of the crime," he said, "is matched only by the enormity of the injustice [done] to this man." The judge set aside the conviction and ordered Richardson released.

Richardson, who learned to read and write in prison, filed suit against DeSoto County for wrongful conviction. He was awarded a settlement of $150,000, most of which went to his lawyers. Having spent nearly twenty-two years of his life in prison, he was ineligible for Social Security benefits. Under Florida's compensation statute, he would be entitled to a payment of $50,000 for each year he spent behind bars. But the statute requires DNA evidence and none was available. As of 2014, at age seventy-nine, Richardson was still pursuing legal remedies that would make him eligible for compensation.

He and his wife, who had stuck with him during his years of imprisonment, were later divorced. Richardson, who had suffered two severe heart attacks, remarried and he and his wife, Theresa, took residence on the ranch of his cardiologist in Wichita, Kansas. Bessie Reese died of Alzheimer's disease at the nursing home in 1992.

Commentary: Shades of Kafka

In a criminal justice system fraught with corruption and riddled with invitations to error, there is no testimony as toxic as that of a jailhouse snitch. According to the Midwest Innocence Project, an informant or jailhouse snitch testified against the defendant in more than 15 percent of wrongful conviction cases overturned by DNA testing. Statements by people with incentives to testify, whether members of the law enforcement community or convicts already serving time, are invariably suspect. Yet, such statements are often the central evidence in convicting innocent people. The situation is aggravated by the fact that the jury is generally unaware that the witness is being rewarded for his testimony. Defendants have been wrongfully convicted in cases in which snitches have been paid to testify; have offered testimony in exchange for early release from prison; or where they claim to have heard the defendant confessing to the crime. Unfortunately, perjured testimony is not confined to convicts and fellow inmates. Law enforcement officials also have an incentive, on occasion, to seek a conviction on manufactured evidence. Police officers and prosecuting attorneys, after all, have staked their careers on arresting and convicting criminals, and all too often, they are ready to cut a deal here or there in order to obtain a conviction in a case where the forensic evidence is none too convincing. In many instances, law officers do not testify themselves, but seek out potential informants and feed them the information needed to provide false testimony.

Soliciting snitch testimony is all too easy, for the snitch has nothing to lose. At worst, he will fail to get what the state has promised him; at best, he might receive a reduced sentence, lesser charges, better accommodation while serving the rest of his sentence, or possibly an early release. Added to the mix is that jailhouse prisoners are not likely to be overly devoted to the truth. High-security prisons would not be the place of choice for one who, like Diogenes, was searching for an honest man.

A 2005 report by the Center on Wrongful Conviction at Northwestern University in Chicago profiles thirty-eight death-row defendants convicted on the false testimony of snitches whose convictions were later overturned. According to the report, snitch testimony is the leading cause of wrongful conviction in capital cases, where the stakes are highest. Judges in two such cases—one in Georgia, the other in Pennsylvania—have described such proceedings as Kafkaesque.

James Creamer
Georgia

James Creamer and six co-defendants were convicted of murdering two physicians in Marietta, Georgia, in a 1973 trial that a US district court judge said "bordered on the Kafkaesque." He was not exaggerating. The judicial proceeding was tainted from the start and included perjured testimony from an accomplice, prosecutorial misconduct, and junk science, including the introduction of evidence secured during sessions of hypnosis.

Drs. Warren and Rosina Matthews were found shot to death in their home in May 1971 in what looked like an attempted robbery gone awry. Creamer and six other suspects were taken into custody and prosecuted almost entirely on the word of Deborah Ann Kidd, who said she had accompanied the men to the Matthews' home. Testifying under a grant of immunity, Kidd named Creamer as the shooter. The seven suspects were found guilty by a Cobb County jury. Six were given life sentences. Creamer, the presumed shooter, was sentenced to death. In 1974, the Georgia Supreme Court unanimously upheld all the convictions and sentences.

The case began to unravel a year later following an investigation by the *Atlanta Constitution*. The newspaper's probe revealed that Kidd initially had claimed that she had been high on drugs the day of the crime and was unable to recall any of the events that took place. Later, in a hypnotic state induced by a police-appointed hypnotist, she said she remembered that Creamer had committed the murders, with the other six defendants serving as accomplices. The prosecution had intentionally withheld from the defense the transcripts of the statements Kidd had made prior to testifying. The transcripts revealed she had offered a number of conflicting descriptions of what had transpired at the crime scene. The identity of the shooter changed from one version to another and so did her identification of those who were present. At one point, she confessed to having shot the victims herself. The *Constitution* also discovered that Kidd was romantically involved with one of the detectives assigned to the case.

Charging the prosecution with willful destruction of the taped testimony, District Court Judge Charles A. Moye ordered all the convictions to be reversed. The state appealed, but its case was dissolving rapidly. Kidd admitted she had lied in her trial testimony. To clinch matters, Billy Birt, a prisoner already on death row for another crime, confessed that he and two other men—one who was in federal prison and another who was then a fugitive—had murdered the two doctors. Charges against all seven men were dropped and they were released in 1975. The district attorney, however, said he was not convinced of their innocence and he declined to prosecute Deborah Kidd for perjury.

Neil Ferber
Pennsylvania

A jailhouse snitch was instrumental in getting Neil Ferber, a thirty-nine-year-old furniture salesman, convicted of carrying out a gangland-style hit on a Philadelphia mobster in 1981, but not without some help. There was the mistaken testimony of two eyewitnesses and a police conspiracy that a judge called a "Kafkaesque nightmare" and a "malevolent charade."

On the evening of May 27, 1981, Chelsais "Steve" Bouras, a well-known underworld figure, was gunned down by two men while dining in the Meletis Restaurant in South Philadelphia. His dinner companion, Jeanette Curro, also was slain. A month later, Ferber was arrested after being identified by two eyewitnesses—a man and his wife—who said they saw the killer run out of the restaurant, remove a ski mask, and flee down the street. The woman identified Ferber in a police photo spread, only to change her mind after seeing him in person in a police lineup. Her husband, however, maintained that Ferber was the man he saw that night.

At the trial, the most incriminating testimony was provided by Gerald Jordan, a former cellmate of Ferber's at the Philadelphia Detention Center. Jordan, who had spent much of his adult life serving time for petty crimes, told the jury that Ferber had admitted being one of two gunmen who had shot Bouras and Curro. No further evidence was presented and none was needed. Ferber was convicted and sentenced to death.

The district attorney's office, as well as some Philadelphia homicide detectives, appeared to have lingering doubts regarding the case that was presented. About two years after Ferber was convicted—years he spent on death row—the DA's office told the court that Jordan had failed a lie-detector test concerning Ferber's guilt, a bit of information that had not been shared with the defense. At around the same time, Jordan recanted his testimony and said he never believed Ferber had had anything to do with the murder. On January 3, 1986, his last day in office, District Attorney Edward G. Rendell asked Common Pleas Judge

Robert A. Latrone to grant Ferber a new trial. Latrone immediately threw out Ferber's conviction, and Rendell's successor, Ronald D. Castille, declined to retry him. He was freed the following day.

Ferber did not lose much time in filing suit against the city, contending he had suffered bleeding ulcers and a nervous breakdown as a result of his unjust imprisonment. In 1993, a Common Pleas Court jury awarded him $4.5 million. As reported in the *Philadelphia Inquirer*, the jury found that Ferber had been framed by homicide detective Daniel Rosenstein and a police sketch artist, Dominic Frontino. The award was overturned by Common Pleas Judge John Herron because of technical changes in the liability laws. But the judge made it clear that he believed Ferber had been railroaded by corrupt officials and noted that the wronged man could seek further recourse in federal court. Herron described Ferber's trip through the criminal justice system as a "Kafkaesque nightmare of the sort which we normally characterize as being representative of the so-called justice system of a totalitarian state." He found that police had manipulated witnesses, "withheld important information, tampered with identification evidence, and misled judicial officers."

Ferber declared his intention to press his case for damages, but in 1996 the city agreed to a settlement. Ferber was granted $1.9 million, a sum Rendell called "fair and appropriate, and a fraction of what a jury would have awarded." In settling the civil suit, the city did not acknowledge any impropriety in its handling of the case.

Willie Brown and Larry Troy
Florida

Willie Brown and Larry Troy were already in prison when they were convicted in 1981 of stabbing to death Earl Owens, a fellow inmate, at Florida's Union Correctional Institution. The two men were held as suspects in solitary confinement for seventeen months before they were formally charged with the crime. Then, three inmates came forth and identified Brown and Troy as the murderers. Since two of the inmates were known to have mental problems, the word of the third man, Frank Wise, became the pivot of the state's case. Wise was not a prosecutor's ideal witness. He was doing time for murdering Troy's cousin and was quoted before the trial as saying that he hated Brown and Troy so much that he would like to see them executed whether they were guilty or not. He now had the opportunity to fulfill his wish. Wise testified at the trial that he saw both men leaving the victim's cell shortly before the body was discovered. His testimony resulted in Brown and Troy being convicted and moved from the prison's general population to death row.

Salvation, at least for the time, came to the pair in the form of a German anti-death-penalty activist, Esther Lichtenfels. In the course of her work, Lichtenfels visited Florida's death row on several occasions, and she and Brown fell in love. She was determined to help free him, and over the next several years invested $70,000 in her own investigation of the case. Her efforts were given impetus in 1987 when the state supreme court reversed the convictions because the prosecutors did not share with the defense statements they received during prison interviews.

While awaiting a new trial, Lichtenfels managed to set up a sting operation that freed both men from death row. Wearing a legally authorized tape recorder and fitted with a hidden microphone, she recorded Wise saying that he had lied in his testimony and offering to recant and tell the truth in exchange for $2,000. On the basis of the recorded admission, all charges against Brown and Troy were dropped, and Wise was charged with committing perjury.

Brown, who was also serving twenty years on a robbery charge, left prison in 1988 and had hardly tasted freedom when he and Lichtenfels were married. Neither they nor Troy lived happily ever after. Troy, who had been serving a twenty-five-year sentence for another murder, was released in 1990, but he was not free for long. Seven months after leaving prison, he was arrested for selling cocaine and was sent to the Charlotte Correctional Institution in North Carolina. Brown's life continued to be driven by drug use and robberies. He was returned to prison for robbing a bank in Springfield, Massachusetts, and later arrested for holding up a bank in Dunedin, Florida, brandishing the handle of a broomstick, then leading police on a high-speed chase in a stolen car.

Brown insisted that the authorities had unfairly made him a target. "In their eyes, I was never exonerated," he said from jail. "There's enough pain in this stuff to last a lifetime."

Walter McMillian
Alabama

Walter "Johnny D" McMillian came close to becoming a victim of Southern justice in 1988 when he was sentenced to death for killing a white eighteen-year-old store clerk in Monroe County, Alabama. McMillian, a black logger, was railroaded in a trial that took less than two days and convicted on the testimony of three criminal suspects. The death sentence was imposed by the judge, who overrode the jury's recommendation that McMillian be given a life term in prison. Fittingly enough, the judge was named Robert E. Lee Key Jr. It took the efforts of a zealously committed defense attorney, Bryan Stevenson, under the bright light of publicity provided by the television show *60 Minutes,* to save McMillian's life.

McMillian was convicted of killing Ronda Morrison while robbing the shop in which she worked. Arrested with him was Ralph Myers, who agreed to testify against McMillian in return for consideration from the state. The prospect of just treatment looked dim for McMillian from the outset. The fact that he had a white girlfriend and his son had married a white woman did not sit well in that part of the country. Shortly after his arrest, the Monroe County sheriff told him, "I ought to take you off and hang you like we done that nigger in Mobile, but we can't." Nonetheless, what followed was in every sense the equivalent of a judicial lynching.

Two weeks after his arrest, McMillian was placed on death row, although he had no prior criminal record. Amnesty International believed that no other defendant in the United States had ever been placed in a death row cell while still awaiting trial. On a change of venue, the trial was moved from Monroe County to Baldwin County, the locale of *To Kill a Mockingbird*, Harper Lee's well-known novel about Southern racism.

The trial, a caricature of criminal justice, was, in Thomas Hobbes's phrase, nasty, brutish, and short. The core of the state's case was the perjured testimony of three witnesses, including a convicted murderer, who placed McMillian at the scene of the crime. The defense, by contrast, produced twelve black witnesses who testified that McMillian was at a church fund-raising fish fry when the murder occurred. The jury returned a verdict of guilty and voted seven-to-five against the death penalty. However, Judge Robert E. Lee Key Jr. thought the jury too forgiving. He imposed the death penalty, and McMillian officially took his place as a denizen of death row. The case attracted the attention of the ubiquitous Bryan Stevenson, a Montgomery, Alabama, attorney and director of the Equal Justice Initiative of Alabama. Stevenson had been representing condemned inmates in the South for thirteen years, and as he began to look into McMillian's case he discovered much that was amiss. The prosecution, he learned, had hidden exculpatory evidence, including the existence of a witness who had seen the victim alive after the time she was presumed to have been murdered by McMillian. There also was an unedited police tape which differed markedly from the one given to the defense and appeals teams. It contained a statement by a prosecution witness complaining that the police wanted him to frame an "innocent Johnny D." For added measure, all three prosecution witnesses recanted their testimony and admitted they had lied.

Despite the mounting evidence of official misconduct, state courts denied appeals on four occasions. At that point, Stevenson decided to go public. He took McMillian's story to CBS-TV and was interviewed by Ed Bradley on *60 Minutes*. With the story now in the open, the Alabama Court of Criminal Appeals reversed the conviction. The county district attorney acknowledged that the case had been bungled and joined the defense in getting the charges dropped. McMillian finally was freed in 1993 after serving nearly six years on death row. "Often times," Stevenson said, "obtaining evidence suppressed by prosecutors or police can take many years of litigation."

In 1997, Stevenson argued before the US Supreme Court that McMillian should be permitted to sue the county sheriff who suppressed evidence that would have benefited his defense. The court ruled against him, but McMillian settled with other parties involved in the case for an undisclosed sum. In 2001, Alabama passed a statute granting compensation to prisoners who have been exonerated.

"No man who has had to withstand the psychic trauma of sitting on death row should have to go through such rigmarole to get reimbursed," Stevenson said. "The presumption should be, if you were exonerated, the state should compensate you for the time you were in prison and to help make your transition easier into the real world. I think that's something society owes someone who has been deprived of the liberties we take for granted."

Curtis Kyles
Louisiana

Curtis Kyles became something of a career defendant, having been tried five times for the same crime and imprisoned for fourteen years before being freed on a federal writ of habeas corpus. At one point he had come within thirty hours of execution.

Kyles was arrested in 1984 for the murder of Dolores Dye during a car theft in a store parking lot in Gretna Parish, Louisiana. The case against him hinged on the testimony of four eyewitnesses and some strong physical evidence: the murder weapon, a spent cartridge, and the victim's purse were found in his apartment. Nevertheless, his first trial, in November 1984, ended in a hung jury. A month later, he was retried, convicted, and sentenced to death. His appeals to state courts won him a remand for an evidentiary hearing, which would determine whether the existing evidence was sufficient to sustain the verdict, but the state trial court denied relief. He then took his appeal to the State Supreme Court which rejected his application for discretionary review.

During the appeals process, one of the eyewitnesses recanted, stating in an affidavit that she had not seen the killer's face but had identified him under pressure from police and prosecutors. One prosecutor, she said, told her that "all the other evidence pointed to [Kyles] as the killer." To assure that she would be able to pick out the defendant in the courtroom, she was told that "the murderer would be the guy seated at the table with the attorney and that [he] was the one I should identify," the affidavit said. It was also discovered that the state had withheld critical information about another witness—a paid informant who might have been the actual killer. While the informant had given detailed testimony implicating Kyles, there was undisclosed evidence indicating that the snitch himself had had possession of the victim's belongings and might well have planted the incriminating items in Kyles's apartment. In addition to deflecting suspicion from himself, the informant, who fit another eyewitness's description of the murderer, might also have been motivated by a reward offered in the case.

Having lost all his appeals in the state courts as well as the US Court of Appeals for the Fifth Circuit, Kyles found relief from the US Supreme Court on a habeas corpus petition in April 1995. In a decision rendered just a few days before he was to be executed, the high court remanded the case based on failure of police and prosecutors to turn over exculpatory evidence to the defense before the trial and denounced the "uncritical readiness" of the prosecution to accept the informant's questionable story. The court ruled that Kyles was entitled to a new trial because there was "reasonable probability" that the disclosure of the concealed evidence would have produced a different result.

But Kyles's long journey into the night of the criminal justice system was far from over. His third trial, in October 1996, ended in a deadlocked jury, and subsequent trials in the next two years had the same result. After the fifth trial and fourth mistrial, prosecutors decided to drop the charges and Kyles was released.

Though Kyles suffered the oppressive indignities of wrongful conviction, he might count himself fortunate that his petition for habeas corpus came as early as it did. A few years later, the bar for habeas petitions was raised in deference to the jurisdiction of state courts. Had the strict time lines and standards of the Anti-Terrorism and Effective Death Penalty Act, passed in response to the 9/11 attack, been in effect in 1995, Kyles might well have been returned to Louisiana's death row to await execution.

PART V

False Confession

No EVIDENCE IS more compelling than a suspect's confession. Rarely is anything else needed to convict, for why would anyone confess to a crime he did not commit? Yet false confessions have become legion in the criminal justice system. Of the convictions that have been reversed on the basis of DNA evidence—those in which there is no doubt of error—20 percent involved a false or coerced confession. Studies indicate that about 75 percent of juries will vote to convict when the defendant has confessed, even if convincing physical evidence and the testimony of other witnesses suggest that the defendant is innocent. Such confessions have become a growing national problem, particularly in cases involving minors or the mentally ill; they result not only in the wrong person being imprisoned or possibly executed, but in the guilty party remaining at large.

People confess to crimes they did not commit for reasons that run the spectrum from plea bargains or police coercion to psychological compulsions whose complexity is not easily gauged. The old rubber-hose, third-degree treatment made famous in grade-B movies of the forties and fifties was outlawed nationally by the US Supreme Court in 1933. It has been replaced by more subtle, psychological techniques that often enlist attrition as an ally. Detectives take turns interrogating

198 ~ Convicting the Innocent

a suspect until, twenty or thirty hours later, a confession might seem a small price to pay for a ticket home or a night's rest. Those more open to suggestion, like the young or mentally retarded, might in fact come to believe that they committed the crime after all. "The difference between the third degree and psychological interrogation," Peter Carlson wrote in the *Washington Post*, "is akin to the difference between getting mugged and getting scammed."

When a crime has been highly publicized and the suspect is likely to be familiar with the details of the case, a technique of hypothetical questioning can sometimes pry loose a confession that includes some telling details. For example: "Let's just say you were going to commit this crime, what type of weapon would you use? You wouldn't use a gun, would you, because that would have attracted too much attention, right? Yes, you would use a knife, and if you used a knife, what would you have done with it after you killed her? Of course, you would have disposed of it, but first you would wipe the blood off, wouldn't you?" Each time the suspect agrees, the noose is drawn tighter, and if he begins to agree to details that would be known only to police and the person who committed the crime, he is that much closer to confessing.

Sometimes suspects can be tricked into offering a confession. Alleged accomplices are often questioned separately, with each being told that the others have implicated him in the crime. On other occasions they are told they failed a "voice stress" test that showed they were lying. Under such circumstances, wrote crime reporter Jim Dwyer in *The New York Times*, social scientists say "a false confession may seem like an exit ramp from an impossible predicament, just as a bear might chew off its own foot to escape from a trap."

The issue of false confession came into sharp focus in 1963 with the well-publicized "career-girl murders" on New York's Upper East Side. Police questioned hundreds of suspects but had gotten nowhere until, six months later, James Whitmore Jr. was arrested and interrogated in another case. Whitmore, who was mentally slow, voluntarily went into detail on how he had stabbed to death Janice Wylie and Emily Hoffert while burglarizing their apartment. It was soon discovered that

Whitmore was elsewhere at the time of the murders, and the actual killer, Richard Robles, was later convicted and sentenced to twenty years to life.

But at the time of his confession, the double charge of capital murder made Whitmore a likely candidate for Sing Sing's electric chair and produced some lasting changes in the justice system. The prospect of an innocent man being executed was instrumental in the New York State Legislature's decision to abolish capital punishment in 1965. On the national level, the Supreme Court also took note. The tactics used by police to elicit Whitmore's confession were cited extensively in the court's 1966 Miranda ruling which required police to advise suspects of their right to remain silent or have an attorney present when they are questioned.

Four decades later, false confessions again were at the center of debate when five teenagers who had confessed to raping a young woman, who later became known as the Central Park Jogger, were found to be innocent of the crime. The confessions of the youths were videotaped and played on television regularly, and they appeared to be as authentic as one could wish. But another man confessed thirteen years after the crime was committed, and DNA tests proved that he had raped the victim and the Central Park Five had not.

Since 1963 there have doubtless been scores, perhaps hundreds, of instances of false confession. It is impossible to estimate the true number because the cases are hidden from view until brought to light, usually by a chance occurrence. But we know for certain that a number of innocent people have been dispatched to death row on the basis of confessions that turned out to be false. The following have been well documented.

Henry Lee McCollum and Leon Brown
North Carolina

The deck had been stacked against Henry Lee McCollum and his half brother, Leon Brown, right from the start. When arrested for the brutal rape and murder of an eleven-year-old girl in rural North Carolina in

1983, both were still in their teens and they were mentally disabled, Brown's IQ registering as low as fifty-one. McCollum, who had grown up in Jersey City, was in North Carolina temporarily, visiting his mother and was looked upon as an intruder. Perhaps most critical of all, they were going to be tried by a district attorney who was listed in the *Guinness Book of World Records* as the world's "deadliest prosecutor," having won nearly fifty death sentences during his tenure. Once convicted, they would spend the next thirty years of their lives in prison—McCollum on death row—for a crime they did not commit and for which there was virtually no evidence tying them to the case.

The victim, Sabrina Buie, had been raped and suffocated with her underwear crammed down her throat, her body found in a soybean field in Red Springs, a town of fewer than 4,000 people in the southern part of the state. On the night of September 28, McCollum, who was nineteen, and Brown, fifteen, were picked up by police on a tip from a local teenager. There was no physical evidence implicating them and no eyewitness testimony.

As described by Jonathan M. Katz and Erik Eckholm in *The New York Times*, the two youths were questioned for five hours with no lawyer present. McCollum's mother waited outside in the hallway, not permitted to see her son. McCollum apparently concocted a story of how he and three other youths attacked and killed Sabrina. In an interview with *The News & Observer* shortly after their release from prison, McCollum said, "I had never been under this much pressure, with a person hollering at me and threatening me. I just made up a story and gave it to them so they would let me go home." Later that night, having been told that his half brother had confessed and that he could be executed if he did not cooperate, Brown also signed a confession.

At trial, both defendants recanted, saying that their confessions had been coerced. The other two men mentioned in McCollum's confession were never arrested. The prosecutor, Joe Freeman Britt, turned out to be as good as his reputation. Described in *The Times* as a "six-foot-six, Bible-quoting district attorney," Britt was later profiled on the television show *60 Minutes* as the country's "deadliest DA," reinforcing *Guinness's* designation. McCollum and Brown were found guilty solely on the basis of their confessions, in a brief, cursory trial, in which they received little in the way of defense. Both defendants were initially sentenced to death, but in new trials ordered by the State Supreme Court, Brown was convicted only of rape and his sentence reduced to life in prison. McCollum remained on death row.

In 1994, the US Supreme Court turned down a request to review the case. In a dissent, Justice Harry A. Blackmun observed that McCollum had the mental age of a nine-year-old and that "this factor alone persuades me that the death penalty in this case is unconstitutional." Justice Blackmun later went a step further. He announced that he was opposed to capital punishment in all circumstances. Justice Scalia expressed a very different viewpoint, saying that the Buie crime was so heinous it would be hard to argue against lethal injection. It was in reference to the Buie case that he had described lethal injection as an "enviable" and "quiet" death.

It appeared that the string had run out for McCollum until 2011 when the Center for Death Penalty Litigation, a non-profit legal group in North Carolina, took up the case. Working with private law firms, lawyers from the Center began searching for new evidence. They learned that three days before the trial began, police had requested that a fingerprint found at the crime scene be tested for a match with a man named Roscoe Artis, who lived a block from where the victim's body was found and who had a history of convictions for sexual assault. The test was never performed and prosecutors never revealed the request to the defense. They also discovered that statements in the two confessions were inconsistent with each other and with the known facts in the case. Most significantly, they turned up a cigarette butt near the murder site. Testing by the North Carolina Innocence Commission, an independent state agency, found a match, but it was not to either McCollum or Brown; it was a match to Artis. Just weeks after the murder of Sabrina, Artis had confessed to the rape and murder of an eighteen-year-old girl in Red Springs.

He was convicted and sentenced to death, later reduced to life, and was still in prison throughout the trial of McCollum and Brown.

Remarkably, despite the similarity between the two crimes, Artis was never questioned in relation to the Buie murder.

Finally, an evidentiary hearing was held on September 2, 2014. The only witness at the hearing was Sharon Stellato of the Innocence Inquiry Commission. Questioned by the defense attorneys, she noted the lack of evidence connecting the two men to the crime and the DNA findings implicating Artis. The new district attorney, Johnson Britt, a distant relation to the original prosecutor, said he had no evidence to the contrary. Citing his obligation to "seek justice," not simply gain convictions, the DA said he would not try to prosecute the men again because the state "does not have a case." The two men, now fifty and forty-six years old, were declared innocent and ordered released.

Unfortunately, their release did not mark the end of their woes. Each man received $45 upon release from prison. For the next few months they barely got by on charity in one form or another. A report in the *Times* by Alan Blinder, said they lived at a home in Fayetteville, North Carolina, where McCollum slept on a mattress and box spring in one room, while Brown slept on a couch in another. They subsisted on a meager diet that often consisted of no more than canned potatoes and pork and beans. It was not what they had expected when they left the penitentiary. They were told that under North Carolina law, each would be paid $750,000 because he had been wrongfully convicted and spent decades in prison. But the payment was contingent upon receiving a "pardon of innocence" from the governor. As it turned out, that was not so easy.

According to the *Times* report, Governor Pat McCrory had taken a "deliberate approach" to granting the pardon. It was not clear to what extent, if any, opposition to granting the pardon was responsible for the delay in ruling on the application for pardon. The prosecutorial Britt was quick to register his hard-line view. He said, "There is no doubt in my mind that they're not entitled to a pardon, and there is no doubt in my mind that they're not entitled to compensation by the taxpayers." Scott Brettschneider, an attorney for the defense, said he hoped "there isn't something more here than just bureaucracy."

In March 2015, a local bank, judging that the delay was indeed due to the bureaucratic tangle, granted the men a large enough loan that enabled them to rent a home in which each had a bedroom. McCollum, who from force of habit sometimes referred to a room as a cell, chose one at the top of a stairwell. "This is my room right here," he said. "This is my room."

Ronald Kitchen and Marvin Reeves
Illinois

Ronald Kitchen and Marvin Reeves were among the many victims of the reign of terror that was the Burge Era in Cook County, Chicago. They confessed to five murders in 1988 after being beaten and tortured, reputedly by Detective Michael Kill, an underling of Police Commander Jon Burge. The coerced confessions were part of a pattern of brutality that corrupted the Chicago police force and judicial system through the eighties and early nineties. Burge and Kill were both forced to retire in 1993 for engaging in the systematic torture of scores of African American criminal suspects. Burge later served four and a half years after being convicted of perjury and obstruction of justice. He was released on parole in February 2015.

The five victims—two women and their three children—were discovered on July 27, 1988, in a burning home on the South Side of Chicago. Kitchen and Reeves became implicated when a jailhouse informant named Willie Williams contacted a Chicago police officer with a tip that Kitchen had told him he had committed the crime with Reeves as his accomplice. The admissions came, according to Williams, during two telephone calls that he made to Kitchen. However, telephone records indicated that Williams had made no such calls on the dates cited. Nonetheless, police obtained a court order allowing them to tap into all future calls that Williams made to Kitchen. Between August 12 and 22, police tracked thirty-six such calls, but none of them contained any information that might have implicated either Kitchen or Reeves in the fatal fire. Neither was there any physical evidence connecting them to the case.

But police deemed such evidence to be unnecessary. Kitchen was arrested on August 25 and taken to the station house where he was interrogated by a team led by Detective Kill. After sixteen hours of alleged torture, during which Kitchen said he was repeatedly beaten, including an assault on his testicles with a blackjack, he signed a confession prepared by Cook County Assistant State's Attorney Mark Lukanich.

At his first court appearance after being charged, Kitchen told Judge Richard J. Fitzgerald he had been tortured and coerced into confessing. There was physical evidence to support his claim. Fitzgerald found a number of marks of abuse on various part of Kitchen's body and ordered him sent to a hospital where he was treated for testicular trauma and various other injuries.

Based solely on his confession and the testimony of Williams, Kitchen was found guilty on September 19, 1990, and sentenced to death by Judge Vincent Bentivenga. Reeves was tried separately a year later and sentenced to life by the same judge. His conviction was based primarily on Kitchen's alleged admission to Williams. However, a judge of the Illinois Appellate Court reversed Reeves's conviction on the grounds that Williams's hearsay account of events should not have been admitted. Reeves was retried and again sentenced to life.

Over the years, as it became increasingly apparent that the Chicago criminal justice system was rotten at its core, the cases of Kitchen and Reeves attracted increased attention. In 2003, Judge Paul Biebel Jr., the presiding judge of the Cook County Circuit Court Criminal Division, removed the Cook County State's Attorney's Office from all post-conviction proceedings involving allegations of torture. The judge found a conflict of interest because Dick Devine, the State's Attorney, while in private practice, had represented Burge in some civil suits regarding charges of torture. Judge Biebel assigned Illinois Attorney General Lisa Madigan to take over the cases. Madigan joined with attorneys from the Bluhm Legal Clinic at Northwestern University School of Law and the law firm of Baker & McKenzie to reinvestigate the Kitchen-Reeves case. Upon her recommendation, Judge Biebel vacated the convictions on July 7, 2009, and dismissed all charges against both men. Six weeks later, Biebel granted them certificates of innocence, qualifying each for $192,000 in compensation through the Illinois Court of Claims.

Kitchen, who had spent a total of twenty-one years in prison—thirteen of them on death row until Governor George Ryan commuted his death sentence—filed a lawsuit in 2010, alleging that he was arrested on a false tip, deprived of food and sleep, and repeatedly tortured by Burge, Kill, and their associates. On September 6, 2013, the Finance Committee of the City of Chicago approved payment of a $12.3 million settlement to be divided equally between Kitchen and Reeves.

Robert Springsteen and Michael Scott
Texas

In Austin, Texas, the crime became known as the Yogurt Shop murders, invariably preceded by the term "notorious." The nude bodies of four teenage girls, all tied up and shot in the back of the head, were found on December 6, 1991, in a back room of the I Can't Believe It's Yogurt Shop. The discovery was made by firefighters who had responded to a fire that apparently had been set to cover up the crime. The four victims were: Eliza Thomas and Jennifer Harbison, both seventeen; Sarah Harbison, fifteen; and Amy Ayers, thirteen. The crime was called one of the most infamous in Austin history. Nearly a quarter of a century later, it remained unsolved. Compounding the gravity of the murders, two innocent teenagers, both seventeen at the time, served long, hard prison terms before being exonerated and released.

The two wrongfully convicted youths were Robert Springsteen and Michael Scott, both seventeen. Two of their friends—Maurice Pierce, sixteen, and Forrest Welborn, fifteen—also were initially implicated but were cleared before being tried. The four teenagers became suspects when one of them was found carrying a .22-caliber revolver in a shopping mall. Three of the victims had been shot with .22-caliber ammunition, the other with a .33-caliber gun. When a ballistics test on the gun confiscated by police failed to match the bullets taken from the victims, all four youths were released.

More than six years passed. The crime, which had shaken Austin to its roots, had become a cold case but, given its grisly details and the publicity it had attracted, police decided to take another look. On September 9, 1999, Scott was brought to the station house for a new round of questioning. The interrogation lasted twelve hours, and at one point Scott said he knew the identities of the killers. The interrogation resumed the following day and, in a pseudo-confession, Scott said he had fired a gun once and had *probably* shot one of the girls. He also said he had set the fire. He was brought back again on September 13 and said he remembered seeing Pierce with one of the girls in a separate room in the yogurt shop. He said he thought Pierce had gagged one of them with paper towels or napkins.

He then brought Springsteen into the case, saying that the .22-caliber pistol came from him. He recalled little about the other weapon but thought it was a semi-automatic .38 caliber. Springsteen, now twenty-three, was arrested in Charleston, West Virginia, where he was living. In a videotaped interrogation, he confessed to sexually assaulting and killing one of the victims. At that point, police charged all four suspects with capital murder, but the charges against Pierce and Welborn were later dropped.

Springsteen was tried first and, although he had recanted his confession and said it had been coerced, he was convicted on May 30, 2001, chiefly on the basis of the videotaped confession. He was sentenced to death, but the sentence was reduced to life in 2003 when the US Supreme Court ruled that the execution of people who were under eighteen when the crime was committed constituted cruel and unusual punishment in violation of the Eighth Amendment.

Scott was convicted on September 22, 2002, based almost entirely on twenty hours of videotaped interrogation during which he admitted participating in the crime. He also claimed that his confession was coerced and that he was in fact innocent. Scott was sentenced to life when the jury failed to unanimously agree on a death sentence.

Both Springsteen and Scott embarked on a series of appeals that would end in their exoneration and release from custody. In 2006,

Springsteen's conviction was overturned when the Texas Court of Criminal Appeals ruled that Scott's confession should not have been allowed into evidence because it violated Springsteen's Sixth Amendment right to cross examine witnesses. A year later, the same court set aside Scott's conviction on the same grounds regarding Springsteen's videotaped statements at Scott's trial.

While the state proceeded to prepare for retrials, defense lawyers requested that DNA tests be performed on physical evidence found at the scene, as DNA testing had become more precise in the seventeen years since the crime was committed. The prosecution complied, and biological evidence taken from two of the victims—Ayers and Jennifer Harbison—produced the profile of someone other than Springsteen and Scott. Pierce and Welborn also were excluded. The DNA of another man was found on clothing used to bind the wrists of a third victim, Eliza Thomas. A partial profile of yet another perpetrator was found on Jennifer Harbison.

All charges against Springsteen and Scott were dropped on October 28, 2009. Since then, Springsteen has been exploring various ways to clear his name with a declaration of "actual innocence." He has filed civil suits in federal court and in Bexar County District Court, but as of 2014 without success. Because he is no longer incarcerated, Springsteen cannot prove his innocence via the appeal process and he has exhausted all administrative remedies. Texas courts have long held that it is "improper for a civil court to issue preemptive declarations of guilt or innocence." In his suit, Springsteen has maintained he is due more than $700,000 in compensation and other benefits. Without a judicial declaration of innocence, he contends, there is no recourse for the wrongfully accused or convicted.

Damon Thibodeaux
Louisiana

Almost nothing about Damon Thibodeaux's confession matched the facts of the case. One of the crimes he confessed to had not even been committed. Yet, he was convicted of murder and rape and spent sixteen years in prison, fifteen of them on death row.

The crimes involved the killing and alleged rape of his fourteen-year-old step-cousin, Crystal Champagne. The girl had left her apartment in Marrero, Louisiana, at around 5:15 on the afternoon of July 19, 1996, to go to a nearby supermarket. When she failed to return home after more than an hour, her parents and twenty-one-year-old Thibodeaux went looking for her. The following afternoon, her partially naked body was found on a levee near the Huey P. Long Bridge. A piece of red extension cord was wrapped around her neck and the right side of her head and face had been beaten. Her shirt had been pulled up and her shorts were down between her knees and ankles, suggesting the possibility of sexual assault.

Before the girl's body had been discovered, investigators from the Jefferson Parish Sheriff's Department had begun interviewing people who had been with her before she disappeared. An officer was questioning Thibodeaux, who was at her home when Crystal left for the store, when word came that her body had been found. At that point, the questioning was turned over to a homicide detective. Thibodeaux initially said he knew nothing of the crime. He agreed to take a polygraph test which police said indicated a degree of deception regarding Crystal's death. After nine hours of questioning, of which only forty-five minutes was recorded, Thibodeaux confessed to raping and murdering Crystal. He told the police that he had picked the girl up at the supermarket and driven her to the levee in his car. He said they began having consensual sex but that he "snapped" when she "started hollering 'Ouch, it hurts! Take it easy.'" He began strangling her with his hands, he said, and then completed the job by wrapping a wire around her neck.

His confession, however, was at odds with several details of the crime. The detectives fed Thibodeaux information that had not been made public, but on his own, he often provided embellishments that were inconsistent with the facts. He said, for example, that he had strangled Crystal with a white or gray speaker wire from his car when the murder device was a red electrical cord that had been burned off a section of cord found hanging from the tree above her body.

While extracting his confession, police had no other evidence linking Thibodeaux to the crime. Hairs and fibers vacuumed from his car did not match samples taken from the victim. Nothing on his clothing or hers provided a connection. Although investigators said he had told them specifically that he had ejaculated into and onto Crystal's body, no semen was recovered from her body.

Immediately after his interrogation, Thibodeaux was arrested and charged with rape and murder. Later, given an opportunity to eat and rest, he recanted his confession, but he was nonetheless on his way to trial.

A week after the crime was committed, detectives questioned two women they found walking on the levee. They told police that on the evening of the murder they had seen a man pacing aimlessly around the scene of the crime. Both picked a photo of Thibodeaux from a photographic lineup and identified him as the man they had seen, and both testified for the prosecution at the October 1997 trial. The only other evidence presented by the state was the confession, which the defense contended was coerced and elicited by detectives who suggested facts of the crime during interrogation. The defense staked its claim on an alibi provided by his mother and sister, who testified he was with them at the time the crime was committed. On October 3, 1997, a jury convicted Thibodeaux of first-degree murder and rape. At the punishment phase of the trial, Judge Patrick McCabe sentenced him to death, given the aggravating circumstance that the murder had occurred during the process of rape.

Thibodeaux's attorneys filed motions for a new trial and a post-verdict judgment of acquittal. Both were denied by the trial court. They then appealed to the Supreme Court of Louisiana, arguing that Thibodeaux's confession was false and unreliable and should not have been admitted. They further contended that Thibodeaux was psychologically fragile and open to suggestion, which the detectives were eager to provide. The Court upheld his conviction on September 8, 1999.

In 2007, pro bono attorneys from the Innocence Project of New York, the Capital Punishment Post-Conviction Project of Louisiana, and the Minneapolis law firm of Fredrikson & Byron persuaded Jefferson Parish District Attorney Paul Connick Jr. to reopen the investigation. Forensic geneticist Edward T. Blake found that DNA testing established conclusively that Crystal had not been raped. A DNA profile of a man other than Thibodeaux was found in blood on a piece of wire similar to that used to strangle Crystal which had been hanging from a tree near the crime scene. As for the two women who had testified to seeing Thibodeaux pacing the levee near the crime scene, investigators learned that they had seen a photo of him in the news media before identifying him in the police photo lineup. Furthermore, they could not have seen him at all because on the night in question, Thibodeaux was already in custody.

All told, the reinvestigation established that Thibodeaux's confession was false. He admitted raping Crystal when, in fact, no sexual assault had occurred. He said he had used a gray speaker wire to strangle her when it was a red cord that had been used. At this point, the prosecution summoned a forensic psychiatrist who was an expert in false confessions, Dr. Michael M. Weiner. Dr. Weiner concluded, along with the defense, that the confession was the result of police pressure, exhaustion, psychological pressure, and fear of the death penalty.

On September 29, 2012, Judge McCabe, who had sentenced Thibodeaux to death, granted a motion to vacate his conviction and death sentence and dismiss the charges against him. That afternoon, Thibodeaux was released directly from death row at the Louisiana State Penitentiary at Angola. He was the three hundredth person to be exonerated by DNA, eighteen of whom had been sentenced to death.

Commentary: The Central Park Jogger

When it comes to false confession, there is one case that defines the genre. More than twenty-five years later, it still gets prominent headlines in the New York press; it still is the subject of television discussions and interviews. Many of the elements of the case were unusual if not unique. It involved five teenagers all confessing individually to the same crime on the same night. All five were in custody and being interrogated by police before it was even known that the crime for which they would later be convicted had been committed. Their separate confessions differed from one another in critical details. The victim in the case became a citywide celebrity long before anyone knew who she was.

Nameless, her identity no more than a shadow cast across the conscience of a troubled city, she nonetheless became a part of the language of her time. For fourteen years, she was known simply as the Central Park Jogger. Her presumed assailants—four black men and one Hispanic—also became monuments to a tarnished system of justice whose inequality was being etched more deeply in the awareness of a customarily indifferent public. They became known as the Central Park Five.

The jogger, a twenty-eight-year-old investment banker at the Wall Street firm of Salomon Brothers, was violently attacked on the evening of April 19, 1989, while out for a jog in New York's Central Park. She had been raped and left for dead. Her skull had been caved in with a heavy object. Her temperature was 84 degrees and she had lost 75 percent of her blood. She was in a coma for twelve days. Her gradual recovery was regarded by some as nothing short of a miracle. She was the most notable victim among many during a night of marauding by about forty teenagers. The maddening romp introduced a new term into the vernacular of oppression. It was called "wilding."

The attacks unleashed a firestorm of outrage throughout the city. The police felt the pressure for a quick resolution to the case and dozens of youths were herded into the stationhouse for questioning. Among them were five Harlem teenagers who would forever be joined in a tableau that traced a broken system of criminal justice. All between the ages of fourteen and sixteen, their names were: Anton McCray, Kevin Richardson, Raymond

Santana, Kharey Wise, and Yusef Salaam. All five initially denied having taken part in the attack or even being aware of it. But it was a long night and an even longer day ahead, and gradually each of the suspects began to give way. Finally, they all confessed to having been involved to one degree or another.

The prosecution made much of the fact that their confessions had been videotaped, but the cameras were not turned on until April 21, after the suspects had been in custody and questioned for as much as twenty-eight hours. The youths' confessions were inconsistent with one another and at variance with the facts as they were known. There were conflicts about when, where, and how the rape took place, and differing descriptions of the clothing the jogger was wearing.

The confessions, flawed as they were, were nonetheless the backbone of the prosecution's case. The only physical evidence was hairs on one of the boys that were said to be consistent with the hair of the jogger. In two separate trials, all were found guilty, with charges ranging from rape, to attempted murder, to the lesser charges of sexual abuse and assault. Their sentences varied from five-to-ten to five-to-fifteen years. Throughout their prison terms, the youths maintained they were innocent. They said they were tricked into making false admissions and often were responding to promises of leniency or threats of harsher treatment if they failed to comply. The authorities paid little attention. They even ignored the testimony of a DNA expert who, more than a year later, on July 13, 1990, testified in a Manhattan court that analysis of the semen found in the victim did not come from any of the five convicted of the crime. "That means," he said, "there was another rapist who is still at large." In fact, there was and he was the only one to have committed the crime.

In January 2002, a convicted murderer and serial rapist by the name of Matias Reyes, who was serving a term of thirty-three and a third years to life in the Clinton Correctional Facility in upstate

New York, confessed to raping the jogger. He explained that he had found God and felt compelled to confess that he, and he alone, was guilty of the crime. Reyes's confession was compelling. He recreated the details of the crime with startling accuracy. Four months later, a DNA test matched his semen to that taken from the victim's body. The office of Manhattan District Attorney Robert M. Morgenthau began reexamining the evidence in December. Two weeks later, on December 19, in a ruling that took just five minutes, State Supreme Court Judge Charles J. Tejada vacated all convictions against the five men, now between the ages of twenty-eight and thirty. They had all completed their prison terms of between seven and thirteen years.

Now fully recovered, the jogger went public on April 19, the fourteenth anniversary of the event that propelled her into the headlines. Her name was Trisha Meili, and she had just told her story in a memoir entitled *I Am the Central Park Jogger: A Story of Hope and Possibility*.

In September 2014, the city finally approved a settlement with the five men of $41 million, approximately $1 million for each year of their imprisonment. The suit, which had been filed in 2003, was opposed by the administration of then-mayor Michael Bloomberg but was reopened when Mayor Bill de Blasio took office. The wording of the settlement appears to absolve the city of any wrongdoing in the case. In the carefully crafted terms of the legal profession, it reads: "The City of New York has denied and continues to deny that it and the individually named defendants have committed any violations of law or engaged in any wrongful acts concerning or related to any allegations that were or could have been alleged." Mayor de Blasio expressed a different point of view. The settlement, he said, arose from "a moral obligation to right this injustice," which he added, was "long overdue."

The idea of one confessing to a major crime which he did not commit appears to be counter-intuitive. The greater likelihood is that one would deny committing a crime of which he is actually guilty. But false confessions come in multiple forms and diverse variations. Most often, those who confess falsely are mentally handicapped or entirely naïve with respect to their legal rights and the intricacies of a criminal justice system that serves best those who are trained to use it to their own advantage.

Gary Gauger
Illinois

The case of Gary Gauger was a classic example of a confession extracted by hypothetical prompting. Gauger, an organic vegetable farmer who lived and worked on his parents' farm in McHenry County, Illinois, near the Wisconsin border, was charged with killing his parents at their home on April 8, 1993. His induced confession was offered up after he was interrogated for sixteen hours without a lawyer being present. He was convicted and sentenced to death by lethal injection.

The Gaugers, Morris and Ruth, both in their seventies, were found dead with their throats slashed, and Gary was taken into custody for questioning. He was interrogated through the night, and the authorities came away with what they claimed was a confession. Gary insisted on his innocence and denied having confessed. He said he had offered, at the urging of the police, a hypothetical account of how he might have committed the double murder. He had been told that he failed a polygraph test and that clothes soaked in his parents' blood had been found in his room. Neither statement was true, but Gary had no way of knowing that. If indeed the bloody clothes were found in his room and he flunked the lie-detector test, how might he account for that? His interrogators asked him to consider the possibilities, just hypothetically of course. Gary responded that if he had in fact killed his parents, it must have been during a blackout because he remembered nothing about it. That was enough of a confession for the sheriff's deputies. Gauger was charged with the crime, and on May 5 a grand jury returned an indictment on two counts of murder. At a pretrial hearing, Gary described his interrogation and explained how he had been maneuvered into speculating about his guilt, but a motion to suppress the confession was denied.

The confession formed the backbone of the prosecution's case, and the deputies filled in the details at the trial. They testified that Gary told them he had come upon his parents from behind, pulled their heads back by the hair, and cut their throats. Additional state's evidence was offered by a pathologist who performed autopsies on the bodies and a forensic scientist who examined loose hairs found near Ruth's body. The pathologist, Dr. Lawrence Blum, testified that the wounds were consistent with the prosecution's account of how the victims' throats were cut. Under cross-examination, however, he acknowledged that it was equally likely that the Gaugers had been bludgeoned first. The forensic scientist, Lurie Lee, said that the hairs found near Ruth's body and presumed to be hers had been stretched and broken in a manner that was consistent with the prosecution's version of the murder. But as with Blum, Lee conceded under cross-examination that the hairs also could have been broken during combing or brushing. The state then dusted off and presented to the jury a jailhouse snitch named Raymond Wagner who was a fellow inmate of Gary's at the McHenry County Jail when he was awaiting trial. A twice-convicted felon, Wagner testified that Gary often described how he had gone about killing his parents.

The state's jerry-built case was good enough for the jury. Gauger was found guilty on both charges. He waived his right to be sentenced by the jury that convicted him and heard his death sentence pronounced by Judge Henry L. Cowlin on January 11, 1994.

Gauger was fortunate enough to have his case taken on appeal by Northwestern Law School Professor Lawrence Marshall, and nine months later Judge Cowlin reduced his sentence to life in prison. Two years later, his prospects grew even brighter. On March 8, 1996, the Appellate Court for the Second District in Illinois unanimously reversed his conviction and remanded the case for retrial because Cowlin had failed to grant the motion to suppress Gauger's confession. The court declared the entire interrogation unconstitutional, and ruled that since the arrest itself was made without probable cause, any statements made by Gauger should not have been admitted at trial. Without the confession, the state had no case. All charges were dropped, and Gary was set free.

The issue of his actual innocence, however, was not completely resolved until June 1997 when officers of the US Bureau of Alcohol, Tobacco and Firearms came across a wiretap recording that cleared Gauger of any involvement in the crime. Investigating a conspiracy among members of a Wisconsin motorcycle gang called the Outlaws, federal officials heard a tape recording in which one of the gang members, Randall E. Miller, said that the authorities had nothing to link him to the Gauger murders because he had been careful to leave no physical evidence. A federal grand jury in Milwaukee indicted Miller and another gang member, James Schneider, for thirty-four acts of racketeering, including the murder of the Gaugers. Schneider pleaded guilty to the crime in 1998; Miller was convicted in US District Court in 2000.

Robert Lee Miller Jr.
Oklahoma

The "confession" that led to the conviction of Robert Miller for the rape and murder of two elderly women in Oklahoma City was based on the contents of a dream that he shared with detectives who were questioning him about the crime in 1988. For Miller, the dream soon turned into a nightmare that ended with him spending seven years on death row. For most of that time, the state had and withheld DNA evidence that would have established his innocence.

Zelma Cutler, a ninety-two-year-old widow who lived alone in a corner house in the Military Park section of Oklahoma City, was found dead in her bed four months after another widow, Anna Laura Fowler, eighty-three years old, had suffered a similar fate. Both women had been raped. No property was taken from their homes.

There was no murder weapon. Both women appeared to have been suffocated by the weight of the man who attacked them. The murders were part of a crime spree that had begun in 1987 and spread panic through the neighborhood. A task force of twelve detectives was assigned to the case. The only hard evidence they had to go on was the identification of A-positive blood types in the semen of the rapist and what was described as three "Negroid" hairs found on the sheets covering Mrs. Cutler's body.

Police questioned more than one hundred black men in the area. Blood samples were taken from twenty-three of them. One of those with A-positive blood was Robert Miller, a twenty-seven-year-old, unemployed heating and air-conditioning repairman. When questioned, Miller told police he was eager to help in any way he could. He was taken in for questioning, and his nightmare was about to begin. Miller was a drug user given to an occasional hallucinatory dream, and he made the mistake of describing one for Detectives Jerry Flowers and David Shupe. His revelations were recorded on nearly twelve hours of videotape. During those hours, Miller told the detectives that he dreamed about the murders and proceeded to regale his interrogators with an array of dreams and visions that regularly invaded his sleep, offering premonitions, paranoid warnings, and insights into events that had already occurred. They were clearly the detached fragments of a mind not fully in control, but the detectives believed they were on to something. They worked Miller hard, coaxing, cajoling, suggesting various scenarios of the murders until one would ignite Miller's imagination. Finally, they thought they had gotten enough. Miller, they said, had given them details of the crimes that only the killer would know. He was charged with the murders of the two women.

The prosecution went to trial with an A-positive blood sample, three hairs that an expert witness said were Negroid and could have come from Miller, and a twelve-hour videotape played for the jury that sounded nothing like a confession. The district attorney, Robert Macy, also pulled from his bag of tricks a pair of Fruit of the Loom underpants that had been left at the murder scene. It was the same brand Miller wore, and the prosecution contended that when Miller was questioned he knew such an item of clothing had been left behind.

There was little of consequence the defense could present by way of rebuttal, as the prosecution's case was void of substance. The blood was one of the most common types, and the hair samples were not specifically matched to Miller's. The secret details of the crimes that Miller was presumed to have knowledge of were actually known to many people in the neighborhood, according to at least one defense witness, a neighbor of Miller's who described him as a peaceful man who often performed helpful chores for others in the area. On the videotape, which was the core of the state's case, Miller was heard proclaiming his innocence. But in its way, the trial was over before it began. The all-white jury convicted Miller in 1988 of two murders, two rapes, and two burglaries. He was sentenced to two death penalties plus 725 years in prison.

Robert Miller's case, however, was a long way from decided, as shown in a detailed description and analysis in *Actual Innocence*, a book by Barry Scheck and Peter Neufeld, founders and directors of the Innocence Project, and by Jim Dwyer, at the time a reporter and columnist for the *New York Daily News*. Lee Ann Peters, a young appellate lawyer in the Oklahoma City public defender's office, had been following the case with more than casual interest because her grandmother lived in the Military Park area. Now, assigned to handle Miller's appeal, she noticed that while twenty-three black men had undergone tests for their blood types, twenty-four had been checked for their hair. The man whose blood had not been sampled was named Ronald Lott, and, as it developed, his omission from the blood list was apt to be more than just an oversight.

Working with retired homicide detective Bob Thompson, Peters discovered that the Military Park crime spree had not ended with Miller's arrest. Two other elderly women were attacked later in precisely the same manner. Both in their seventies, they survived the attacks, and nothing was stolen except for a handgun which the intruder had taken away from one of his victims. A few days later, Lott was arrested for the two rapes. The stolen gun was in his possession and his fingerprints were found in the home of the other victim. Blood tests turned up A-positive. He should have been considered a prime suspect in the Cutler-Fowler murders for which Miller was then being prosecuted. Furthermore, Peters and Thompson learned that the same prosecutor, Barry Albert, was handling both cases. Lott pleaded guilty to the two more recent rapes at precisely the same time pre-trial hearings were being conducted in Miller's case. Albert said later that he had informed the judge that the existence of a suspect such as Lott constituted exculpatory evidence in Miller's behalf. The judge was unmoved. Albert withdrew from the case and was replaced by Macy and Assistant District Attorney Ray Elliott. Lott's arrest and guilty plea in almost identical crimes were kept secret throughout Miller's trial.

Peters in the meantime pressed on. She had the physical evidence against Miller tested for DNA, and the results cleared him conclusively; they did not exclude Ronald Lott. Peters presented her findings to the district attorney, who was not particularly moved. The only thing the DNA tests proved, he maintained, was that Miller did not rape the victims. They did not prove he was absent from the scene. The explanation was elementary: Lott had raped the women, but Miller killed them. He had confessed, hadn't he?

An examination of the interrogation transcript was a revelation. There were more than one hundred inconsistencies regarding what Miller said about his dream vision and his accounts of events, and he was incorrect about dozens of details. Also, when the detectives referred to the killer in the third person while describing their hypothetical scenarios, Miller went along with them. When they switched to the second person, substituting "you" for "he," Miller invariably balked and corrected them, saying "It's not me." The questioning technique was at its shabbiest when detectives tried to elicit an admission that Miller had left a pair of his underwear at the scene. When asked what the killer had left behind, Miller suggested a variety of items including a shoe, a knife, hair, a shirt, "probably a knife" in a second guess, his hat, a ski mask, and gloves, as well as the possibility of underwear. But the detectives kept coming back to the underwear, finally asking at which of the two houses it was left and what brand of underwear it was. Miller replied, "I don't know." That was admission enough for the police.

By 1994, Lee Ann Peters had left the public defender's office, and the new PDs handling Miller's appeal suggested he take a deal with the DA's office and accept a sentence of life without parole. Miller, who had been on death row since 1988, declined, and in 1995 the district attorney agreed that a new trial was warranted. The state's case this time would be even less compelling than the first, for little of its evidence was still available. The DNA showed that Miller was not the source of the sperm; the jailhouse snitch had recanted his testimony and disappeared. All that remained was the videotape of Miller's interrogation.

At a hearing to determine whether there were grounds for holding Miller for retrial, Judge Larry Jones made short work of the state's last piece of evidence. "There is nothing in these statements by defendant which would in any way be considered a confession," he said. "I get the impression . . . that Mr. Miller was attempting to tell the detectives what he believed they wanted to hear. And it is evident from the video that the detectives are directing many of the responses."

The issue should have been decided right there, but the DA's office was not ready to let go. The prosecution appealed to a higher judge who it felt was likely to be of a different mind. Judge Karl Gray, though conceding that the confession was at best weak, ruled that enough of Miller's statements were accurate to justify probable cause. He decided that Miller could be held for retrial.

At this point, a friend of Miller's brother called Barry Scheck at the Cardozo School of Law in New York City. Scheck recommended that they contact an attorney named Garvin Isaacs, who had built a reputation as an attorney for the damned, taking and often winning cases whose prospects had long been abandoned. Isaacs took the case for one dollar and went to work immediately. He had Miller take a polygraph test, which he passed. He then filed a series of motions. Early in 1998, all charges against Miller were dropped.

Elliott, who seemed determined to get Miller one way or another, offered Ronald Lott a deal. Lott was already serving a forty-year sentence for the two other rapes, and, given the presence of his semen at the Cutler and Fowler murder scenes, his outlook was not bright. Elliott made Lott an offer he thought he could not refuse. If he agreed to implicate Miller, Elliott would take the death penalty off the table and present Lott with the gift of a straight life sentence which could result in his walking free in thirty to forty years. Lott declined the offer. Elliott now had nowhere else to go. He decided not to retry Miller, and Miller was released on January 22, 1998. Later that year, Elliott was elected a judge in Oklahoma County.

David Keaton
Florida

David Keaton, an eighteen-year-old star football player with plans to enter the ministry, became famous in his hometown of Quincy, Florida, for events not of his making. He and four others became known as the "Quincy Five," all accused of a murder they did not commit; only Keaton did time on death row before he was exonerated.

The Quincy Five were charged with killing an off-duty deputy sheriff during the holdup of a grocery store in 1971. About four months after the crime, local authorities were ready to file charges against six local black men, although there was no physical evidence linking them to the murder. What kept the Quincy Five from becoming the Quincy Six, however, was the inconvenient discovery that one of the suspects was in jail when the killing took place. One of the remaining five was found incompetent to stand trial, charges against another were dropped, and a third was tried and acquitted. Keaton and a young man by the name of Johnny Frederick were found guilty. Frederick was sentenced to life in prison; Keaton, the alleged trigger man, was sentenced to death.

Although he had an alibi, Keaton was held in custody for more than a week. During that time, he later maintained, he had been threatened, lied to, and beaten until he confessed. He believed that despite the confession, no jury would convict him when they heard his alibi which placed him elsewhere when the murder was committed; he was wrong. The coerced confession was buttressed by the false testimony of five eyewitnesses, whose identification was prompted by photos they were shown by police. The jury found Keaton guilty.

The case became something of a cause célèbre, with local activist groups proclaiming his innocence, but Keaton remained on death row for two years. On appeal, the State Supreme Court reversed the conviction when the judge learned that exculpatory evidence had been withheld by the prosecution. A new trial was ordered, but it turned out to be unnecessary. Through an improbable series of events, three other men, all from Jacksonville, were arrested for killing the deputy. The evidence that implicated them included their fingerprints being found at the crime scene. Two of the men confessed and all were convicted. Keaton and Frederick were released in 1973.

Keaton was the first prisoner to be exonerated from death row. Once free, he devoted his time to helping others who had fallen victim to the indiscretions of a flawed system of justice. In 2003, Keaton became one of the founding members of Witness to Innocence, a non-profit group that works to abolish the death penalty and to support people who have been exonerated from death row. Despite a history of heart problems, he continued to address groups and lawmakers about the hazards of capital punishment. He died in July 2015, at the age of sixty-three.

Johnny Ross
Louisiana

False confessions from juveniles are commonplace in the criminal justice system. Teenagers rarely are acquainted with their rights, they are generally open to suggestion, and are easily intimidated. As tough and streetwise as they might be, juveniles also tend to be uncertain and easily led in situations where they are clearly overmatched.

Johnny Ross, a sixteen-year-old black youth from Louisiana, was roused from sleep by police early one morning in 1975 and told he was suspected of having raped a white woman. He was taken to the scene of the crime and then to the stationhouse for questioning. Without an adult being present, he waived his right to an attorney and subjected himself to intense interrogation. When the questioning was concluded, police came away with what they said was a confession. Ross contended that he had signed a blank piece of paper only after being beaten by the police. He was nonetheless charged with rape which, at the time, was a capital crime in Louisiana.

Ross's trial lasted all of three hours. The prosecution's case consisted of a signed, four-page confession and the tentative identification by the victim. No alibi evidence was presented in the defendant's behalf. Ross was convicted and sentenced to death under Louisiana's aggravated rape statute, which precluded consideration of mitigating evidence and made the death penalty mandatory. The conviction was upheld on appeal, but the death sentence was vacated when the US Supreme Court ruled that the mandatory sentencing statute was unconstitutional. The case was remanded with instructions to impose a twenty-year sentence.

The Southern Poverty Law Center intervened in an effort to obtain a new trial. In 1980, tests revealed that the blood type of the sperm found in the victim did not match Ross's. Confronted with the new evidence and a writ of habeas corpus, the New Orleans district attorney agreed to drop the charges and Ross was released a year later.

PART VI

Long-Term Confinement

PRISONS ARE A part of America's mythology. The names, the tales, the legends that swirl about them are the common property of schoolboys and scholars, the stuff of which novels, ballads, and a whole generation of movies were made. We are a nation whose greatest pride is the idea of our own freedom. We will make all variety of sacrifice, endure any hardship, and even surrender a measure of that freedom if circumstances are such, but we will never let go of the idea that we are a free people, for that idea itself is the nutrient that staffs the American Dream. It is no accident that America was the first country to make imprisonment—the loss of freedom—the standard punishment for convicted criminals. And it should come as no surprise that the United States has the largest prison population of any country in the world.

As of 2013, there were approximately 2.4 million people behind bars in the US, according to the International Centre for Prison Studies. Second was China with about 1.6 million although its total population was more than four times that of the United States. While the US represents about 4.4 percent of the world's population, it houses 22 percent of the world's prisoners. The US also leads the world in the rate of incarceration with about 716 per 100,000 of the national population. The rate in China is 121 people per 100,000.

Of course, the prison population is apt to grow a degree or two as states abolish capital punishment. In the past ten years, five states—Connecticut, Illinois, Maryland, New Jersey, and New Mexico—have brought the total to eighteen states as well as the District of Columbia. In Nebraska, the legislature voted to abolish capital punishment in June 2015, but four months later a petition drive by proponents of the death penalty mandated that a referendum on the issue be held in November 2016. In addition, Kansas and New Hampshire have carried out no executions since 1976, which amounts to a de facto moratorium on the death penalty. Governor Tom Wolf of Pennsylvania declared a moratorium on all executions in February 2015. A number of states—Tennessee, Ohio, Georgia, Oklahoma, Florida, and Alabama—had placed a stay on the death penalty, which was lifted in June 2015 when the Supreme Court voted 5-4 that lethal injection did not violate the constitution.

But as the number of executions declines, prison terms necessarily grow longer. Life without the possibility of parole, or LWOP as it is called, invariably is the sentence that replaces death and helps account for the growth of the prison population. The exceptional length of sentences imposed, again longer than any other industrialized nation, came into focus gradually as a number of long-term prisoners were exonerated after serving unconscionably long terms—twenty years, thirty years—sometimes even longer. In some jurisdictions, the longer sentences appeared to be accompanied by an unusually high rate of conviction. In Brooklyn, New York, it was exceptionally high, especially in the precinct of a detective by the name of Louis Scarcella.

The Scarcella Factor
New York

By all accounts, Louis J. Scarcella was a homicide detective of legendary dimensions. Scarcella, who retired in 2000 after serving for twenty-six years on the New York City police force, earned the Chief of Detectives' Award for Outstanding Police Investigation several times and was deemed by his colleagues in Brooklyn's 90th Precinct to have no equal when it came to closing a case. More often than not, Scarcella got a confession from the suspect with a conviction to follow. He maintained his status as a cop's cop thirteen years into his retirement, but in 2013 things started to go wrong. In just a few years Scarcella was accused of being a "dirty cop" who framed innocent people, using every illegal trick at his disposal, from forced confessions to witness tampering, not excluding physical abuse that resonated from the long-ago past when the so-called "third degree" was looked upon as standard practice.

By the spring of 2015, more than a dozen of Scarcella's cases had either been overturned or ended in exoneration of those convicted. It appeared to be just the beginning. Brooklyn District Attorney Kenneth Thompson had ordered the review of a total of seventy-one convictions involving Scarcella. It all began in March 2013 when a man convicted of murdering a rabbi was released from prison after serving more than twenty-three years.

David Ranta
New York

In 1991, David Ranta was convicted of fatally shooting Rabbi Chaskel Werzberger, a Holocaust survivor and prominent Hasidic rabbi in the Williamsburg section of Brooklyn. The shooting occurred in the early morning hours of February 8, 1990, in a robbery gone wrong. Chaim Weinberger, a jewel courier, was hurrying toward his car carrying a suitcase filled with fifty pounds of uncut jewels worth some $250,000 when he noticed that he was being followed by a man with a pistol. Weinberger jumped into his car and sped away, knocking the gunman down as he fled. Rabbi Werzberger was nearby, warming up his own car, when the killer turned, shot him in the face, and took off in his car. Werzberger died four days later.

The police had no viable suspects until two men being held on criminal charges in other cases offered up the name of Ranta, said to have been an unemployed drug addict. One of the men was a convicted rapist, the other a convicted drug user with five open robbery cases pending. Both reportedly implicated Ranta in an effort to get a break on their legal troubles. Scarcella hunted down Ranta, who was then interrogated by Scarcella and his partner, Stephen Chmill. On the basis of their testimony and a purported signed confession, Ranta was convicted and sentenced to thirty-seven and a half years in prison. Twenty-three years later, he was released under the most unusual circumstances.

In 2013, Brooklyn prosecutors asked a judge to turn Ranta loose. After two decades of opposing Ranta's appeals, Kings County (Brooklyn) district attorneys reevaluated the case and determined that he should never have been locked up. A recently formed Conviction Integrity Unit began reviewing the case in 2011, and events turned in Ranta's favor when one of the witnesses who had testified against him— the convicted rapist—told investigators that Scarcella had coached him and suggested he identify Ranta from a police lineup. The detective, he said, had told him to "pick the guy with the big nose," which happened to be Ranta. The other witness also recanted. All that was left now was the uncertain testimony of a young teenage boy who said he saw two suspicious-looking men sitting in a station wagon at the scene of the crime around the time Werzberger was shot, and a presumed confession Ranta had signed. The youth also said that he had been told to "pick the guy with the big nose." As for the confession, Ranta had denied confessing right from the start. His statement was written on the face of a manila file folder which, he said, was blank when he signed it. He said he thought he was signing a form that would allow him to make a phone call. Following his release, Ranta agreed to a $6.4 million settlement from the City of New York.

The Ranta case, described in detail in an article written by Sean Flynn in the August 14, 2014 issue of *GQ* magazine, pried the lid off a Pandora's box of tainted cases involving Detective Scarcella. Almost immediately, other inmates began insisting that they, too, had falsely confessed to crimes they had not committed under pressure of one sort or another applied by Scarcella. Reporters for *The New York Times,* poring over old court records, discovered that a number of presumed confessions in Scarcella's cases began with similar terminology and sounded as if they had been composed by the same person. They also found that a crack-addicted prostitute by the name of Teresa Gomez was a key witness, sometimes the only witness, in six Scarcella cases. In May 2013, the DA's office announced that it would review fifty-seven trial convictions of inmates arrested by Scarcella, and that number continued to grow.

Scarcella, retired more than thirteen years at the time of Ranta's release and living on Staten Island, denied having framed anyone or forcing a confession. According to *GQ*, he told *The New York Times*: "I have to be a pretty smart guy to lock someone up, get it through the DA's office, get it through a trial and jury, and convict a guy. I'm not that smart. It's not a Louie Scarcella show." But in a larger sense it was, and it was just beginning.

Derrick Hamilton
New York

By the spring of 2014 it had become an epidemic. Between March 2013 and April of the following year, *The New York Times* had, according to Sean Flynn, carried thirty-four articles dealing with Scarcella and his arrests. Ironically enough, it was a convict serving big time who was the first to notice a disturbing pattern in Scarcella's arrests. He seemed to be involved in an unusually high number of cases in which those convicted claimed they had been coerced into confessing; also, the same eyewitness was used to provide critical testimony of their guilt. Derrick Hamilton, forty-nine years old, was convicted of murder in 1991 and sentenced to twenty-years-to-life in prison. As it happened, he served twenty-three years of that sentence, but while in prison he did not waste his time. He studied hard, and in the process of becoming a jailhouse lawyer he freed himself and turned the light on the corrupt practices of Detective Scarcella.

He was on parole for manslaughter when he was arrested and charged with the fatal shooting of a man by the name of Nathaniel Cash in the Bedford-Stuyvesant section of Brooklyn. He was clearly guilty of violating his parole at the time because Hamilton owned a hair salon in New Haven, Connecticut, and was not allowed out-of-state. What brought him to Brooklyn was a going-away party for a friend who was about to depart for prison on a drug conviction. The state's chief eyewitness was the victim's girlfriend, Jewel Smith, who initially told police she had not seen the shooting. Later, however, questioned by Scarcella, she said she had seen the murder and implicated Hamilton. She subsequently changed her story again, saying she had been pressured by Scarcella who threatened her with a charge of perjury and the possibility of jail time if she did not identify Hamilton. The defense countered her testimony with eight witnesses, including a former New Haven police officer, who testified that Hamilton was still in Connecticut at the time of the shooting, but it was of no help to Hamilton.

From the start, he had insisted on his innocence and was determined to prove it. The story of his autodidactic embrace of the law and his successful campaign to free himself is recounted by Stephanie Clifford in *The New York Times*, January 10, 2015.

Hamilton led a group of similarly inclined inmates which met weekly in the law library at the Auburn Correctional Facility in upstate New York. They called themselves the "actual innocence team." Hamilton took a paralegal course while in prison and began researching his case on his own and with the help of outside lawyers. He got a job in Auburn's law library where he met with other members of what became the "actual innocence team" who were working to overturn their convictions, many of which involved the detective work of Louis Scarcella. They organized themselves into an efficient work team.

Daniel Rincon, convicted of a 1991 quadruple murder in Manhattan, wrote the letters in which he would summarize the cases in concise narratives and send them to journalists and lawyers.

Shabaka Shakur, convicted of a 1998 double murder in Brooklyn which Scarcella investigated, was the researcher. He looked up case law and crafted the legal arguments.

Nelson Cruz, convicted of a Brooklyn murder in 1998 in a Scarcella-Chmil case, was the artist. He would sketch out crime scenes indicating where witnesses and victims stood.

One afternoon a week they would write their names on the law library sign-in sheet and take their seats at tables with a security officer stationed above them. Hamilton would put up a chalkboard and distribute handouts that summarized what they would work on that day. They received instructions on how to use the legal-research service Westlaw and proceeded to draft legal motions, letters, or responses to arguments. Hamilton's efforts finally bore fruit when he was granted parole in December 2011.

His fortunes improved even more in 2014 when Kenneth Thompson was elected as Brooklyn district attorney. Thompson, who had earned a reputation as a champion of civil rights, defeated Charles J. Hynes in the Democratic primary, having run on a platform of judicial reform. He wasted no time in showing he was as good as his word. Shortly after taking office, he formed the Conviction Review Unit and ordered the review of around one hundred cases where questionable conduct was involved. Hamilton's was one of the first cases to be investigated. The Conviction Review Unit found that the forensic evidence, such as the path of bullets and where the victim's bleeding occurred, was inconsistent with the testimony of the eyewitness and determined that she was not credible. Members of the unit journeyed to North Carolina to interview Jewel Smith and, according to prosecutor Mark Hale, they found her to be "unreliable, incredible and for the most part untruthful. They had to depend on her credibility to convict Mr. Hamilton," he said, and as a result, "his due process rights were violated." On January 9, 2015, Hamilton was exonerated.

From the time of his parole, Hamilton has been active in campaigning to root out cases of wrongful conviction. On a spring morning in 2014, he championed a massive rally at the steps of City Hall in Lower Manhattan. Most in attendance were ex-cons and the friends and relatives of those still in prison who claimed to be innocent. Hamilton passed out black baseball caps with white stitching that read "wrongfully convicted" above the brim and "victims of detective scarcella" on the right temple. The rally was organized by Lonnie Soury, a consultant who works on cases of wrongful conviction and false confessions. At the rally, Soury described Scarcella as "a symptom of a deadly disease." The real problem, he said, was not one detective, but the sprawling system that supported and rewarded him.

The Three Brothers
New York

Three half-brothers hold the distinction of being the first of Scarcella's presumed "victims" to be exonerated. Two of the brothers were convicted as accomplices in the same murder, the third in a separate one. But they all had two things in common: They were arrested by Scarcella and convicted on the basis of testimony offered by Teresa Gomez.

The 1985 murder of Ronnie Durant had gone unsolved for two years until Detective Scarcella entered the case. Magically, a witness by the name of Teresa Gomez emerged who said she saw two of the brothers—Alvena Jennette and Darryl Austin—rob and kill a man. Durant's nephew told police that Jennette and Austin had committed the crime, but two other witnesses told a different story. They said that although the two men were at the scene, they had nothing to do with the shooting. The statements of those two witnesses remained secret for nearly thirty years.

The third brother, Robert Hill, was implicated in another murder about two years later. A drug dealer by the name of Donald Manboardes was murdered in the Crown Heights section of Brooklyn. A tip from none other than Teresa Gomez led to Hill's arrest, but he was released after being questioned. A week later, Gomez entered the scene again. Still insisting that Hill had killed Manboardes, she now told Scarcella that Hill was also responsible for the murder of one Bruce Siblings in December 1986, a month before Manboardes was slain. With Scarcella in control, Hill was arrested and charged with both crimes. Now on a roll, Scarcella began looking into the murder of Durant. With Gomez acting as his virtual partner, Scarcella arrested Jennette and Austin and charged them with Durant's slaying.

In 1988, Hill went on trial for the Siblings murder. At the trial, Gomez testified that she was hiding in a closet in a crack house and, watching through a keyhole, had seen Hill put a pillow over Siblings's head and shoot him. The defense called to the stand an investigator who had visited the scene of the shooting and testified there was no keyhole in the door of the closet through which Gomez could have witnessed the shooting.

Hill was acquitted in the Siblings case and was then tried for the Manboardes murder. Gomez again was on hand to deliver her version of events. In the Siblings trial, she had testified under cross-examination that she had not seen that shooting, but now she told the jury she had seen Hill and Manboardes arguing on the street about drugs. Then, she said, Hill drew a pistol, shot Manboardes and, together with another man, dragged him into a taxi. The taxi driver said that a man who claimed to be Manboardes's brother did in fact put him in the cab and directed the driver to take Manboardes to a hospital. But now, the driver said he was unable to identify the man. Another witness for the prosecution said she had heard Hill, in a conversation with an acquaintance, say he had killed one man and was not afraid to kill again. It was later revealed that Hill's attorney was told that three other witnesses who were present at the shooting would testify that while they had seen Hill put Manboardes in the taxi, he was not the shooter. However, none of the three was called by the defense to testify. Hill was convicted of second-degree murder and sentenced to eighteen years-to-life in prison.

Shortly after Hill's trial was concluded, Jenette and Austin went on trial together for the murder of Durant. Both were convicted almost entirely on the basis of Gomez's testimony. Police notes indicating that a witness to the shooting said neither man was the gunman were not shared with the defense. Jenette and Austin were convicted of second-degree murder and given the same sentence as Hill.

More than twenty years after the fact, the cases of the three half-brothers came under the scrutiny of DA Thompson's Conviction Review

Unit. The investigation of Scarcella's involvement was given impetus by a report in *The New York Times* accusing Scarcella of misconduct in as many as fifty-seven cases involving fabricating evidence, coercing witnesses, and concealing evidence of defendants' innocence. It was not long before the convictions Austin, Jennette, and Hill were overturned. In a statement on May 6, 2014, Thompson said: "Based on a comprehensive review of these cases, it is clear that testimony from the same problematic witness undermined the integrity of these convictions and resulted in an unfair trial for each of these defendants."

In a rarely seen sequence of events, it was on the initiative of a motion by the district attorney's office that charges against all three defendants were vacated and dismissed. Jennette had been paroled in 2007 after serving thirteen years of his sentence. Hill, who was scheduled to be paroled in less than a month, was released immediately after spending twenty-seven years in prison. It was too late for Austin. He died in prison in 2000 after serving thirteen years.

In June 2014, Hill and Jennette filed a lawsuit seeking $150 million from the City of New York, alleging that they had been framed by Scarcella. Austin's mother filed a similar suit on behalf of his estate. In January 2015, the City agreed to settle the three claims for a total of $17 million. The money was distributed on the basis of time spent incarcerated: Hill received $7.5 million; Jennette, $6 million; and $3.85 million went to Austin's estate.

Upon their release, Jennette reflected on their ordeal and told the *Times* in an interview: "The last time I saw my brother was at sentencing (twenty-seven years earlier); the next time I seen him was in a casket. This is the thing that really, really troubles me. He could not be here to share this. He was always optimistic that we would get out some day and that a wrong would be righted."

Rosean S. Hargrave
New York

New ground was broken in the Scarcella saga in the spring of 2015. For the first time, his name was introduced in proceedings leading to the release of a man who had served twenty years in prison for a crime of which he was innocent. The 1991 crime was the fatal shooting of a correction officer, an offense which invariably is treated with more urgency than one involving a civilian. The accused, Rosean S. Hargrave, was given short shrift. He was arrested one day after the shooting and his trial lasted just two days. At the time of the murder, Hargrave was seventeen years old. Arrested with him was a fourteen-year-old youth by the name of John Dwayne Bunn.

The shooting occurred on the night of August 13, 1991. As the story unwound in trial testimony, Rolando Neischer and Robert E. Crosson, both probation correction officers, were sitting in a parked car in the Kingsborough housing projects in Brooklyn when two youths on bicycles approached the car and ordered them to get out in an attempted carjacking. A gun battle ensued in which Neischer was fatally shot. Crosson, who survived, initially described the assailants as "light-skinned" black males in their twenties. It was a description that fit neither of the defendants. All the same, Scarcella, presumably acting on an anonymous tip, arrested Hargrave and Bunn the following day. Crosson then identified both boys as the killers, and it was his testimony on which the defendants were convicted. Ballistics and body fluid evidence recovered from the scene were not tested. Fingerprints that were found inside the car did not match those of either youth. Still, both were convicted without much fanfare. The defense had little to offer. Such evidence that might have helped their case was withheld by the prosecution. Hargrave was sentenced to thirty years-to-life. Sentenced as a juvenile, Bunn was given nine years-to-life.

It was the investigation of Scarcella's cases that brought attention to Hargrave's plight. After twenty years, he was still under lock and key in the Southport Correctional Facility, a maximum-security state prison reserved for inmates with severe behavioral problems. Bunn, turned down for parole three times, was finally released in 2009. *The New York Times*, which had been conducting its own investigation, included Hargrave's case in a series of articles examining Scarcella's record. In September 2014, a hearing was held on a defense motion to vacate

Hargrave's conviction. It was here that Brooklyn Supreme Court Justice ShawnDya Simpson delivered a scathing critique of Scarcella's role in the defendant's conviction.

Justice Simpson began by noting that Scarcella had become something of "a legend" for his record of convictions. But, she said, "There's an old saying, when it's too good to be true, it usually is." She then cited five previous wrongful convictions in which Scarcella played a key role.

"It has been established," she said, "that the cases of David Ranta, Derrick Hamilton, Robert Hill, Alvena Jennette, and Darryl Austin were comprised of the intentional acts of Detective Scarcella, which led to the extinguishment of the judgment and sentence in those cases by the decision of the district attorney's office. In each of those cases, Detective Scarcella procured identification testimony that was false and predominantly the basis for their conviction." She went on to say, "The scant evidence that convicted the defendant makes the new-found wrongdoing of Detective Scarcella significant." Since the end of the trial, she noted, "potentially exculpatory evidence" had been destroyed, further undermining the possibility that Mr. Hargrave could find justice.

The hearing came to a moment of TV-like drama when Scarcella took the stand to testify before a muted courtroom. His testimony, however, offered little in the way of new insights. He began by telling the court that he had played only "a minor role" in the Hargrave case. According to *Times* reporter Stephanie Clifford, he uttered some version of "I don't recall" more than twenty times. In about an hour's worth of testimony, he emphasized that he did not work alone on investigations and that the prosecutor shared the responsibility. Under cross-examination by defense attorney Pierre Sussman, he said that the practice in Brooklyn at the time was for prosecutors to authorize all arrests. Questioned about his consistent use of Teresa Gomez as a witness, Scarcella said, "The district attorney interviewed her extensively and used her as a witness." Detectives were told to "bring it to the district attorney's office." Sussman asked if Gomez was a crack abuser and if Scarcella had given her money and food. He answered "yes" to each question. Noting that Scarcella shared a New York Police Department card with his partner, Stephen Chmil, he asked if it was true that the words "adventurers, marathoners, regular guys, and mountain climbers" were printed in the corner. Scarcella responded, "It's a fact that three of four things we stated were definitely true. The mountain climbers part of it was because it sounded good. It was a funny card." The hearing ended on a potentially explosive note when Hargrave and Bunn followed Scarcella into the hallway. "Scarcella," one of them shouted, "why you do it, man? Why you frame me?"

In April 2015, Judge Simpson ordered Hargrave to be released from prison. In summary, she observed that the defense has not been able to conduct its own investigation as the evidence "cannot now be located and may have been destroyed." She further noted that the only evidence the prosecution relied on was the eyewitness testimony of the victim's partner which, she continued, could have been supported or contradicted had the evidence available been tested. She also cited the brevity of the legal proceeding. "It appeared," she said "to be a summarily tried case, with missing evidence and a rushed process." She concluded, "The finding of this court is that retired Detective Louis Scarcella was, at the time of the investigation, engaged in false and misleading practices. The pattern and practices of Detective Scarcella, which manifested disregard to the rules, law and truth, undermine our judicial system."

The relation of Scarcella's activities to the structure of the criminal justice system as a whole was summarized nicely by David A. Love on the Grio website:

> Police officers such as Louis Scarcella give good cops a bad name, this much is certain, but he is merely the tip of the iceberg. Remember that such individuals are allowed to operate in the criminal justice system because they are part of a larger web of corruption. The Detective Scarcellas of the world are unmonitored, given the reign to commit their wrongdoing, and are even awarded medals for it.

Moreover, Scarcella never convicted or sentenced innocent people; he merely arrested them. And he was on the force at a time of high crime, the crack epidemic, when public officials wanted to show they were taking bold steps to control crime, even if they were secretly framing people. Dirty cops, corrupt prosecutors and unscrupulous judges join forces with ineffective defense lawyers and gullible juries to create this problem.

Shabaka Shakur
New York

By 2015, the name Louis Scarcella had become part of the lexicon of New York's criminal justice system. It was as if his specter inhabited every space of what was commonly known as the halls of justice, leaving behind the taint of moral corruption. Curiously enough, it was Scarcella's reputation for manipulating the truth that allowed Shabaka Shakur to go free after being wrongly imprisoned for twenty-seven years. But then that just leveled the scales because it was Scarcella's apparent penchant for framing the innocent that had sent him to prison in the first place.

Shakur was convicted in 1989 of murdering two of his acquaintances—Stephen Hewitt and Fitzgerald Clarke—the previous year following a dispute over payments on a car. The basis for his conviction was a statement that Scarcella said he took from Shakur which said in part: "They were going to kill me. I know C [Clarke] and Steve for about two years. They deserve to die." Shakur denied ever having made the statement. The only eyewitness was Clarke's brother who fingered the defendant as the killer. Although the evidence was slight, Shakur was convicted in a three-day trial and sentenced to two consecutive terms of twenty years to life.

The case came under review some twenty-five years later as part of Brooklyn District Attorney Kenneth P. Thompson's investigation of Scarcella's cases. In 2014, Thompson's Conviction Review Unit looked into the case and decided to uphold the conviction, saying that the work of the police and prosecution was not faulty and that the evidence was properly handled at the trial. A year later, with Ronald L. Kuby and Leah Busby serving as defense counsel, Shakur was granted a hearing at which Justice Desmond A. Green, of State Supreme Court, ordered a new trial for Shakur, saying there was "a reasonable probability that the alleged confession of defendant was indeed fabricated." The judge went on to say that Scarcella's account of how he got the confession "is particularly troubling and causes serious doubts." He cited in particular Scarcella's "propensity to embellish or fabricate."

In his motion for a new trial, Shakur presented two alibi witnesses who did not testify at his trial. Justice Green noted that the two witnesses "would have impacted the decision of the jury in favor of the defendant." He concluded: Scarcella "did not show defendant a statement and ask him to read it. He did not read a statement to defendant. He did not ask defendant if he was willing to be videotaped. No one from the district attorney's office came to the precinct with video equipment to talk to the defendant. According to defendant, the next time he saw Detective Scarcella was at the pre-trial hearings." While finding Scarcella's statements to be unreliable, Judge Green did not find Shakur's to be entirely trustworthy either. He said he was unconvinced that the defendant's claim of actual innocence was necessarily supported by the facts.

A day after a new trial was ordered, DA Thompson said he would not retry or appeal the case. "Our ability to retry has been compromised by a number of factors," the judge said, "including the death of the main eyewitness (Clarke's brother). Therefore, I have decided not to prolong Mr. Shakur's incarceration with a lengthy appeal or retrial and will consent to his release."

The following day, the indictment against Shakur was dismissed and he walked free.

Upon his client's release, Kuby, said, "Twenty-seven long years. That's a long time to take away from a human being. It's a tragedy, but an avoidable tragedy. For every wrongful conviction, there is a guilty person walking around free. There's an innocent person whose life has been destroyed. And there's a justice system that has lost some of its legitimacy."

Martin Tankleff
New York

Scarcella was hardly unique. In one of the most bizarre cases in recent history, a corrupt cop railroaded a seventeen-year-old youth into confessing, albeit briefly, to the murder of his parents. The young man, Martin Tankleff, ended up spending seventeen years in the Clinton Correctional Facility in Dannemora, New York, on not a shred of evidence except for a trumped-up confession. The case received nationwide publicity. It was the subject of a book published twenty years after the crime and several television specials, including an episode of *48 Hours* on CBS. Right from the start, the story had all the subterranean shades of doubt and wonder that would have been nutrient for the imagination of Franz Kafka.

Martin Tankleff awoke one morning in his comfortable home in Suffolk County, Long Island, to find his parents had been murdered. It was September 6, 1988, and Martin was preparing to begin his senior year in high school. Events intervened. Moving through the silence of the house, he found his father, Seymour, slouched in a chair in his home office, unconscious and bleeding heavily. After dialing 911, he found his mother, Arlene, lying dead in her bedroom. She had been stabbed and bludgeoned brutally.

When the police arrived, it did not take them long to finger Marty as the prime suspect. The lead detective, James McCready, did not believe Marty could have slept through the mayhem undisturbed. He also said the son did not look properly aggrieved at the sudden loss of his parents. McCready went for the quick kill. He took Marty to the stationhouse where he was interrogated without a lawyer or an adult present. He was not read his Miranda Rights. The detective suggested that Marty had blacked out and did not recall committing the murders. To clinch his case, McCready told the suspect that his father had come out of his coma briefly and named his son as the killer. Obviously stung and well out of his depth in dealing with the aggressive questioning, Marty hesitantly confessed, wondering whether he indeed might have blacked out; then, deciding otherwise, he recanted almost immediately.

In the meantime, McCready had drawn up a written confession that Marty never signed but that was nonetheless introduced by the prosecution at his trial. There was no physical evidence. The defendant's oral confession was elicited by McCready on the strength of a flat-out lie. In fact, Seymour Tankleff had never regained consciousness before dying. Martin was framed by a corrupt cop, run through a morally tarnished criminal justice system, convicted of murdering both parents, and sentenced to two twenty-five-year terms.

Eager for a quick resolution to the case and apparently indifferent to the call of justice, the police never so much as considered the possible involvement of the most obvious suspect. The Tankleffs had hosted a card party on the evening of the murders. Among the guests was Seymour's business partner, a man by the name of Jerry Steuerman who owed him half a million dollars. Steuerman, who was believed to have criminal connections, was the last to leave the party. Shortly after the killings, he faked his own death and fled to California using an alias. But none of this was revealed until 2004, fourteen years after Martin was convicted, when he was finally granted an evidentiary hearing.

From the time he was arrested, Martin had the unwavering support of dozens of friends and relatives, including the sisters and brother of his parents. He also attracted the pro bono efforts of a number of attorneys, including former prosecutors; a private investigator; a retired New York City homicide detective; and several organizations devoted to weeding out cases of wrongful conviction, among them Barry Scheck and the Innocence Project and the National Association of Criminal Defense Lawyers. Dozens of witnesses testified on his behalf at the hearing. It was there that Steuerman was first identified as the overlooked suspect.

According to defense witness testimony, Steuerman's son had sold cocaine out of the bagel stores owned by the partners. The son's enforcer had bragged over the years about having taken part in the Tankleff murders. The drug enforcer's records contained the name of an accomplice who admitted having been the getaway driver on the night of the murders. Perhaps most tellingly, Tankleff presented evidence, unchallenged by the prosecution, that McCready and Steuerman were acquaintances and business associates prior to the murders. McCready had denied any association with Steuerman during the trial. McCready was further discredited when a scathing report by the New York State Investigation Commission on corruption and misconduct in Suffolk County law enforcement disclosed that he had perjured himself in a previous murder trial.

On December 21, 2007, the Appellate Court vacated Tankleff's conviction and ordered a retrial "to be conducted with all convenient speed." Six days later, Martin was released following a bail hearing. On January 12, 2008, then Governor Eliot Spitzer appointed Attorney General Andrew Cuomo (who would later replace Spitzer as governor) as special prosecutor in the case. On June 30, Cuomo's office announced that it would not retry Tankleff, citing insufficient evidence to prove his guilt. A month later, all charges against him were dismissed. He later was awarded $3.4 million by the state after settling his wrongful conviction lawsuit.

By the time he was released, Tankleff had spent nearly half his life in prison. Now, at age thirty-six, he was ready to start anew. The law, which had betrayed him in his youth, would become his accomplice as he approached middle age. He earned a bachelor's degree in sociology from Hofstra University and a law degree in 2014 from Touro Law School on Long Island. He soon joined with Barry Scheck in forming a Long Island organization that would mirror the work of the Innocence Project on behalf of those wrongfully convicted. Scheck, noting that he is "tremendously proud" of Tankleff, said: "The terrible injustice he endured has no doubt given him a unique understanding of the flaws in the system that will make him a powerful advocate for those trying to prove their innocence. As he knows all too well, we can certainly use more great litigators willing to take on this extremely difficult work."

Married now and the father of an eighteen-year-old stepdaughter, Marty has even grander plans for the future. In May 2015, he announced that he was considering running for Congress in his Long Island district against the Republican Peter King who has held the seat for more than twenty years. He would run as an Independent rather than as a Democrat. "That way," he said, "my allegiance is to the people; it's not to a political party . . . Think about the impact I could have on the criminal justice system by being in Congress."

Ricky Jackson
Ohio

Ricky Jackson holds the record. The fifty-seven-year-old exoneree owns the unenviable distinction of serving the longest time in prison—thirty-nine years, three months, and nine days—of any defendant exonerated in US history. Jackson and two other men—the brothers Wiley and Ronnie Bridgeman—were sentenced to life terms for the 1975 murder of a money-order salesman outside a convenience store in Cleveland. The Bridgeman brothers were eventually paroled, Wiley in 2002, Ronnie a year later. Jackson was not released until he was exonerated in 2014. All three men were convicted solely on the eyewitness testimony of a twelve-year-old schoolboy who, as it developed, was not an eyewitness at all.

When fifty-nine-year-old Harold Franks left the neighborhood store on May 19, he was confronted by two men who demanded he turn over his briefcase. When he resisted, one of his assailants clubbed him on the head with a pipe and splashed acid in his face. The other robber then shot him twice in the chest and fired a second shot through the store's glass front door which struck the fifty-eight-year-old co-owner of the store, Ann Robinson, who survived. The two thugs fled with the briefcase containing $425 in a green car that was parked a short distance down the block.

A few days later, twelve-year-old Eddie Vernon went to the police and told them he was on a school bus near the scene when the murder occurred and that he knew who the culprits were. He identified Jackson, eighteen at the time, as the shooter and the Bridgeman brothers as accomplices. None of them had a criminal record. All three were arrested six days after the crime. They were charged with aggravated murder, aggravated attempted murder, and aggravated robbery. They went on trial separately in August. Vernon's testimony was the pivot of the state's case, but it was somewhat flawed. Initially, he had told police that he was on the bus coming home from school when he saw the two men attack Franks as he got out of his car and walked to the store. At the trial he said he had already gotten off the bus when he saw Franks attacked as he left the store. Ann Robinson testified that she was unable to identify the robbers.

The defense seemed to have a stronger case. A sixteen-year-old neighborhood girl testified that she had entered the store just before the attack took place and saw two men just outside. Neither of the men, she said, was Jackson or the Bridgeman brothers. Several of Vernon's schoolmates who were on the bus with him said they had heard gunshots, but none of them was able to see who did the shooting. Despite the frailty of the prosecution's case, the three men were convicted and sentenced to life in prison.

The case was already thirty-six years old and Jackson well into his middle years when it came to the attention of Kyle Swenson, a reporter for *Cleveland Scene* magazine. In a detailed article published in 2011, Swenson noted the inconsistencies in Vernon's testimony, the absence of any physical evidence, and that Vernon had been paid fifty dollars by Ann Robinson's husband in exchange for his testimony. Swenson contacted Vernon and asked for an interview, but Vernon demurred. Ever persistent, Swenson reached out to Vernon's pastor, Arthur Singleton, and sent him a copy of the article. Singleton approached Vernon but without success. In 2013, Singleton visited Vernon, now in his fifties, in a hospital, where he was being treated for high blood pressure. Later, in a sworn affidavit, Singleton said he again asked Vernon about the article. This time, Vernon opened up. "Edward Vernon told me that he lied to the police when he said he had witnessed the murder in 1975," Singleton said in the affidavit. "He told me that he tried to back out of the lie at the time of the lineup, but he was only a child and the police told him it was too late to change his story." Vernon broke down and wept, Singleton said. "I could see the weight . . . being lifted from his shoulders."

With the pastor's statement on the record, events began to turn in Jackson's favor. Brian Howe and Mark Godsey, attorneys with the Ohio Innocence Project, filed a petition for a new trial in Jackson's behalf. Similar petitions were later filed on behalf of Wiley and Ronnie Bridgeman. Ronnie had since changed his name to Kwame Ajamu. The Innocence Project's investigation uncovered new evidence that placed the burden of the wrongful conviction on corrupt police practices. It found that when Vernon tried to recant his identification of the three defendants, the police intimidated him into testifying falsely. The defense never was told that the witness had asked to recant his accusations. Police reports obtained by the Project also indicated that the police had considered two other men—Paul Gardenshire and Ishmael Hixon—as suspects but cut short their investigation when Vernon made his identifications. The license plate on the getaway car was matched to a vehicle belonging to Hixon, whose police record included a robbery and shooting a year earlier. In 1976, a year after the Franks murder, Hixon pled guilty to more than a dozen counts of aggravated robbery,

At a hearing in November 2014 before Judge Richard McMonagle in which Jackson asked for a new trial, Vernon came clean. "I don't have any knowledge about what happened at the scene of the crime," he said. "Everything was a lie. They were all lies." Vernon told the judge he was on the bus when he heard two pops that sounded like firecrackers. The bus was close to the crime scene but not near enough for him to see what was happening. His identification of Jackson and the Bridgeman brothers was based on a rumor he heard on the streets. "I'm thinking, 'I'm doing the right thing,'" Vernon said. "I told the officer, 'I know who did it.'" He told the court he tried to recant, but detectives took him into a room and told him that it was too late. They told him that although he was too young to go to jail, they would arrest his parents for perjury if he denied his statement. It was because of these threats, he said, that he agreed to testify at the trials. "All the information was fed to me," he said. "I don't have any knowledge about what happened at the scene of the crime."

On November 21, Jackson's conviction was vacated and he was set free. Released along with him was Wiley Bridgeman, who was paroled in 2002, then returned to prison on a parole violation. In February 2015 a judge declared them innocent. Jackson was awarded $1 million in compensation. Bridgeman and Ajamu were to split $1.6 million between them. In May 2015, Jackson filed a federal civil rights lawsuit against the City of Cleveland and former police officers.

May was not a good month for Cleveland's police force. The US Department of Justice, following a long investigation, imposed tough new standards on the city's police. The agreement was part of a settlement over what federal officials have called a pattern of unconstitutional policing and abuse. A review released in late 2014 found that police officers had used stun guns inappropriately, punched and kicked unarmed people, and shot at people who posed no threat. Such occurrences often went unreported. None of this was new. Following instances in which several unarmed victims were fatally shot by police, a Criminal Incident Review Committee had been formed in 2013. From that point until Jackson was freed, seventy-two police officers were suspended without pay, one supervisor was fired, and two more demoted.

Michael Morton
Texas

Michael Morton celebrated his thirty-second birthday in August 1986 at a restaurant with his wife, Christine, and their three-year-old son, Eric. The celebration ended earlier than Morton had hoped. At night's end, Christine declined his offer of sex and Morton made his disappointment known the next morning with a note on the bathroom vanity. Whatever displeasure he expressed, however, was softened at the end when he signed off with "I love you." Then, at 5:30 a.m., he left for work as manager of a supermarket in Austin, Texas. He could not have had the slightest notion that the note he had left behind would, in short order, change his life forever.

When he returned home, he found his house encircled by yellow police tape. The police told him that Christine's body had been found in their bed. She had been bludgeoned to death with what appeared to be a wooden object. The sheets on the bed were stained with what later was found to be semen. Morton was taken into custody on the spot. The next day, Christine's brother, John, found a bloody bandana at a construction site not far from the Morton home and he turned it over to the authorities.

Christine's mother told the police that Eric had been in the house at the time of the murder. She said he told her that he saw a "monster with a big mustache" hit his mother. He described the murder and the crime scene in detail and specifically said, "Daddy was not at home" at the time. Questioned by police, several of the Mortons' neighbors said they had seen a man park a green van on the street behind the Morton house and walk off into the nearby woods. Police records also showed that Christine's missing credit card might have been recovered in a San Antonio jewelry store and that an officer there said he could identify the woman who tried to use it. None of that evidence was shared with the defense.

Defense attorneys suspected that significant information was being withheld. That feeling was reinforced when they learned that the prosecution did not intend to call the chief investigator, Sergeant Don Woods, to testify. They informed the trial judge of their suspicions and he ordered the prosecution to turn over all of Woods's reports. What he discovered was that all evidence regarding Eric's eyewitness account, the green van, and Christine's credit card was not included in the records. At trial, the prosecution offered no physical evidence and called no witnesses that linked Morton to the crime. They based their entire case on the note Morton left and surmised that he had killed his wife because she refused him sex the night before. On February 17, 1987, Morton was found guilty and sentenced to life in prison.

In 2005, the Innocence Project, along with the law firm of Raley & Bowick, filed a motion requesting DNA testing of items found at the scene of the crime. The prosecution opposed the request and the court split the difference. It allowed testing of evidence found directly at the scene but excluded the bloody bandana found near the Morton home. The tests, including samples taken from the bed, were inconclusive. Five years later, in 2011, the court finally permitted tests to be performed on the bandana and hair taken from the bandana. DNA matches were found from Christine and an unknown male. The unknown male, identified through the CODIS data bank (a DNA system), turned out to be a convicted felon from California by the name of Mark Norwood. At the time of the crime, Norwood was living in Texas, where he also had a criminal record. Investigation by Morton's attorneys in conjunction with the Travis County district attorney, implicated Norwood in a similar crime. A hair from the new suspect was found at the Travis County scene of the murder of Debra Masters Baker who, like Christine, was bludgeoned to death in her bed. Her murder took place two years after Christine's, while Morton was being held securely in state prison.

Morton was released on October 4, 2011, after spending nearly twenty-five years in prison. He was officially exonerated two months later. Norwood was convicted of Christine's murder. During the course of Morton's post-conviction litigation, his attorneys filed a Public Information Act request and obtained the prosecution's file. They found that the file contained documents indicating Morton's innocence, which had been withheld at trial. In response to a brief filed by the Innocence Project, the Texas Supreme Court issued a rare order for a Court of Inquiry to determine whether Ken Anderson, the prosecutor who had tried the case and later became a judge, was guilty of misconduct. The Court of Inquiry concluded there was probable cause that Anderson had violated criminal laws by concealing evidence and charged him with criminal contempt. The State Bar of Texas also brought ethics charges against Anderson. In November 2013, Anderson agreed to serve a ten-day jail sentence. He resigned his position as district court judge and permanently surrendered his law license.

After his release, Morton moved in with his parents in Liberty City, Texas, then rented a house in nearby Kilgore. In March 2013, he married Cynthia May Chessman, whom he met in the church he had been attending since his exoneration.

Dewey Bozella
New York

On October 11, 2011, Dewey Bozella won his first and last professional boxing match, earning a four-round decision over Larry Hopkins in Staples Center, Los Angeles. Bozella was fifty-two years old at the time; officials believed he was the oldest fighter ever licensed to box in California. His ring career was late getting started because he had spent half his life—twenty-six years—in the legendary Sing Sing Correctional Facility in Ossining, New York. It was at Sing Sing that he learned to box. The ring was in the building that once housed the prison's storied electric chair, and it was there that Bozella won the institution's light-heavyweight championship. He was, at the time, serving a twenty-year-to-life sentence for a brutal murder of which he was innocent.

The murder victim was ninety-two-year-old Emma Crapser who was slain in her apartment in Poughkeepsie, New York, in 1977. The elderly woman had just returned home from a church bingo game to find an intruder already present. The burglar hit her, tied her up, and stuffed linens down her throat. She died of suffocation.

The most immediate suspects were two brothers, Lamar and Stanley Smith, and Bozella, all of whom had records of petty crime and were known to hang around the area. The Smith brothers initially denied any knowledge of the crime, but they turned on Bozella when police lied to them, saying that he had accused them of committing the murder. Lamar was the first into the breach. He told the police that he had seen Bozella and another man, Wayne Mosley, on the front porch of the victim's house trying to break in. Stanley added that he had spotted Bozella, Mosley, and a third man in a nearby park shortly before the burglary.

Bozella and Mosley denied any involvement in the crime and a grand jury declined to return an indictment. But the prosecutors continued to level their sights on Bozella. They offered Mosley immunity for testifying against him as well as for committing perjury. They sweetened the pot by agreeing to reduce the length of the jail sentence he was already serving.

In 1983, six years after the murder, a new grand jury issued an indictment, and Bozella was tried and convicted, largely on the testimony of Mosley and the Smith brothers, and was sentenced to twenty years to life. His conviction was overturned a few years later when the defense appealed on the grounds that the prosecutor had used his peremptory challenges during jury selection to exclude black jurors. But the reprieve was of short duration. Although Stanley Smith had recanted and refused to testify at a second trial, Bozella was again convicted and given the same sentence.

Over the next few years, Bozella continued to maintain his innocence. Prior to trial, he had turned down a plea bargain and during his incarceration he had refused to admit any guilt before the parole board which denied him parole on four occasions. In 2007, he contacted the Innocence Project which referred the case to Ross E. Firsenbaum, an attorney at the law firm of WilmerHale, [*sic*] who agreed to take the case pro bono. Firsenbaum wasted no time in getting started. He questioned a retired police lieutenant who had been the lead investigator in the case and had kept a file on the Crapser case because he had doubts about the way it was handled.

The file contained witness accounts that had not been turned over to the defense which would have raised doubts about Bozella's guilt. One was the testimony of a neighbor who said that on the night of the murder she had heard garbage cans rustling in the alleyway, near a window of the Crapser home. Police had found a fingerprint at that spot that belonged to man named Donald Wise. Wise had been convicted of killing another elderly woman in the same manner and in the same general location. The location was significant because prosecutors said Bozella had entered the building through the front door rather than through the alleyway. Yet, police never followed up on Wise's possible involvement. There was other evidence that police failed to pursue and some that it suppressed. In addition, by this time, Lamar Smith also had recanted on his testimony. On October 28, 2009, Supreme Court Justice James Rooney of Putnam County overturned Bozella's conviction, based on the prosecution's mishandling of evidence, and he was released. In January 2015, a federal civil rights suit he filed in 2010 was settled for $7.5 million.

While in prison, Bozella earned a bachelor's degree from Mercy College and a master's from New York Theological Seminary. When he was released, he worked with youths at a local gym in Newburgh, New York, teaching them about boxing and the dangers of joining gangs. After the gym closed, he took his message to various youth organizations.

In 2011, during a ceremony in which he accepted an award for his service, Bozella told a reporter for ESPN that he still dreamed of having at least one professional fight. It was a dream that finally came true. On the night before the fight, he received a phone call from President Obama wishing him luck. On October 12, 2011, the day after he won the decision over Larry Hopkins, Dewey Bozella retired undefeated.

Juan Rivera
Illinois

The case of Juan Rivera, convicted in three separate trials and sentenced to life in prison each time, was a study in just about every violation of civil rights that can lead to wrongful conviction. It involved eyewitness error, false confession, false accusation, and official misconduct.

On March 20, 2015, Juan Rivera was awarded $20 million by Lake County, Illinois authorities for serving twenty years in prison—$1 million for each year of incarceration—for a depraved crime he did not commit. It was the largest wrongful conviction settlement in history but not nearly sufficient under the circumstances. As Rivera said when the award was announced, "I still would prefer my twenty years back [rather than] the $20 million."

The twenty years was part of a life sentence that Rivera received following each of three trials. The crime he was convicted of was as brutal as one can imagine. On August 17, 1992, eleven-year-old Holly Staker was raped and stabbed to death while babysitting for two young children in their Waukegan, Illinois home. Ten weeks later, police received a tip from an informant implicating Rivera, a nineteen-year-old former special education student who had been convicted of a burglary and was on electronic home monitoring at the time of the murder.

Detectives took him into custody and questioned him for four days, starting on October 26. He continued to protest his innocence until around midnight on the fourth day when the interrogation became increasingly aggressive. Finally, he was alleged to have broken down and nodded his head when asked if he had raped and murdered the young girl. At that point, the questioning picked up intensity. At around 3 a.m., investigators left to draft a statement for Rivera to sign. Minutes later, he was said to be seen beating his head against the wall in what was later termed a psychotic episode. As dawn approached, Rivera signed the typed confession that had been drawn up for him. Much of the statement turned out to be inconsistent with the details of the crime and Lake County States Attorney Michael Waller ordered the investigators to resume questioning Rivera until the inconsistencies were resolved. The interrogation resumed on October 30. It produced a second signed confession which was a credible account of the crime and matched the known facts of the case.

The trial began on November 1, 1993 and lasted slightly more than two weeks. The prosecution made its case largely on the second confession. On November 19, the jury returned a verdict of guilty. A month later, Judge Christopher C. Starck sentenced Rivera to life in prison. Three years later, the Illinois Appellate Court reversed the conviction on the basis of the cumulative effect of prosecutorial errors made at trial. The Court remanded the case for a new trial.

Rivera's second trial began on September 16, 1998. Again, the prosecution relied primarily on the signed confession. But this time it also came up with an eyewitness who identified Rivera as the man who stabbed Staker. The witness, Taylor Englebrecht, was about as reliable as Rivera's first confession. He was one of the two children for whom Staker was babysitting on the night she was attacked. Taylor was two years old at the time. Nonetheless, after thirty-six hours of deliberating over four days, the jury found Rivera guilty, and, for the second time, Judge Starck sentenced him to life. On December 12, 2001, the Illinois Appellate Court affirmed the conviction. But yet a third trial lay ahead for Rivera.

On May 24, 2005, DNA evidence taken from a rape kit excluded Rivera as a source of the semen recovered from the victim. Given the new evidence, Judge Starck vacated the conviction and ordered a new trial. Despite the DNA findings, Lake County State's Attorney Michael Waller chose to retry the case. At the trial, which began on April 13, 2009, Assistant State's Attorney Michael Mermel offered two somewhat farfetched arguments calculated to discount the DNA evidence. The first was the possibility that Staker, at age eleven, was sexually active and the DNA might have come from one of her sex partners. The second was the slightly more plausible view that the DNA actually belonged to Rivera but was mishandled by lab technicians. On May 8, the jury found Rivera guilty and Judge Starck sentenced him to life for the third time.

Rivera's third appeal was led by Lawrence C. Marshall, a Stanford University Law Professor and co-founder of the Center on Wrongful Convictions. Other attorneys from the Center acted as co-counsel along with the law firm of Jenner & Block. The defense argued that the evidence presented by the prosecution was insufficient to establish guilt beyond a reasonable doubt. It contended that Rivera's confessions should have been suppressed because they were coerced and that Rivera had been denied his right to present a viable defense when Judge Starck refused to allow his attorneys to offer evidence rebutting the false claim by police that Rivera knew facts about the crime that only the perpetrator would know.

On December 9, 2011, the Illinois Appellate Court ruled that Rivera's conviction was "unjustified and cannot stand." This time,

Waller declined to retry the case and announced that the state would dismiss the charges. "Today," he said, "I believe the right thing to do is to bring to a conclusion the case against Rivera by electing not to appeal the reversal of his conviction." Rivera was released from prison in January 2012. He filed his federal wrongful conviction lawsuit against Lake County law enforcement officials in October, alleging that they had framed him. Three years later, he was awarded the $20 million in settlement.

Locke Bowman, an attorney who represented Rivera through Northwestern University's MacArthur Justice Center, called Rivera's conviction "a stellar example of miscarriage of justice."

United States v. Criminal Justice

K ALIEF BROWDER SPENT three years in New York's City's Rikers Island jail although he was never sentenced to serve time. He was never convicted of a crime; he was never even tried in a court of law. Yet, make no mistake: Kalief Browder was executed by the state, as surely as if a stream of drugs had been spewed into his veins or if he had been burned to death strapped to a chair that served only that purpose. And he never was granted the opportunity to offer a defense and be judged by a jury.

Starting in 2010, at age sixteen, Browder spent those three years in what many consider to be the toughest, most corrupt penal institution in the jurisdiction. He was awaiting trial for stealing a backpack, a charge he continued to deny. Two of those years were spent in solitary confinement, a practice that, along with capital punishment, appears to be losing favor with the public as well as with members of the judiciary. Prisoners in solitary are isolated from the general population. They are held for twenty-three hours a day in windowless cells as small as six-by-nine feet. New York City Mayor Bill de Blasio has since banned the use of solitary for prisoners under the age of eighteen. But it came too late for Browder.

Browder's case came to light in October 2014, following an article in *The New Yorker* by Jennifer Gonnerman. Browder told her that he was repeatedly beaten by correction officers and abused by fellow inmates. He attempted to commit suicide on several occasions. By 2013, prosecutors had lost touch with the only witness against him. They dropped all charges and Browder was released. He moved back into his parents' house not far from the Bronx Zoo and tried putting his life back together. He earned a high school equivalency diploma and began attending community college.

But the specter of his years spent in solitary confinement continued to haunt him. According to Gonnerman, as reported by Michael Schwirtz and Michael Winerip in *The New York Times*, once home, "he almost recreated the conditions of solitary," shutting himself in his bedroom for long periods of time. He was very uncomfortable being around people, especially in large groups. He grew increasingly paranoid. He threw out his television because he feared he was being watched. In December 2014, he was hospitalized on a psychiatric ward at Harlem Hospital Center. Back home, his condition worsened. On Saturday, June 6, 2015, Browder hanged himself. He pushed an air-conditioning unit out of a second-story window in his parents' apartment, wrapped a cord around his neck, and pushed himself out feet-first. His mother heard a noise, went outside and saw her youngest child hanging limply alongside the wall of the building. Kalief Browder was twenty-two years old.

Browder's story was not entirely unique. He languished in jail on a minor charge because he could not come up with the relatively modest bail of $3,000. According to a report by the Vera Institute of Justice, about half the people in New York City's jails are being held on $2,500 bail or less, most of them for misdemeanors. The ostensible purpose of bail is to ensure that the defendant would remain in place and not disappear before he is tried. At age sixteen and in circumstances approaching poverty, Browder did not appear to be a high risk to flee to a far-off sanctuary.

If Browder's confinement suggests a malfunction in the legal system, one might consider the extended period for which he was held. The speedy-trial laws require that a defendant must be tried within six months of arrest or be released from custody. But, as pointed out by *Times* columnist Jim Dwyer, "the courts use a special kind of arithmetic that allocates blame for the delay; the calendars ordinarily used by humans to measure the passage of time are of no relevance. So after three years at Rikers Island, Kalief Browder still had not reached the six-month deadline."

Upon such random intricacies are lives damaged or lost. It has become the fashion for traditionally law-and-order politicians and ranking members of the judicial hierarchy to describe the criminal justice system in the United States as "broken." It is a convenient term but a far too modest assessment of the truth. To state the facts baldly, America's system of criminal justice is unjust, inefficient, racist, and corrupt at its core. It is a blight on the national conscience that begins with the practice of capital punishment. The uneasy truth is that the United States remains the only industrialized country in the West that still carries out state executions, and at a rate that places it in company with China and a handful of authoritarian regimes in the Middle East such as Iran and Saudi Arabia.

Nonetheless, the taste for the death penalty has diminished in recent years. The annual survey by the Death Penalty Information Center (DPIC) found that twenty-eight people were executed in 2015, seven fewer than the previous year. The number has been declining steadily since 1999 when there were ninety-eight executions. Only six states carried out executions in 2015, led by thirteen in Texas, six in Missouri, and five in Georgia. Florida had two and Oklahoma and Virginia, one each. The number of death sentences also has been dropping sharply. The forty-nine handed down in 2015 were twenty-three fewer than the previous year, which was the lowest number in the modern era of capital punishment, dating back to 1974. All told, death sentences have declined by nearly 80 percent since 1996.

The growing distaste for the death penalty is due largely to the advent of DNA testing and the diligent work of organizations like the Innocence Project. The startlingly large number of death row exonerations—154 between 1973 and June 2015—brought attention to the fallibility of a system that was sending innocent people to the death chamber. A 2014 study by the National Academy of Sciences estimated that 4.1 percent of death-row defendants are wrongfully convicted. It is not possible to know how many of them were executed but estimates run as high as 10 percent.

All available statistics suggest that the death penalty simply does not work. It is not a deterrent and serves no useful purpose. Every year since 1991, states without capital punishment had consistently lower murder rates than those with the death penalty. Still, despite the evidence of its ineffectiveness and its apparent loss of favor, it continues to mar an already tarnished criminal justice system. As of April 2015, there were 3,002 prisoners awaiting their fate on death row. Only a small fraction of them will be executed. The numbers in that regard are staggering. The average resident of death row will spend more than eleven years in solitary confinement before he is either executed or set free. Since 1973, the beginning of the modern era of capital punishment, the most likely outcome of a death sentence is that it will be overturned. Of the 8,466 death sentences handed down since 1973, only 1,359—about 16 percent—were carried out. Almost three times the number of those sentenced to death will see their sentences overturned on appeal or reduced to a lesser penalty than will be executed. Of the 8,466 convicts condemned to die since 1973, 3,194 had their sentences overturned on appeal; 509 died on death row from suicide or other causes; 392 saw their sentences commuted by the governor to life in prison; 33 were removed from death row for other reasons; 2, 979 were still on death row as of the start of 2014; 1,359 were executed.

The statistics reflect the public's growing dissatisfaction with the death penalty. It has become increasingly clear that it serves little purpose while the possibility of error is greater than conscience might allow. A 2015 poll by the Pew Research Center found that 56 percent of Americans still favor capital punishment for those convicted of murder, a decrease of 6 percent since 2011. Throughout the 1980s and 1990s, support for the death penalty often exceeded 70 percent. In 1996, 78 percent of the public favored it while only 18 percent opposed it. In the latest Pew poll, 38 percent opposed it.

Unfortunately, the Supreme Court is often a decade or two behind the public on such issues, and the only realistic way to abolish capital punishment nationally would be for the US Supreme Court to rule it a violation of the Eighth Amendment's prohibition of cruel and unusual punishment. While over the years the Court has voted to continue the practice of capital punishment in one form or another, it is not altogether unthinkable that, given the right case and favorable circumstances, it might vote in favor of abolition. In 2015, the Roberts Court seemed to suggest that the nation's entire criminal justice system should come under closer scrutiny.

It is not unusual for Supreme Court justices to recalculate their views on constitutional issues that tweak the conscience while on the Court or even in retirement. Such was the case with three justices—John Paul Stevens, Lewis Powell, and Harry Blackmun—who had cast key votes to maintain capital punishment while they were on the bench but reconsidered years later, each supporting its abolition. It is conceivable that Kennedy might do likewise. The four justices on the 2015 court who oppose the death penalty appear to be taking a more vigorous approach in their position. In a case that closed out the term in a flurry of critical decisions in its last few days—some of them surprising in their turn to the left—the Court approved the use of an execution drug used in Oklahoma. Kennedy supplied the deciding vote in a 5-4 decision, but that case was decided on extremely narrow grounds—whether the use of the drug midazolam was likely to cause excruciating pain. The dissent, written by Justice Sonia Sotomayor, offered a sharp criticism of the Court's opinion, but Justices Stephen P. Breyer and Ruth Bader Ginsburg delivered a more sweeping, detailed dissent that indicated they were ready to put the very concept of capital punishment on trial.

As reported by Adam Liptak in *The New York Times*, Breyer wrote, "Rather than try to patch up the death penalty's legal wounds one at a time, I would ask for full briefing on a more basic question: whether the death penalty violates the Constitution." In a forty-six-page dissent that included charts and maps, he said, "it is highly likely that the death penalty violates the Eighth Amendment." He said there was evidence that innocent people have been executed, that death-row exonerations were frequent, that death sentences were imposed arbitrarily, and that the capital justice system was warped by racial discrimination and politics. He further noted that there was little reason to believe that the death penalty deterred crime and that long delays between death sentences and executions might themselves violate the Eighth Amendment.

Not surprisingly, Justice Scalia, waddling about in an antediluvian stupor, called Breyer's critique "gobbledygook," which was more coherent than the rest of his argument. He explained that the death penalty is "contemplated" by the Constitution, and complained that it is not carried out quickly enough. By way of illustration, he absurdly said that the situation "calls to mind the man sentenced to death for killing his parents, who pleads for mercy on the ground that he is an orphan."

Scalia, who seems to believe that time stopped at the precise moment when the ink on the Constitution dried, considers himself to be an advocate of "original intent," a doctrine that contends that the words, as written at the time, are sacred and are to be followed explicitly without regard to progress or change. Joseph J. Ellis, a noted historian of the Revolutionary period and author, most recently, of *The Quartet*, responds to that argument with words from Thomas Jefferson himself:

"Some men look at constitutions with sanctimonious reverence and deem them, like the Ark of the Covenant, too sacred to be touched. They ascribe to the preceding age a wisdom more than human . . .

"But I know also, that laws and institutions must go hand in hand with the progress of the human mind."

Yet, even Scalia, as staunch an advocate of capital punishment as one might find, has conceded that its days might be numbered. Addressing the subject at the University of Minnesota Law School in October 2015, he noted that recent decisions by the Court have made it "practically impossible to impose it." He went on to say that "it wouldn't surprise me" if the Court would one day declare it to be unconstitutional, but made it clear that such a decision would have to come without his support. He described the Constitution as an "enduring" document that should not be open to interpretation, expressing his displeasure that some of his colleagues deemed it to be flexible.

As hard-line as he is on the criminal justice system, Scalia has made clear his outrage at the length of time some prisoners spend on death row before their cases wind down to conclusion. "How has it gone on this long?" he asked a lawyer for the state of Florida when he learned that Freddie Lee Hall had been on Florida's death row for more than three decades. At the same time, Justice Kennedy noted that the last ten people executed in the state had spent an average of almost twenty-five years on death row. "Do you think that that is consistent with the purpose of the death penalty?" he asked the lawyer, "and is it consistent with the sound administration of the justice system?"

The situation was not particular to Florida. In California, more than two hundred inmates in Pelican Bay, the state's toughest prison, have spent more than a decade in solitary which, in that institution, is an eight-by-twelve-foot cell, for twenty-two hours a day. Dozens more have been held there for fifteen years or longer. A federal judge in Oakland raised the possibility that holding prisoners in such isolation might qualify as cruel and unusual punishment, violating their Eighth Amendment rights. The ponderous barbarism of California's death-penalty system was alluded to by United States District Judge Cormac Carney, an appointee of George W. Bush, in July 2014. Overturning the death sentence of Ernest Dewayne Jones, who had been sentenced in 1995 for the murder of his girlfriend's sister, Judge Jones noted that of the more than nine hundred people California had sentenced to death since 1978, only thirteen have been executed. More than 40 percent of the rest have been on death row for at least nineteen years, and the backlog continues to grow. The delays, the judge said, are not due to repeated appeals of the inmates, but to the state's own plodding efforts in moving forward and its impoverished defense system.

As the death penalty edges its way, ever so slowly but inexorably, into the past, the length of sentences and the growing prison population are becoming increasingly critical issues. Prisons are expensive to build, difficult to maintain, and troublesome to locate as no one wants a penal institution located anywhere near a residential area. The growing popularity of LWOP, life without the possibility of parole, adds significantly to the burden. A nineteen-year-old who commits a brutal murder that might otherwise have resulted in a death sentence might now spend fifty, sixty years, or even longer in a penitentiary at public expense toward no reasonable purpose. All studies indicate that the teenager could have been returned to society decades earlier at negligible risk. Most advanced countries have more practical penal systems than the United States which heads the list for long-term incarceration. One of the most interesting systems is found in Norway, as described in *The New York Times* by Dana Goldstein, a staff writer at the Marshall Project, a non-profit news organization that specializes in the coverage of criminal justice.

In Norway, the maximum prison term for a crime, no matter how grave, is twenty-one years. But that is just the initial sentence. At the end of the term, judges have the option of adding an unlimited number of five-year extensions if the prisoner is deemed a danger to the public. As recounted by Goldstein, the case for such a system was made by Marc Mauer, the director of the Sentencing Project, an advocacy group, in March 2015 before a congressional task force on reforming the federal prison system. Such a policy, Mauer said, would control costs in a system that is now 40 percent over capacity and would "bring the United States in line with other industrialized countries."

Mauer's argument, supported by statistics, was powerful. Studies show that all but the most violent criminals mature out of criminal activity before middle age, indicating that long sentences do little to prevent crime. Homicide and drug arrests peak at age nineteen, according to the Bureau of Justice statistics, and forcible rape peaks at eighteen. Some crimes, such as vandalism, crest even earlier, at age sixteen, while arrests for forgery, fraud, and embezzlement reach their summit in the early twenties. For most of the crimes tracked by the FBI, more than half of all offenders will be arrested by the time they are thirty. Criminal careers tend to be short. For the FBI's eight most serious crimes— murder, rape, robbery, aggravated assault, burglary, larceny-theft, arson, and auto theft—five to ten years is the typical life-span for adults who commit those crimes, as measured by arrests. More than 10 percent of federal and state inmates, a total of nearly 160,000, are serving life sentences; 10,000 of them have committed non-violent crimes. Since 1990, the prison population over the age of fifty-five has increased by 550 percent to a total of 144,500 inmates. As a consequence of an aging population, the state and federal prison systems spend about $4 billion on health care.

Keeping dangerous people off the streets is just part of the rationale for imprisonment. The other part is the inclination to punish offenders. But, Mauer asks, "How much punishment is enough? What are we trying to accomplish, and where does redemption come into the picture?" Criminology Professor Alfred Blumstein, of Carnegie Mellon, commenting on the significance of aging in the sentencing process, noted that "we went crazy in the 1980s and 1990s. Lots of people, as they age, they are no longer a risk. We are keeping people in prison who are physically unable to represent a threat to anyone."

The most harrowing aspect of long-term confinement is the specter of solitary confinement. It is likely that solitary will disappear from America's justice system even before capital punishment. One can hardly question the cruelty of a system that places a human being in a cell sometimes not much larger than the mattress he is given to sleep on, while he is virtually denied human contact, and kept under those conditions for years, sometimes decades. Longevity records on such issues can be elusive, but it is generally conceded that the forty-three years Albert Woodfox has been held in isolation in Louisiana's infamous Angola Prison is longer than any prisoner in the nation's history.

Woodfox was one of the notorious Angola 3, which consisted of members of the Black Panther Party, a revolutionary black left-wing organization formed in 1966. He was still being held in solitary in

November 2015, awaiting a decision on whether he would be tried a third time for the 1972 killing of a prison guard. On November 9, a three-judge panel of a federal appeals court reversed, by a margin of 2-1, a lower court ruling ordering Woodfox's release and barring a third trial. He had been convicted twice for stabbing to death Brent Miller, a twenty-three-year-old prison guard, but both convictions were overturned on constitutional grounds. The other two men of the Angola 3 were Robert King, who was released in 2001, and Herman Wallace, who was released in 2013 and died three days later of liver cancer.

Clearly, the Angola 3, who maintained their innocence from the start, might have suffered their judicial fate at least in part because of their affiliation with the Black Panthers. Nineteen seventy-two, after all, was not a time of social tranquility in America. Richard Nixon was about to be reelected, Watergate was just coming into focus, the Vietnam War was still ablaze, the revolutionary temper of the times was in full flourish, and three black men could not reasonably expect to receive anything resembling justice in the state of Louisiana.

Of course the concept of Louisiana justice would remain a myth long after the turmoil of the late sixties and early seventies. Glenn Ford (whose case is discussed earlier in the book) spent nearly twenty-nine years on Angola's death row before his conviction and death sentence were overturned in March 2014. His freedom did not last long. He died of lung cancer on June 29, 2015, at a home provided by Resurrection After Exoneration, a non-profit group that assists prisoners who have been freed. He was sixty-five years old. Ford's attorney, Glenn Most, said that a medical test given to Ford at Angola had revealed a cancer marker, but he was denied the opportunity to see an oncologist.

Ford's case had a marked effect on A.M. "Marty" Stroud III, the prosecuting attorney who helped convict him. Months before Ford died, Stroud wrote a letter to the *Shreveport Times* in which he apologized for his role in getting Ford convicted and said he was "full of grief and sorrow." He further explained: "In 1984, I was thirty-three years old. I was arrogant, judgmental, narcissistic and very full of myself. I was not as interested in justice as I was in winning."

From there, Stroud went on to call for the abolition of the death penalty. "The really sad part for me," he wrote, "is that as much as I would like to believe that this case will advance the cause of abolition of the death penalty, I am afraid that Louisiana is too steeped in the culture of death to abolish voluntarily capital punishment.

"I do believe, however, that the day will come when the Supreme Court will finally make note of all the innocents, like Glenn Ford, who have been released from death row and come to the conclusion that our society is incapable of administering a fair system of capital punishment."

After apologizing to Ford, his family, the family of the victim who were denied closure, the members of the jury and the court for not having done a more thorough job, he closed his letter on a plaintive note: "I end with the hope that providence will have more mercy for me than I showed Glenn Ford. But I am also sobered by the realization that I certainly am not deserving of it."

Months before Ford died, he and Stroud had a face-to-face meeting in which Stroud, his voice a bit unsteady, apologized to Ford and asked his forgiveness. Ford, to his credit, replied in a matter-of-fact tone. He said he could wish Stroud the best in his future but no, "I can't forgive you." It was an altogether proper response, a refreshing contrast to the treacly sentimental offers of forgiveness that have become the custom for the victims of horrendous crimes to bestow upon their predators.

Stroud's turn of heart was not of course representative of Louisiana's law enforcement community. In fact, not long after Ford's death, Dale Cox, the acting district attorney of Caddo Parish, in the northwest corner of the state, explained to *The Shreveport Times* exactly what was required to bring order and justice to Louisiana. Capital punishment, he said, is primarily and rightly about revenge and the state needs to "kill more people. Retribution is a valid societal interest." Then, as if trying to dispel any doubts that he might be at least marginally crazy, he offered an illustration: "What kind of society would say that it's okay to kill babies and then eat them, and in fact we can have parties where we kill them and eat them, and you're not going to forfeit your life for that? If you've gotten to that point, you're no longer a society." Cox went on to offer assurance that thus far he had not seen any case involving cannibalism. But, he warned, it would be the next logical step given what he called the "increase in savagery" in society.

Despite Cox's primitive view of the world around him, Stroud's call to end capital punishment is the more likely cast of the future, yet another small turn in the direction of abolition. The United States is a country infused with a culture of violence and a thirst for retribution. It has been that way from the very start, in matters both domestic and global. Change comes slowly but, it seems, inexorably. The propriety of capital punishment, both in its moral aspect and its merit as part of a criminal justice system, has been a matter of national concern for at least the better part of a century. It came into sharp focus in 1924 when Clarence Darrow put the concept itself on trial while defending Nathan Leopold and Richard Loeb in a bench trial that has become ingrained in American folklore.

Leopold and Loeb, teenage intellectual whiz-kids from prominent Chicago families, had killed young Bobby Franks for the thrill of it. Each was being fitted for the hangman's noose when Darrow, the wondrous and eloquent freethinker, entered the case. He pleaded his clients guilty and asked that the trial to determine their sentences be conducted without a jury. Darrow, best known perhaps for his clash with William Jennings Bryan in the Scopes "monkey trial," could bring magic to bear upon a jury, but here, he said, he wished the fate of the defendants to be decided by the judge alone; the responsibility for hanging two teenagers would not be divided by twelve.

In a dazzling closing argument that spanned several days and covered nearly one hundred pages in transcription, Darrow took on the death penalty before such sentiment had become the fashion. As in most matters, Darrow was decades ahead of the flow. "I never saw so much enthusiasm for the death penalty as I have seen here," he said. "It's been discussed as a holiday, like a day at the races."

In his plea to the judge, Darrow introduced elements of psychology and philosophy; he reviewed a bit of the history of capital punishment, contending that as its use diminished, so then did the crimes for which it was applied. He quoted liberally from the Persion poet Omar Khayyam. Near the end, he summed up the case against the death penalty: "I am pleading for the future," he told the judge and the world. "I am pleading for a time when hatred and cruelty will not command the hearts of men; when we can learn by reason and judgment and understanding and faith that all life is worth saving, and that mercy is the highest attribute of man."

The lives of Leopold and Loeb were spared. They were sentenced to life plus ninety-nine years. For a brief time, capital punishment became a popular, though largely intellectual, subject of debate. There were few abolitionists who felt compelled to act upon their views. The death penalty was used increasingly during the following decade, and it was not until the seventies and beyond that countries around the world began to take it off the books. France tore down its guillotine in 1972; Sweden did away with capital punishment the same year and the United Kingdom a year later. Many more countries dropped it in the eighties, and two dozen nations set it aside in the nineties. By the turn of the century, the United States was the only industrialized country in the West that persisted in performing state-sanctioned executions.

All the same, while the use of the death penalty is certain to diminish in frequency, it is not likely to disappear any time soon. America's criminal justice system—unjust, corrupt, and odious as it is—appears to be embedded, by now, in the national character. Critics can bemoan the "broken" criminal justice system, but there seems to be little impetus to do much about it, no sense of outrage at the persistent inhumanity that is at the core of the machinery of justice.

David Swanson, author of *War Is a Lie*, sees it this way: "Civilization is something we no longer seem to aspire to. The United States locks up more people and a greater percentage of its people than anyone else. We lock them in training centers for anger and violence. We subject them to rape, assault, humiliation, and isolation. We throw the innocent in with the guilty, the young with the old, the nonviolent with the violent, the hopeful with those who've lost all interest in life. And we routinely subject numbers of prisoners to the torture of isolation. We lock human beings in little boxes for twenty-two or twenty-three hours per day." Then, he asks, "Where is the outrage."

The outrage always is slow in coming. When finally it arrives, it seems to have happened all at once, for it tiptoes in, as Sandburg wrote, "on little cat feet." It happened that way with women's right to choose, and even more so with gay rights and same-sex marriage. But if one looks back far enough and carefully enough, the roots of the outrage and finally the change it inspired can be found in incandescent markers that one failed to heed. How many little noted events led to President Obama's taking on the criminal justice system in July 2015, midway through the seventh year of his presidency? He became the first president to visit a federal correctional facility when he walked through the gates of the El Reno prison in Oklahoma. There, he peered into a cell measuring 9-by-10 feet that contained three bunks, a toilet with no seat, a night table with books, a small sink, prison clothes on a hook, and some metal cabinets, according to the description offered by Peter Baker in *The New York Times*. Obama wasted no time in calling for a sweeping bipartisan effort to fix "a broken system" of criminal justice that has locked up too many Americans for too long, especially a whole generation of young black and Hispanic men. Not long after the president made his declaration, as if programmed in a time zone still uncharted, Pope Francis stirred some of the deepest waters of the national conscience when he toured the United States and voiced his unyielding opposition to capital punishment. To many, it seemed to be the most dramatic fusion of state and church since the Emperor Constantine brought Christianity to Rome.

It suggested that the day may not be far off when America no longer executes its citizens. Other reforms of the criminal justice system are likely to precede the abolition of capital punishment. The use of solitary confinement, as old as the system itself, has just recently begun to stimulate the kind of outrage that produces change. It is almost certainly on the way out, along with the dungeon-like death-row cells, the increasing length of sentences, and the swelling rate of incarceration. It is not unreasonable to assume that the day of the legendary prison fortress is fading into the past, there to be mused upon by scholars and saints of a later day, much as we now muse upon the use of the rack and the lash.

If we look far enough into the future, as hopeful as prudence allows, we might hope to find that prisons as we now know them will no longer mar the landscape; no new ones will be built and those still standing will be razed or turned to more lofty purposes. Penologists of a far distant time might yet look back and know that today we stood on new ground and at a new time, and that when the battle was over, like Joshua at Jericho, the walls came tumbling down.

Author's Note

T HE COMPLETION OF this book required the aid and understanding of a great many people. The conclusion was in sight when I was diagnosed with a condition that required emergency surgery. I was hospitalized for a month and then went home for a lengthy period of recuperation during which I was unable to work. Herman Graf, my longtime friend and publisher, thoughtfully extended my publication date and called regularly without ever asking when I could get back to work. While I was mending, Kimberley Lim, assistant editor at Skyhorse, line-edited the portion of the manuscript that was already complete with care and precision. Jessica Diaz, my research assistant, performed spectacularly, finding what I needed promptly and efficiently.

Many of the events recounted in this book were evolving as I was working. I kept pace as best I could, trying to remain as current as possible. The factual information was culled from a great many sources. I have endeavored to credit all of them and apologize for any omissions. The opinions and views expressed throughout, unless otherwise noted, are those of the author alone.

I would be remiss not to mention the array of medical people who got me through an extremely difficult time. At the top of the list are Drs. Charles Glassman, Marc Zimmerman, and Rakesh Shreedhar. The staffs of Good Samaritan and Helen Hayes Hospitals, in North Rockland County, also earned my appreciation for their kindness and care. Once home, I was provided with several months of care by Nyack Hospital Home Care services. I offer my thanks to all those skilled nurses and aides who helped restore me to a condition resembling normalcy.

Unable to get around for many weeks, I thrived on the regular visits and phone calls from my devoted family: my children, Linda and Steve; their wonderful spouses, Greg and Monique; and my magnificent grandchildren, Michael, Jessica, Sammi, and Matt.

Finally, the book would never have been completed and I would not likely be sitting here today were it not for the round-the-clock ministrations of my wife, Betty. She sacrificed all varieties of leisure and entertainment, including a long-planned trip to Europe, to provide me with the kind of care worthy of a professional nurse. Even more critical was the love and emotional support that kept me going when my spirits flagged.

My undying love and appreciation to them all.

Source Notes

Introduction

Devine, Daniel James. "Execution, Not Surgery." January 26, 2008. www.worldmag.com.

Eckholm, Erik and John Schwartz. "Oklahoma Vows Review in Botched Execution." *The New York Times,* May 1, 2014.

Gibbs, Renwick. Letter to Stanley Cohen. June 22, 2004. Raleigh, North Carolina.

"Over 4% of US Death Row Prisoners Are Innocent, Finds Study." April 29, 2014. http://www.countercurrents.org/cc290414A.htm.

Randall, Kate. "Texas Death Row Inmate Granted Last-Minute Stay of Execution." May 14, 2014. www.wsws.org.

Richard, Heather, Austin Sarat, and Robert Henry Weaver. "Bad Drugs, Veins and Policy: Oklahoma Fits a Pattern of Botched US Executions." May 2, 2014. Theguardian.com.

"State Killing: Scalia Doesn't Care Whether You're Innocent, You Get Executed Anyway." August 20, 2009. http://deathpenaltynews.blogspot.com/2009/08/state-killing-scalia-doesnt-care.html.

The Editorial Board. "Don't Be Cruel, Justice Scalia." January 7, 2008. Theboardblogs.nytimes.com.

"The Supreme Court and Lethal Injection: When Is it Cruel and Unusual?" Abcnews.go.com.

Tosch, Chris. "State: Justices Ask About Pain of Execution." *Tampa Bay Times*, April 27, 2006. www.sptimes.com.

Ungar, Rick. "Justice Scalia—Executing the Innocent Does Not Violate the Constitution." August 17, 2009. Trueslant.com.

Vining, John B. Letter to Stanley Cohen. October 17, 2005. Raiford, Florida.

Wikipedia.org.

Part I: Official Misconduct

Death Row 10

Kim, Alice & Parkin, Joan. "Meet The Death Row 10; A Victory for the Death Row 10: The Struggle Continues." www.nodeathpenalty.org.

The New Yorker, August 4, 2014.

www.nodeathpenalty.org.

Aaron Patterson

Brant, Martha. "Last Chance Class." *Newsweek,* May 31, 1999. www.truthinjustice.org.

Sherrer, Hans. "Illinois Governor George Ryan Pardoned Four Innocent Men Condemned to Death on January 10, 2003 and the Next Day He Cleared Illinois' Death Row." www.justicedenied.org.

Warden, Rob. "A Tortured Path to Death Row." Center on Wrongful Convictions website. www.northwestern.edu.

Madison Hobley

Kubilus, Stephanie M. "Meet the Death Row 10: Madison Hobley." September 2006. www.nodeathpenalty.org.

Sherrer, Hans. "Illinois Governor George Ryan Pardoned Four Innocent Men Condemned to Death on January 10, 2003 and the Next Day He Cleared Illinois' Death Row." www.justicedenied.org.

Warden, Rob. "Pardoned Based on Innocence in Concocted Confession Case." Northewestern University School of Law Center on Wrongful Convictions website.

Leroy Orange

McNulty, Noreen. "Meet the Death Row 10: Leroy Orange's Fight For Injustice." www.nodeathpenalty.org.

Sherrer, Hans. "Illinois Governor George Ryan Pardoned Four Innocent Men Condemned to Death on January 10, 2003 and the Next Day He Cleared Illinois' Death Row." www.justicedenied.org.

Warden, Rob. Northwestern University School of Law Center on Wrongful Convictions website.

Stanley Howard

Main, Frank. "Cook County Judge Still Faces Claims in Torture Case." October 22, 2008. www.truthinjustice.org.

Parkin, Joan. "Meet the Death Row Ten: Stanley Howard." February 2000. www.nodeathpenalty.org.

Sherrer, Hans. "Illinois Governor George Ryan Pardoned Four Innocent Men Condemned to Death on January 10, 2003 and the Next Day He Cleared Illinois' Death Row." www.justicedenied.org.

Warden, Rob. "The Supreme Court Found Evidence "Overwhelming," but Governor Ryan Found Otherwise." Northwestern University School of Law Center on Wrongful Convictions website.

Glenn Ford

"After Nearly 30 Years on Death row, Glenn Ford is Exonerated." www.washingtonpost.com.

Ford, Dana. "Louisiana's Longest-Serving Death Row Prisoner Walks Free After 30 Years." March 12, 2014. www.cnn.com.

"Glenn Ford, Louisiana Death Row Inmate, Ordered Released After 1984 Murder Conviction is Vacated by Judge." March 11, 2014. www.cbsnews.com.

Possley, Maurice. The National Registry of Exonerations website. www.cbsnews.com

Joe D'Ambrosio

Patterson, Thom. "Unique Skill Set Helps Save Man From Death Row." March 21, 2014. www.cnn.com.

www.witnesstoinnocence.org.

Nathson Edgar Fields

Goldbaum, Nate. "Feedom for Nathson Fields." September 1999. www.nodeathpenalty.org.

Goldbaum, Nate. "Sentenced to Death by a Crook." February 1998. www.nodeathpenalty.org.

Janssen, Kim. "Jury: Wrongfully Convicted Ex-El Rukn Member was Denied Fair Trial." April 29, 2014. www.suntimes.com.

The National Registration of Exonerations. www.law.umich.edu.

Walberg, Matthew. "Judge's injustice is Righted—23 Years Later." April 9, 2009. articles.chicagotribune.com.

"After 11 Years on Death row, Where is the Justice For Nathson Fields?" August 1998. www.nodeathpenalty.org.

Harold C. Wilson

Possley, Maurice. The National Registry of Exonerations. www.law.umich.edu.

"The Story of Harold Wilson: Convicted of Triple Murder Sentenced to Die, Exonerated After 17 Years in Prison." December 20, 2005. www.democracynow.org.

Gordon "Randy" Steidl
Dardick, Hal. "8 Years Later, Freed Man Wins $3.5 Million Award." March 28, 2013. articles.chicagotribune.com.
Paul, Jim. "Ill. Man convicted in Killings Goes Free." May 28, 2004. www.truthinjustice.org.
"Steidl's Exoneration Pushes error Rate in Illinois Capital Cases to More Than 6%." Center on Wrongful Convictions. www.law.northwestern.edu.
Sweeney, Annie. "Wrongful Conviction Case Against Police, Prosecutors Win Appeal." May 30, 2012. articles.chicagotribune.com.
The National Registry of Exonerations. www.law.umich.edu.

Seth Penalver
Olmeda, Rafael. "Jury Finds Penalver Not Guilty in Casey's Nickelodeon Triple Murder Case." December 21, 2012. articles.sun-sentinel.com.
Possley, Maurice. The National Registry of Exonerations. www.law.umich.edu.

Wesley Quick
Gross, Alexandra. The National Registry of Exonerations. www.law.umich.edu.
Irsay, Steve. "After Leaving Death row, an Alabama Man is Tried for Burglary." September 8, 2003. news.findlaw.com.

Lemuel Prion
Gross, Alexandra. The National Registry of Exonerations. www.law.umich.edu.
Innes, Stephanie. "Prion's Siblings Testify of Father's Abuse." June 30, 1999. www.tucsoncitizen.com.
www.deathpenaltyinfo.org.

Daniel Wade Moore
Gross, Alexandra. The National Registry of Exonerations. www.law.umich.edu.

Peter Limone
Butterfield, Fox. "Ex-Prosecutor Tells of Ties Between F.B.I. and Mob." *The New York Times*, December 6, 2002.
"FBI To Be Sued for $300 Million." TalkLeft.com, August 25, 2002. http://www.talkleft.com/archives/000759.html.
Finucane, Martin. "Man Freed After Serving 32 Years." Associated Press, January 5, 2001. Truth in Justice website. http://www.truthinjustice.org/limone.htm.

Lawrence, J.M. "Judge: Lawyer can reveal hit man's confession." *Boston Herald*, December 23, 2000. http://AmericanMafia.com/news/12-23-00_Hit_Mans_Confession.html.

Lawrence, J.M. "Lawyer urges judge to free man jailed in 1965 Mob killing." *Boston Herald*, January 2, 2001.

Limone, Olympia with Kathleen Powers. "My Story: I Knew My Husband Was Innocent." *Good Housekeeping*, October 2002.

Maguire, Ken. "Wrongly Jailed Man Gets Apology." Associated Press. Truth in Justice website. http://www.truthinjustice.org/limoneapology.htm.

May, Allan. "Providence Mob." Court TV's Crime Library: Crimnial Minds and Methods. http://www.crimelibrary.com/gangers_outlaws/family_epics/providence_mob/1.html.

Prothero, P. Mitchell. "FBI 'knew innocent men were jailed'." UPI, 25 April 2001. http://www.gospelcom.net/apologeticsindex/news1/an01042413.html.

Sherrer, Hans. "Four Men Exonerated of 1965 Murder After FBI Frameup is Exposed." *Justice Denied*, Vol. 2, issue 5. http://www.justicedenied.org.fourmen.htm.

The Ford Heights 4: Verneal Jimerson, Dennis Williams, Willie Rainge, Kenny Adams

Armstong, Ken, and Robert Becker. "Record Ford Heights 4 Payout May Not Be End." *Chicago Tribune*, March 4, 1999. Illinois Death Penalty website. http//sun.soci.niu.edu/~critcrim/wrong/ford4-suit.html.

Armstrong, Ken and Maurice Possley. "Reversal of Fortune." *Chicago Tribune*, January 13, 1999. Illinois Death Penalty website. http://sun.soci.niu.edu/~critcrim/wrong/tribpros13.html.

"Former Death Row Inmate Not Angry." Associated Press. http://www.suburbanchicagonews.com/joliet/prisons/executed/williams.html.

Higgins, Dr. Edmund. "Wrongfully Convicted."

"Long Road From Death Row to Freedom." Associated Press. http://www.suburbanchicagonews.com/joliet/prisons/executed/willias.html.

Warden, Rob. Northwestern University School of Law Center on Wrongful Convictions website.

Earl Charles

Death Penalty Information website.

Radelet, Michael L., Hugo Adam Bedau, and Constance E. Putnam. "In Spite of Innocence."

Clarence Lee Brandley

Radelet, Michael L., Hugo Adam Bedau, Constance E. Putnam. "In Spite of Innocence."

Warden, Rob. Northwestern University School of Law Center on Wrongful Convictions website.

Michael Graham and Albert Burrell

Campbell, Ward A. "Innocence' Critique."

Louisiana Coalition to Abolish the Death Penalty website. http://lcadp.org/janfeb01.htm.

Reynolds, David. "DNA Testing Frees Death Row Inmate." *Inclusion Daily Express*, January 3, 2001.

Rimer, Sara. "Two Death-Row Inmates Exonerated in Louisiana." *The New York Times*, January 6, 2001.

Thoming-Gale, Stormy. "Free Men Walking." *Justice Denied*. Vol. 2, Issue 3.

Joaquin Martinez

Campbell, Ward A. "Innocence' Critique."

Nguyen, Dong-Phuong. "Man Once on Death Row Acquitted of 2 Murders." *St. Petersburg Times*, June 7, 2001.

"Spaniard Returns Home After U.S. Death Sentence Quashed." Reuters, June 10, 2001. http://www.gospelcom.net/apologeticsindex/news1/an01061106.html.

Juan Robert Melendez

Berkowitz, Nill. "A Dead Man Walking Toward Freedom?" Working For Change, December 23, 2001. Truth in Justice website. http://www.truthinjustice.org/melendez.htm.

Campbell, Ward A. "'Innocence' Critique."

"Exonerated from Death Row." Australian Coalition Against the Death Penalty.

Karp, David. "Judge Cites Prosecutor Trickery, Orders Retrial." *St. Petersburg Times*, December 6, 2001. http://www.oranous.com/JuanMelendez/cites.htm.

Kerry Cook

Death Penalty Information Center website.

Goldwasser, Amy. "The Exonerated." Salon.com, October 20, 2000. http://dir.salon.com/news/feature/2000/10/20/exonerated/index.html.

Higgins, Dr. Edmund. "Wrongfully Convicted."

Part II: Eyewitness Error & False Accusation

Anthony Porter
Warden, Rob. Northwestern University School of Law Center on Wrongful Convictions website.

Rudolph Holton
Goldman, Lawrence & Mason, Cheney. "Holton Case Shows Need for New Law." January 29, 2003. articles.orlandosentinel.com.

Karp, David. "New Stories Cast Doubt on a Murder Verdict—Witnesses and New Evidence Run Counter to Those Presented at a Man's Homicide Trial in 1986." *St Petersburg Times*, April 24, 2001.

Oprea, Karen. National Registry of Exonerations. www.law.umich.edu.

John Thompson
Fitzpatrick, Anna. "The deep roots of prosecutorial misconduct." May 24,2013. http://floridainnocence.org/content/?tag=john-thompson.

Grinberg, Emanuella. "Life After Death Row: helping break the 'jailhouse mentality'." April 5, 2014. http://www.cnn.com/2014/04/04/05/death-row-stories-thompson/index.html.

Gross, Alexandra. The National Registry of Exonerations. www.law.umich.edu.

"Holding Prosecutors Accountable: A Recent Supreme Court Decision Begs the Question of What, if Anything, Prosecutors Can be Held Accountable For." Innocence Project. www.innocenceproject.org.

Alan Gell
"Current Status of North Carolina's Death Penalty." Home Page for North Carolina Coalition for Alternatives to the Death Penalty.

"NC Will Pay $3.9 Million in Wrongful Conviction Case." October 1, 2009. www.thecrimereport.org.

Neal, David. "Former Death Row Inmate Alan Gell Aquitted—North Carolina Needs a Moratorium on Executions Now." February 18, 2004. Death Penalty Information Center. http://www.deathpenaltyinfo.org/node/1049.

The National Registry of Exonerations. www.law.umich.edu.

Wikipedia, http://en.wikipedia.org/wiki/Alan_Gell.

"With Execution Stalled, N.C. Murder Rate Falls." Home Page for North Carolina Coalition for Alternatives to the Death Penalty website.

Jonathan Hoffman
Gross, Alexandra. The National Registry of Exonerations. www.law.umich.edu.

"Charges Dismissed in case of Wrongfully Convicted Death Row Inmate Jonathan Hoffman." December 11, 2007. Death Watch North Carolina. http://deathwatch.wordpress.com.

Glen Edward Chapman
Gross, Alexandra. The National Registry of Exonerations. www.law.umich.edu.
"Glen Edward Chapman Wrongfully Sentenced to Die in NC." 2014. http:// nccadp.org/stories/ed-chapman.
"The Long Road from Exoneration to Compensation." May 22, 2012. www. innocenceproject.org.

Levon "Bo" Jones
Possley, Maurice. The National Registry of Exonerations. www.law.umich.edu.
"Man Wrongfully Convicted of Murder Released from Jail After 20 Years." August 13, 2013. www.businessinsider.com.

Michael Blair
Innocence Project. http://www.innocenceproject.org/content/Michael_Blair.php.
Gross, Alexandra. The National Registry of Exonerations. www.law.umich.edu.
"Texas Death Row Conviction Overturned." June 26, 2008. www. innocenceproject.org.

Yancy Douglas and Paris Powell
Gross, Alexandra. The National Registry of Exonerations. www.law.umich.edu.

Anthony Graves
Death Penalty Information Center. http://tcadp.org/get_informed/wrongful-conviction.
"Death Penalty." Susan Lee Solar Memorial. http://www.aimproductions.com/ SusanLee/DeathPenalty.html.
"Anthony Graves: The TT Interview." *The Texas Tribune*.
Smith, Jordan. "Holding Prosecutors Accountable: Anthony Graves Seeking Justice for Wrongful Conviction." January 21, 2014. www.austinchronicle.com.
"Anthony Graves, Former Death Row Inmate, Creates Scholarship in Name of Attorney Who Saved His Life." *Huffington Post*, October 17, 2013. http://www.huffingtonpost.com/2013/10/17/anthony-graves-scholarship_n_4118176.html.
Grissom, Brandi. "Comptroller Pays Anthony Graves $1.4 Million." June 30, 2011. www.texastribune.org.

"Texas Wrongful Convictions: The Anthony Graves Story." January 8, 2014. http://www.texascjc.org/texas-wrongful-convictions-anthony-graves-story.

Ryan Matthews
Innocence Project. http://www.innocenceproject.org/content/Ryan_Matthews.Php.
International Justice Project. http://www.internationaljusticeproject.org/juvRMatthews.cfm.

Part III: False Forensics

Anthony Ray Hinton
Chandler, Kim. "Alabama Man Freed after Nearly 30 Years on Death Row." *Yahoo News,* April 3, 2015.
Phillip, Abby. "Alabama Death Row Inmate is Free after 30 Years. How The Case Against Him Unraveled." *Washington Post.*
Silva, Daniella. "Anthony Ray Hinton, Alabama Man Who Spent 30 Years on Death Row, Has Case Dismissed." www.nbcnews.com.
Faulk, Kent. "Anthony Ray Hinton Free After Nearly 30 Years on Alabama Death Row." April 3, 2015. AL.com.
Blinder, Alan. "Alabama Man on Death Row for Three Decades is freed as State's Case Erodes." April 4, 2015: A11.

Timothy Howard and Gary Lamar James
Gross, Alexandra. The National Registry of Exonerations. www.law.umich.edu.
Trimble, Mandie. "Wrongful Conviction Trial Resumes After a One Day Recess." March 14, 2006. Wosu.org.
Trimble, Mandie. "Wrongful Conviction: Jury Deliberates." 14 March 2006. wosu.org.
Trimble, Mandie. "Man Who Wins Million Dollar Settlement in Wrongful Conviction Dies." March 19, 2007. wosu.org.
Stoddard, Teri. "PR: Wrongful Conviction and Prosecutor Misconduct at Issue in Upcoming Hearing for Arkansas Death Row Man." October 23, 2013. www.saveservices.org.

Ernest Ray Willis
Gross, Alexandra. The National Registry of Exonerations. www.law.umich.edu.
"Improving Forensics to End Injustice." Innocence Project. www.innocenceproject.org.

John Ballard
"Collier Double Murder Conviction Overturned." NBC 2 News, February 24, 2006. http://www.nbc-2.com/news/documents/060223_ballard-overturn.pdf.
"More on the Ballard Case and its Impact." *Daytona Beach New Journal Editorial*, February 28, 2006. http://www.tcadp.net/2006/03/02/more-on-the-ballard-case-and-its-impact/.
Radelet, Michael L. "Flight to Avoid Prosecution for Drunk Driving Took Him to the Brink of Execution for Murder." http://www.law.northwestern.edu/wrongfulconvictions/exonerations/wvabaileyrbsummary.html.

Curtis Edward McCarty
Innocence Project. http://www.innocenceproject.org/content/Curtis_McCarty.php.
Massie, Alana. "After 21 Years in Prison—Including 16 on Death Row—Curtis McCarty is Exonerated Based on DNA Evidence." Innocence Project. www.innocenceproject.org.
The National Registry of Exonerations. www.law.umich.edu.

Michael Lee McCormick
Coffey, John Mott. "DNA Evidence Set Clear Two Noxubee County Men Convicted of Rape and Murder." http://truthinjustice.org/kennedbrewer2.htm.
Massie, Alana. "Two Innocent Men Cleared Today in Seperate Murder Cases in Mississippi; 15 Years after Wrongful Convictions." Innocence Project. www.innocenceproject.org.
"Mississippi Exonerations Spark Reforms." Innocence Project. www.innocenceproject.org.
The National Registry of Exonerations. www.law.umich.edu

Paul House
Gross, Alexandra. The National Registry of Exonerations. www.law.umich.edu.
Innocence Project. http://www.innocenceproject.org/content/Paul_House.php.
"Paul House Exonerated in Tennessee." *The New York Times*, May 13, 2009.

Gussie Vann
Possley, Maurice. The National Registry of Exonerations, March 26, 2014. www.law.umich.edu.

Gary Dotson

Warden, Rob. Northwestern University School of Law Center on Wrongful Convictions website.

Kirk Bloodsworth

Campaign for Criminal Justice Reform. http://justice.policy.net/cjreform/wrong/.

Chebium, Raju. "DNA Provides New Hope for Wrongly-Convicted Death Row Inmates." CNN.com, June 16, 2000. http://www7.cnn.com/2000/LAW/06/16/death.penalty.dna.main/.

Chebium, Raju. "Innocence Project Credited With Expanding Awareness of DNA Testing in Law Enforcement." CNN.com, December 22, 2000. http://edition.cnn.com/2000/LAW/12/22/innocence.project.crim/.

Chebium, Raju. "Kirk Bloodsworth, Twice Convicted of Rape and Murder, Exonerated by DNA Evidence." CNN.com, June 20, 2000/http://www.cnn.com/2000/LAW/06/20/bloodsworth.profile/.

Ray Krone

Death Penalty Information Center website.

"History and Timeline." The Ray Krone Story. York Daily Record, 2001. http://www.ydr.com/page/krone/background/.

Wagner, Dennis, Beth DeFalco, Patricia Biggs. "DNA frees Arizona inmate after 10 years in prison: 10 years included time on death row." *The Arizona Republic*, April 9, 2002.

Part IV: Snitch Testimony

"How the False Testimony of Snitches Results in Wrongful Convictions." LawInfo website.

"Snitch Testimony. " Midwest Innocence Project website.

Sonia Jacobs

"Florida's Exonerated Death Row Prisoners." Floridians for Alternatives to the Death Penalty website.

Freedberg, Sydney P. "Freed From Death Row." Death Penalty Information Center website.

Grassroots Investigation Project of Equal Justice, U.S.A. "Reasonable Doubts: Is the U.S. Executing innocent People?" Equal Justice, U.S.A. October 26, 2000. http://www.quixote.org/ej/grip/reasonabledoubt/reasonabledoubt.pdf.

Warden, Rob. Northwestern University School of Law Center on Wrongful
Convictions website.

Joseph Amrine
Gross, Alexandra. the National Registry of Exonerations. www.law.umich.edu.
"State of Missouri v. Joseph Amrine." Death Penalty Information Center. www.
deathpenaltyinfo.org.
The Justice Project- Profile of Injustice. www.victimsofthestate.org.

Laurence Adams
Gross, Alexandra. The National Registry of Exonerations. www.law.umich.edu.
Lawrence, J.M. "Laurence Adams: Man Ends 30 Wrongful Years Behind Bars
Today." *Boston Herald*," May 20, 2014.

Dan L. Bright
Gross, Alexandra. The National Registry of Exonerations. www.law.umich.edu.
Innocence Project New Orleans. http://ip-no.org/exonoree-profile/dan-bright.

Derrick Jamison
Gross, Alexandra. The National Registry of Exonerations. www.law.umich.edu.
"Ohio Inmate Becomes 119th Innocent Person Freed From Death Row."
Death Penalty Information Center. http://truthinjustice.org/jamison.
htm.
Witness to Innocence. http://www.witnesstoinnocence.org/exonerees/derrick-
jamison.html.

Michael Toney
Gross, Alexandra. The National Registry of Exonerations. www.law.umich.edu.
Wrongful Conviction- TCADP. http://tcadp.org/get-informed/wrongful-conviction.

Reginald Griffin
Possley, Maurice, The National Registry of Exonerations, www.law.umich.edu,
October 29, 2013.
Sherrer, Hans. "Reginald Griffin's 1988 Murder Conviction Based on Jailhouse
Snitch Testimony Overturned by Missouri Supreme Court." August 5,
2011. http://justicedenied.org/wordpress/archives/1413.

Nicholas Yarris
Innocence Project. http://www.innocenceproject.org/content/Nicholas_Yarris.php.
The National Registry of Exonerations. http://www.innocenceproject.org.

James Richardson

"Compensating Wrongly Convicted James Richardson." www.wjhg.com.

James Creamer

Georgia Moratorium Campaign. http://www.georgiamoratorium.org/.

Higgins, Dr. Edmund. "Official Misconduct." http://www.dredmundhiggins. com/officialmisconduct.htm.

Higgins, Dr. Edmund. "Wrongfully Convicted."

Radelet, Michael L., Hugo Adam Bedau, and Constance E. Putnam. *In Spite of Innocence*.

Warden, Rob. Northwestern University School of Law Center on Wrongful Convictions website.

Neil Ferber

Equal Justice, U.S.A. "Police Abuses in Philadelphia." http://www.quixote. org/ej/archives/mumia/corr2.html.

"Exonerated from Death Row." Australian Coalition against the Death Penalty.

Fazlollah, Mark, Mark Bowden, and Richard Jones. "City Will Pay $1.9 Million to Man over Unjust Jailing." *Philadelphia Inquirer*, August 15, 1996.

Illinois Death Penalty Education Project. "Summaries of 46 Cases in Which Mistaken or Perjured Eyewitness Testimony Put Innocent Persons on Death Row." IllinoisDeathPenalty.com. Chicago, IL. http://www. illinoisdeathpenatly.com/eyewitness.html.

Warden, Rob. Northwestern University School of Law Center on Wrongful Convictions website.

Willie Brown and Larry Troy

Campaign for Criminal Justice Reform website. The Justice Project.

Campbell, Ward A. "'Innocence' Critique."

Illinois Coalition Against the Death Penalty. http//www.icadp.org/.

Warden, Rob. Northwestern University School of Law Center on Wrongful Convictions website.

Walter McMillian

Amnesty International. "Appendix: Statement of Joseph 'Shabaka' Green Brown." From "Fatal Flaws: Innocence and the Death Penalty."

Halperin, Rick. "Death Penalty News and Updates." http://people.smu.edu/ rhalperi/.

Halperin, Rick. "Death Penalty News: October 1997." Abolish Archives. http://venus.soci.niu.edu/~archives/ABOLISH.

Halperin, Rick. "Death Penalty News: October 2000." Abolish Archives. http://venus.soci.niu.edu/~archives/ABOLISH.

Humes, Edward. *Mean Justice*. New York: Simon & Schuster, 1999. Excerpted on Steven Shurka and Associates. www.crimlaw.org/defbrief63.html.

Illinois Coalition Against the Death Penalty. http://www.icadp.org/.

Protest Net. http://www.protest.net.

Sealey, Geraldine. "Society's Debt: Who Pays When Innocent Men Go to Jail? Sometimes No One." ABCNEWS.com. August 8, 2002. http//abcnews. go.com/sections/us/DailyNews/compensation020808.html.

Warden, Rob. Northwestern University School of Law Center on Wrongful Convictions website.

Weinstein, Henry. "Death Penalty Foes Focus Effort on the Innocent." Los Angeles Times, November 16, 1998. http://www.texas-justice.com/latimes/latimes981116.htm.

Curtis Kyles

Amnesty International USA Death Penalty website.

Campbell, Ward A. " 'Innocence' Critique."

Fight the Death Penalty in the U.S.A. http://www.fdp.dk/uk/released.html.

Illinois Coalition Against the Death Penalty. http://www.icadp.org/.

Illinois Death Penalty Education Project. "Summaries of 46 Cases in Which Mistaken or Perjured Eyewitness Testimony Put Innocent Persons on Death Row."

Lovinger, Caitlin. "Death Row's Living Alumni." *The New York Times*, August 22, 1999. www.protest.net/view/cgi?view=1501.

Robinson, Mary. "Re: Feingold Sponsoring Bill to Abolish Death Penalty." Abolish Archives. http://venus.soci.niu.e4du/~archives/ABOLISH/dec99/0097.html.

"Testimony of Brian A. Stevenson." Post-Conviction DNA Testing and Preventing Wrongful Convictions of the Innocent. United States Senate Judiciary Committee. June 13, 2000. http://judiciary.senate.gov/oldsite/6132000_bas.htm.

Part V: False Confession

Henry Lee McCollum and Leon Brown

Blinder, Alan. "Pardons Elude Men Freed After Decades in Prison". *The New York Times*, March 17, 2015.

Eckholm, Erik & Katz, Jonathan M. "DNA Evidence Clears Two Men in 1983 Murder." September 2, 2014. NYTimes.com.

Eckholm, Erik & Katz, Jonathan M. "DNA Evidence Clears Two Men Convicted In Girls' 1983 Murder" *The New York Times*, September 3, 2014: A14.

Katz, Jonathan M. "From Death Row to Unfamiliar World." *The New York Times*, September 4, 2014: A17.

Oppel Jr., Richard A. "As Two Men Go Free, A Dogged Former Prosecutor Digs In." *The New York Times*, September 8, 2014: A13.

"The Innocent on Death Row." *The New York Times*, September 4, 2014: A26.

Ronald Kitchen and Marvin Reeves

"Burge Victim Ronald Kitchen Latest Illinois Death Row Exoneree." www.law.northwestern.edu.

"Chicago Mayor Rahm Emanuel issues Apology for Police Torture in Decades-long Scandal." http://www.law.northwestern.edu/.

"Finance committee Approves $12.3 Million Settlement with Police." www.law.northwestern.edu.

"Ronald Kitchen sues Burge, Daley, Others for Torture and Wrongful Conviction." August 10, 2010. www.law.northwestern.edu.

Torture Victims Ronald Kitchen and Marvin Reeves." September 6, 2013. www.law.northwestern.edu.

The National Registry of Exonerations. www.law.umich.edu.

Robert Springsteen and Michael Scott

"Lehmberg Answers Springsteen Suit: D.A. argues innocence cannot be declared in civil court." April 11, 2014. www.austinchronicle.com.

Possley, Maurice. The National Registry of Exonerations. www.law.umich.edu.

Smith, Jordan. "Springsteen Sues for Wrongful Conviction." May 31, 2013. www.austinchronicle.com.

Damon Thibodeaux

Gross, Alexandra. The National Registry of Exonerations. www.law.umich.edu.

InnocenceProject.http://www.innocenceproject.org/content/Damon_Thibodeaux.php.

Warden, Rob. "False Confession Sent Him to Death Row; DNA Exonerated Him 15 Years Later." www.law.northwestern.edu.

Kevin Richardson, Yusef Salaam, Kharey Wise, Raymond Santana, Antron McCray

Otis, Ginger Adams. "'Jogger' Wrong Righted: central park five get $40M settlement in '89 rape case." *Daily News*, June 20, 2014.

Weiser, Benjamin. "Settlement Approved in '89 Jogger Case, City Deflects Blame." *The New York Times*, September 6, 2014.

Gary Gauger

Aucoin, Laurie. "Righting Wrongful Convictions." Northwestern Magazine. Spring 1999. http://www.northwestern.edu/magazine.northwestern/spring99/convictions.htm.

Lovinger, Caitlin. "Death Row's Living Alumni." *The New York Times,* August 22, 1999.

Rummel, Carolyn. "Exonerated: Powerful Anti-Death Penalty Theater." *People's Weekly World*, October 19, 2002.

Warden, Rob. Northwestern University School of Law Center on Wrongful Convictions website.

"The Wrongly Convicted." The Patrick Crusade website. http://www.patrickcrusade.org/wrongful.htm.

Robert Lee Miller Jr.

"The 17 Innocent People Who Lived." American Civil Liberties Union website. http://archive.aclu.org/issues/death/17exonerated.html.

Higgins, Dr. Edmund. "Wrongfully Convicted."

"Innocence and the Death Penalty." Death Penalty Institute of Oklahoma website. March 18 2001. http://www.dpio.org/issues/innocence.html.

"News Archives: June 2000." Death Penalty Institute of Oklahoma website. March 18, 2001. http://www.dpio.org/archives/News/News_2000_06.html.

Scheck, Barry, Peter Neufeld, and Jim Dwyer. *Actual Innocence*. New York: Doubleday, 2000.

David Keaton

"Exonerated from Death Row." Australian Coalition Against the Death Penalty.

Floridians for Alternatives to the Death Penalty website.

"The Wrongly Convicted." The Patrick Crusade website.

Johnny Ross

Amnesty International. "Indecent and Internationally Illegal: The Death Penalty Against Child Ofeenders." 25 September 2002. Amnesty International website. http://web.amnesty.org/library/Index/engAMR511442002?Opend-Document&of=COUNTRIES?OpendDocuments&of=COUNTRIES.

Berrigan, Patrick J., and Jennifer Brewer. "Appellants Suggestions as to the Applicability of Aitkens v. Virginia to the Issues in Mr. Simmons' Case." State of Missouri v. Christopher Simmons. Case No. SC84454. 20 July 2002. http://www.abanet.org/crimjust/juvjus/simmonsatkins.pdf.

Campbell, Ward A. "Innocence Critique."

"The Wrongly Convicted." The Patrick Crusade website.

Part VI: Long-Term Confinement

The Scarcella Factor

Bandler, Jonathan. "Deskovic to Get Trial vs. Putnam." *The Journal News*, 29 June 2014.

"Brooklyn D.A. Clears 7th Convict in Case Review." Associated Press, June 3, 2014.

Clifford, Stephanie. "Another Man Freed as Brooklyn District Attorney's Office Reviews Cases." *The New York Times,* June 4, 2014.

"Officials Affirm Conviction in '03 Murder." *The New York Times*, January 13, 2015.

"Take Steps to Prevent Wrongful Convictions." *The Journal News,* June 8, 2014.

David Ranta

Clifford, Stephanie. "Family of Framed Man Sues City and Police." June 19, 2014.

Hays, Tom. "Louis Scarcella, Retired NYPD Detective with Storied Career, Defends Record in David Ranta Case." March 30, 2013. www.huffingtonpost.com.

"Witness Who Helped Put David Ranta in Prison for Murder of Rabbi Werzberger Reveals Why he Recanted Testimony." May 4, 2015. www.matzav.com.

Love, David A. "Dirty Ex-Cop Louis Scarcella's Framing of Innocent Black Men is Costing NYC Millions." January 14, 2015.

Derrick Hamilton

Clifford, Stephanie. "Ex-Detective Defends His Methods Again." *The New York Times*, December 5, 2014.

Clifford, Stephanie. "Wrongly Convicted Man was His Own Best Advocate." *The New York Times*, January 10, 2014.

Flynn, Sean. "Brooklyn's Baddest Cop: Louis Scarcella." *GQ Magazine*, August 14, 2014.

The Three Brothers

Clifford, Stephanie. "Judge Voids Murder Convictions For 3 Half Brothers Linked to Detective." *The New York Times*, May 7, 2014.

Clifford, Stephanie & Robles, Frances. "3 Exonerated in Cases Tied to a Detective." *The New York Times*, May 6, 2014.

Clifford, Stephanie and Weiser, Benjamin. "City Settles Three Brothers' Wrongful Conviction Cases for $17 Million." *The New York Times*, January 12, 2015.

Davis, Lorri & Echols, Damien. *Yours for Eternity: A Love Story on Death Row*. New York: Penguin Random House, 2014.

Hays, Tom and Peltz, Jennifer. "Brooklyn Prosecutor to Re-examine 90 Convictions." *The New York Times*, May 26, 2014.

Love, David A. "Dirty Ex-Cop Louis Scarcella's Framing of Innocent Black Men is Costing NYC Millions." January 14, 2015. www.thegrio.com.

"New York to pay brothers $17 million in wrongful conviction settlements." Reuters, January 2015.

The National Registry of Exonerations website.

"Three Men to be Exonerated in Scarcella Review." The Innocence Project website.

Wikipedia.org.

Rosean S. Hargrave

Clifford, Stephanie. "Court and Brooklyn District Attorney's Office Revisit 2 Contested Convictions." *The New York Times*, September 17, 2014.

Clifford, Stephanie. "Ex- Detective, Defending Work in Disputed '91 Murder Case, Points to Role of Prosecutors." *The New York Times*, September 25, 2014.

Clifford, Stephanie. "Brooklyn District Attorney to Appeal New Trial for Man Convicted in 1991 Killing." *The New York Times*, May 11, 2015.

Love, David A. "Dirty Ex-Cop Louis Scarcella's Framing of Innocent Black Men is Costing NYC Millions." January 14, 2015. www.thegrio.com.

Santora, Marc and Schweber, Nate. "Convicted of 1991 Murder, Man is Ordered Released." *The New York Times*, April 15, 2015.

Troiano, Charisma L. "One Detective's History of Providing False Evidence Gives Grounds for Brooklyn Defendant's New Trial." *Brooklyn Daily Eagle*, April 15, 2015.

"Man Convicted in 1991 Murder Released, Gets New Trial." April 15, 2015. www.UPI.com.

Shabaka Shakur

Clifford, Stephanie. "New Trial is Ordered for Man Convicted in 1988 Killings." *The New York Times*, June 3, 2015.

Clifford, Stephanie. "Prosecutor Won't Retry Man Granted New Trial in 2 Killings." *The New York Times*, June 4, 2015.

Clifford Stephanie and John Surico. "Judge Orders Man Freed after 27 Years Behind Bars." *The New York Times*, June 5, 2015.

Remrick, Noah. "Released After 27 Years, An Ex-Inmate is Mindful of a Detective's Cases." *The New York Times*, June 9, 2015.

Martin Tankleff

Eltman, Frank. "Man Vows to Fight for Justice." *The Journal News,* May 2014.

"Marty Tankleff Considering Run for Congress After Earning Law Degree." CBS New York.

"Martin Tankleff Gets $3.7 Million for Wrongful Murder Conviction." www. huffingtonpost.com.

"Martin Tankleff to Receive Law Degree." *Newsday.*

"Marty Tankleff, Wrongfully Imprisoned NY Man, Settles Suit Against NY State." January 8, 2014. CBS News.

Wikipedia.org.

Ricky Jackson

"Ohio: Man Convicted in 1975 Killing is to be Freed." *The New York Times,* November 20, 2014.

"Ricky Jackson, Wrongfully Convicted of Murder, to be Freed After 39 Years in Prison." November 21, 2014.

Apuzzo, Matt & Smith, Mitch. "Police in Cleveland Accept Tough Standards on Force." *The New York Times,* May 27, 2015.

"Cleveland Police Cited for Abuse by Justice Department." December 4, 2014. NYTimes.com.

Dewan, Shaila & Oppel Jr., Richard A. "Many Errors by Cleveland Police, Then a Fatal One." *The New York Times,* January 23, 2015.

"Prosecutors dismiss 39-year-old Murder Charges against Kwame Ajamu, Wiley Bridgeman and Ricky Jackson." November 20, 2015.

"Ricky Jackson and Wiley Bridgeman: Exonerated Friends Leave Prison After 39 Years Behind Bars." November 20, 2014. Cleveland.com.

The National Registry of Exonerations. www.law.umich.edu.

"Two Men Wrongfully Convicted Released from Prison After 39 Years." WTOC-TV website.

Michael Morton

Kristof, Nicholas. "When They Imprison the Wrong Guy." July, 6 2014.

The Innocence Project website.

Dewey Bozella

Berger, Joseph. "Wrongfully Serving 26 Years, Man Settles Case." *The New York Times,* January 13, 2015.

Denzel, Stephanie. National Registry of Exonerations. www.law.umich.edu.

Wikipedia.org.

Afterword: United States vs. Criminal Justice

"A Lifetime on California's Death Row." *The New York Times*, July 21, 2014.

Douthat, Ross. "The Dannemora Dilemma." June 2015.

"Exonerated Death Row Inmate Glenn Ford Dies of Cancer." KSLA News 12.

"Four Decades of Solitary in Louisiana." *The New York Times*, November 22, 2014.

Goldstein, Dana. "Too Old to Commit Crime?" *The New York Times,* March 22, 2015.

Goode, Erica. "Judge's Decision to Hear Inmates' Case threatens Practice of Solitary Confinement." *The New York Times*, June 4, 2014.

"Justice Kennedy on Solitary Confinement." *The New York Times*, June 20, 2015.

"Justice Kennedy's Plea to Congress." *The New York Times*, April 5, 2015.

Liptak, Adam. "With Subtle Signals, Justices Request the Cases They Want to Hear." *The New York Times*, July 7, 2015.

Robertson, Campbell. "The Man Who Says Louisiana Should 'Kill More'." *The New York Times*, June 8, 2015.

"Steering a 1787 Convention to Produce a Document for Nation-Building." *The New York Times*, June 30, 2015.

Swanson, David. "'The degree of civilization in a society,' said Dosteyevsky 'can be judged by entering its prisons.'." r3volution! News website.

Weber, Bruce. "Glenn Ford, Spared death row, Dies at 65." *The New York Times*, July 3, 2015.

Kalief Browder

Dwyer, Jim. "A Life That Frayed as Bail Reform Withered." *The New York Times,* June 10, 2015

Schwirtz, Michael, and Michael Winerip. "Man Held at Rikers Jail for 3 Years Without Trial Commits Suicide at 22." June 7, 2015.

"Suicide Prompts Remarks by Mayor: Man served time as teen on Rikers Island." Associated Press, June 9, 2015: 11A.

"The Death of Kalief Browder." *The New York Times*, June 10, 2015.

Bail System

Dewan, Shaila. "Poor, Accused and Punished by Bail System: Critics point to debt and ruined lives." *The New York Times*, June 11, 2015.

Incarceration

International Centre for Prison Studies website.

Organization for Economic Cooperation and Development website.
"Prisoners Per 100,000: US Has Highest Incarceration Rate in the World." Wikipedia.org.
Scommegna, Paula and Tysen Tsai. Population Reference Bureau.
"U.S. Has World's Highest Incarceration Rate." Wikipedia.org.
"United States Incarceration Rate." Wikipedia.org.

Albert Woodfox, Angola 3
The Woodfox case proceeded as this book was being written. Articles from day-to-day articles in *The New York Times*, beginning on June 11, 2015, were our chief source of information.
"The Last of the Angola Three still in Prison Waits Again To Be Released, or Retried." *The New York Times,* June 11, 2015.

Glenn Ford
The Glenn Ford case is covered in detail in Part 1. The aftermath—the apology offered by the prosecuting attorney, the state of Louisiana Justice, and finally Ford's death—were covered in *The New York Times* and the *Shreveport Times.*
Swanson, David. "War is a Lie." Published in April. Just World Books.

President Obama
Baker, Peter. "Obama Calls for Effort to Fix a 'Broken System' of Criminal Justice." *The New York Times.*
Baker, Peter. "President Visits Federal Prison: Reflecting on turns he might have taken." *The New York Times,* July 17, 2015.
"Mr. Obama Takes On the Prison Crisis." *The New York Times,* July 17, 2015: A26.

Index

About the Author

S TANLEY COHEN IS a veteran award-winning journalist. For more than
fifty years, he has worked as an editor, writer, and reporter for newspapers, magazines, and an international news service. He also has taught
writing, journalism, and philosophy at Hunter College and New York
University. His work has appeared in numerous publications, including

The New York Times, Inside Sports, and *Sports, Inc.;* he was also a contributing writer for *The Diamond* magazine.

He is the author of ten previous books, including *The Game They Played,* which was ranked among the Top 100 Sports Books of All Time by the editors of *Sports Illustrated,* and *The Wrong Men,* which dealt with the epidemic of wrongful death-row convictions and the scourge of capital punishment. Cohen also served as program consultant for the award-winning television documentary *City Dump,* which dealt with the 1951 college basketball scandal.

In the 1960s, Cohen took part in the campaign to abolish capital punishment in New York State and received a citation from Al Blumenthal, who sponsored the abolition bill in the State Assembly.

He resides in Tomkins Cove, New York, with his wife, Betty. Their two children and four grandchildren also live in the New York metropolitan area.